MW01628539

ARTFUL ADORNMENTS

Jewelry from the Museum of Fine Arts, Boston

YVONNE J. MARKOWITZ

MFA Publications
Museum of Fine Arts, Boston
465 Huntington Avenue
Boston, Massachusetts 02115
www.mfa.org/publications

Support for this publication was provided by Skinner, Inc., and Dorfman Jewelers of Boston, as well as by Michael and Karen Rotenberg.

ISBN 978-0-87846-768-6 (hardcover)
Library of Congress Control Number: 2011922448

While the objects in this publication necessarily represent only a small portion of the MFA's holdings, the Museum is proud to be a leader within the American museum community in sharing the objects in its collection via its Web site. Currently, information about more than 330,000 objects is available to the public worldwide. To learn more about the MFA's collections, including provenance, publication, and exhibition history, kindly visit www.mfa.org/collections.

For a complete listing of MFA publications, please contact the publisher at the above address, or call 617 369 3438.

Cover illustration: Charles Robert Ashbee, *Marsh Bird Hair Ornament* (brooch), 1901–2 (p. 157).

IMAGE CREDITS

All illustrations in this book were photographed by Michael Gould and Greg Heins of the Imaging Studios, Museum of Fine Arts, Boston, except where otherwise noted.

Grateful acknowledgment is made to the copyright holders for permission to reproduce the following works:

pp. 27, 94, 140, 145, 146, 153, 154, 156, 164, 165, 168, 169, 171, 172, 174, 179, 181, 182, 188, 191: Reproduced with permission
p. 47: © 2007 Kiff Slemmons
p. 197: © MFC, Inc.
p. 118: All rights reserved Daniel Jocz
p. 144: CHANEL
pp. 148, 149: © Museum of Fine Arts, Boston
pp. 150, 152: © 2011 Calder Foundation, New York / Artists Rights Society (ARS), New York
p. 160: © 2011 Artists Rights Society (ARS), New York/ADAGP, Paris
p. 167: © Estate of Sam Kramer
p. 173: © Björn Weckström
p. 175: © Bruno Martinazzi
p. 177: © renk
p. 178: © Yoshiko Yamamoto
p. 183: © 2007 Kiff Slemmons
p. 187: © Jan Yager

Edited by Emiko K. Usui and Gail Spilsbury
Copyedited by Dalia Geffen
Designed by Christopher Kuntze
Produced by Terry McAweeney
Printed and bound at Graphicom, Verona, Italy

Available through D.A.P. / Distributed Art Publishers
155 Sixth Avenue, 2nd floor
New York, New York 10013
Tel.: 212 627 1999 · Fax: 212 627 9484

FIRST EDITION
Printed and bound in Italy
This book was printed on acid-free paper.

CONTENTS

Director's Foreword 7

Acknowledgments 8

Artful Adornments 11
JEWELRY FROM THE MUSEUM OF FINE ARTS, BOSTON

Magical Jewels 19

Emblems of Wealth & Power 49

Tokens of Affection & Remembrance 99

Dress & Adornment 121

Jewelry & the Avant-Garde 151

Glossary 193

Further Reading 197

Figure Illustrations 198

Index 200

ACKNOWLEDGMENTS

This book would not have been possible without the assistance and expertise of many curatorial colleagues. At the Museum of Fine Arts, Boston, they include Pamela A. Parmal, Department Head and David and Roberta Logie Curator of Textile and Fashion Arts, and Lauren Whitley, Curator, in the David and Roberta Logie Department of Textile and Fashion Arts; Rita Freed, John F. Cogan, Jr. and Mary L. Cornille Chair, Art of the Ancient World, Denise Doxey, Curator, Christine Kondoleon, George D. and Margo Behrakis Senior Curator of Greek and Roman Art, Mary B. Comstock, Cornelius and Emily Vermeule Curator and Keeper of Coins, Greek and Roman Art, Richard Grossmann, former Mary Bryce Comstock Assistant Curator of Greek and Roman Art and Keeper of Coins and Medals, and Lawrence Berman, Norma Jean Calderwood Senior Curator of Ancient Egyptian, Nubian, and Near Eastern Art in Art of the Ancient World; George Shackelford, Chair and Arthur K. Solomon Curator of Modern Art, Ronni Baer, William and Ann Elfers Senior Curator of Paintings, Art of Europe, Marietta Cambareri, Curator, Decorative Arts and Sculpture and Jetskalina H. Phillips Curator of Judaica, Thomas Michie, Russell B. and Andrée Beauchamp Stearns Senior Curator of Decorative Arts and Sculpture, Art of Europe, and Meghan Melvin, Curatorial Project Assistant, in Art of Europe; Erica Hirshler, Croll Senior Curator of American Paintings, Gerald W. R. Ward, Katharine Lane Weems Senior Curator of American Decorative Arts and Sculpture, Kelly H. L'Ecuyer, Ellyn McColgan Curator of Decorative Arts and Sculpture, Art of the Americas, and Dennis Carr, Assistant Curator of Decorative Arts and Sculpture, in Art of the Americas; and Jane Portal, Matsutaro Shoriki Chair, Art of Asia, Oceania, and Africa and Laura Weinstein, Ananda Coomaraswamy Curator of South Asian and Islamic Art in Art of Asia, Oceania, and Africa.

Many others assisted in the project. The research of Emily Banis, former Research Associate, Textile and Fashion Arts, proved invaluable in the writing of the text; MFA photographers Greg Heins, Manager of Imaging Studios, and Michael Gould, Senior Photographer, created outstanding digital images of objects that often posed special challenges; Richard Newman, Head of Scientific Research, Susanne Gänsicke, Conservator, Objects Conservation, and Michele Derrick, Schorr Family Associate Research Scientist both examined and conducted detailed analyses on select objects. Emiko Usui, Director of MFA Publications, applied her exceptional editorial skills to the text with assistance by Gail Spilsbury, while Production Manager Terry McAweeney and Production Editor Jodi Simpson helped produce the book. Christopher Kuntze added his artistic talents to the book's design, creating a handsome publication. Intern Sarah Richter applied her considerable research skills to the project. Toni Strassler providesd unerring support throughout the project, offering her jeweler's expertise and insights into the materials and techniques used in jewelry making throughout the ages.

Special gratitude is extended to jewelry historians and independent curators Elyse Zorn Karlin, Jeannine Falino, Janet Zapata, Elise Misiorowski, Amanda Triossi, and Gloria Lieberman. All generously offered their insights and expertise on jewelry made in Europe and North America, as did Judy Rudoe and Diana Scarisbrick, noted jewelry scholars in England.

Finally, I am grateful for the support for this publication provided by Skinner, Inc., and Dorfman Jewelers of Boston, as well as by Karen and Michael Rotenberg.

Yvonne J. Markowitz
Rita J. Kaplan and Susan B. Kaplan Curator of Jewelry
Museum of Fine Arts, Boston

Artful Adornments

JEWELRY FROM THE MUSEUM OF FINE ARTS, BOSTON

JEWELRY'S PRESENCE in human society is ancient and ubiquitous, reflecting the values of the people who wore it, the technologies available to produce it, and the trade that fostered it. A single ornament can serve a variety of functions and have multiple layers of meaning. Many early civilizations produced jewelry out of materials believed to safeguard, heal, or confer special powers on the wearer. The sunlike brilliance and corrosion-resistant properties of gold, for example, were often associated with the life-giving qualities of the sun and cosmic deities. To adorn one's body with the magical material was to align oneself with potent supernatural forces that ensured well-being and longevity. Man's desire for ornaments made of this prized substance has been so great that once we exhausted all readily available alluvial sources, we made arduous and often lethal attempts to extract the precious metal from the earth. Gold mining continues at a rapid pace in many parts of the world today, and it uses new technologies to expose fine-grained deposits at previously inaccessible depths.

In most societies, adornments function as signifiers of an individual's rank and position. Jewelry made of rare, costly materials establishes the wearer as a person of wealth and privilege; other adornments such as military decorations and institutional achievement awards indicate one's place or value within a hierarchy. Jewelry can also be a form of portable wealth, especially in times of instability. During the social upheavals associated with the European political revolutions of 1848, wealthy aristocrats sold their gem-set jewels as they fled embattled areas. Leading jewelry firms in the United States were the lucky beneficiaries of those economic crises, for they were able to acquire outstanding ornaments for a new class of wealthy American industrialists.

Heads of state may offer rare and costly jewelry or bejeweled objects as diplomatic gifts. The large number of such lavish presents in the United States' presidential libraries and National Archives shows that jewelry still functions in this capacity in modern democracies. As recently as 2009, Saudi Arabia's King Abdullah presented First Lady Michelle

FACING PAGE

The New Necklace, William McGregor Paxton (American, 1869–1941), 1910, oil on canvas.

Obama with a diamond and ruby jewelry suite valued at $132,000. The ornaments, along with other gifts to the first family, are now part of the collections of the National Archives.

In addition to promoting good relations between countries, jewelry has the potential of serving as political propaganda. When a pharaoh of Egypt's Twelfth Dynasty (1991–1783 B.C.) wore a gold pectoral depicting a scene of the king smiting his enemies, he sent a powerful message to anyone visiting his court. The material culture of modern political movements and armed conflicts has also been replete with decorative objects symbolizing sympathy for a specific cause. Many ornaments in this category, such as the yellow ribbon pins worn in support of U.S. troops fighting in Iraq or Afghanistan, are inexpensive and readily available to the public. Unlike the pharaoh's pectoral, the pins point to the sacrifices made by the armed forces and their families, rather than to one individual's power over others.

Jewelry has always had a close and intimate relationship with clothing. Appliqués, belt and shoe buckles, fibulae, toggles, cloak clasps, chatelaines, and pocket watches are all examples of jewelry dictated by fashion. In some cases, such as garments decorated with elaborate beadwork, the distinction between jewelry and dress is blurred. And, when an ornament typically viewed as a separate object is sewn onto an underlying garment, the textile appears to merely support the dazzling jewelry. Adornments of this latter type were prevalent in Europe during the medieval and Renaissance periods.

The highly personal nature of jewelry is evident in ornaments that serve as an expression of love, loss, and remembrance. Known as "sentimental" jewelry, this type of adornment was especially popular in Europe and North America during the eighteenth and nineteenth centuries. Portrait miniatures, acrostic adornments that incorporated a person's initials or a secret message, and mourning jewelry are examples of this genre. Today jewelry remains a popular gift bestowed on loved ones and friends, especially when celebrating rites of passage, birthdays, and anniversaries.

It was not until the late nineteenth century that artists began to see jewelry as a vehicle for expressing their thoughts on social matters. In England, proponents of the arts and crafts movement saw art as a spiritual and moral endeavor with profound aesthetic and cultural ramifications. They denounced mass-produced goods in favor of well-designed, decorative objects made by hand. Jewelers formed guilds and worked with simple, humble materials such as copper, enamel, and semiprecious stones. A similar situation occurred in France and Belgium, where art nouveau jewelers rejected prestigious diamond and platinum, working instead in gold, enamel, glass, and exotic, natural materials such as horn. Although trained under the traditional apprenticeship system, they experimented with new techniques, creating ornaments with dramatic imagery and poetic symbolism influenced by new theories about the power of the unconscious mind. These ideas would later resonate with studio jewelers in the United States and Europe after World War II.

The Museum of Fine Arts, Boston, has an extraordinary collection of jewelry amassed over more than a century. The ornaments span nearly six thousand years of civilization over five continents and represent a wide array of materials, techniques, and functions. They include stellar beadwork from Egypt's Pyramid Age; spectacular jewels from royal burials of ancient Nubia; an exceptional assortment of Greek gold; a world-class collection of ancient Near Eastern cylinder seals and carved gemstones from the classical world; several Neolithic Chinese belt ornaments of jade; a choice selection of medieval pendants; the William D. Boardman collection of European finger rings; fine examples of nineteenth-century revivalist jewelry; a magnificent assemblage of ancient American goldwork and jade; arts and crafts ornaments by Boston makers; important examples of Native American adornments; several dozen Mughal ornaments dating to the eighteenth and nineteenth centuries; American and European high-style adornments; and one of the world's most comprehensive collections of studio jewelry.

The Museum acquired its first works of jewelry, primarily Egyptian scarabs, amulets, and beads, shortly after incorporating in 1870. It also acquired numerous antiquities, including jewelry, by subscription to the London-based Egypt Exploration Fund for several decades beginning about the same time. The Joint Egyptian Expedition of Harvard University and the Museum of Fine Arts, Boston (also known as the Harvard-Boston Expedition), began operations in 1905, resulting in startling discoveries of extraordinary jewelry at Giza, and then later at other sites along the Nile Valley and in the Sudan. The royal ancient Nubian jewels found by the expedition are now considered among the best in the world, important not only for their fine quality but also for the documented context in which they were found—the detailed maps, plans, notes, diaries, and inventories of the excavation team provide scholars with a means of understanding how, where, and why the jewelry was worn. The excavations lasted several decades, adding several thousand ornaments to the Museum's collection.

During the early twentieth century, Denman Waldo Ross, a Harvard University professor of design, Museum Trustee, and avid collector of Asian art, purchased and then donated enameled and gem-set jewelry from Jaipur, and gold head ornaments, earrings, bangles, and necklaces from western and southern India. Ross often collaborated with Ananda Coomaraswamy, the Museum's first curator of Indian art (and the first curator of Indian art in the United States). Both scholars viewed jewelry as an integral part of the culture of India and hoped that the MFA's collection could represent the range of adornment worn in that vast and complex country. Ross acquired both provincial examples made of modest materials and ornaments fabricated from precious materials in leading urban centers.

Fig. 1. Cameo with Livia holding a bust of Augustus, Roman, early Imperial period, A.D. 14–37, turquoise with a modern gold setting.

The Museum's collection also includes outstanding examples of carved cameos and engraved gems from ancient Greece and Rome. Many of these once belonged to George Spencer, 4th Duke of Marlborough, who resided at Blenheim Palace near Oxford in the eighteenth century. The Duke's collection of approximately eight hundred such jewels was the most important assemblage of its kind in eighteenth-century England. When the collection was dispersed in 1899, nearly two dozen cameos and gems were purchased by Edward Perry Warren of Boston, who later donated them to the MFA. They included an exquisitely rendered Renaissance shell cameo depicting the death of Meleager (p. 60), a sardonyx cameo of Cupid and Psyche (p. 105), and a pale green turquoise cameo in high relief depicting Livia holding a bust of a laurel-crowned Augustus (fig. 1).

Jewelry by New England artists, especially those with a connection to Boston, is well represented in the Museum's collection. Some of the earliest works date to the eighteenth century and include portrait miniatures, mourning jewelry, sleeve buttons, and shoe buckles. One prized object is an oval gold frame with a miniature of Rachel Walker Revere, second wife of silversmith Paul Revere Jr. (fig. 2). The portrait is attributed to Joseph Dunkerly, a noted Boston miniaturist who rented his house in North Square from Revere. The celebrated silversmith also occasionally made jewelry, especially for friends and family. He made his wife's simple gold wedding ring, which bears the engraved inscription "Live Contented" inside the band (fig. 3).

Fig. 2. Miniature portrait of Mrs. Paul Revere (Rachel Walker) mounted as a pendant; painting attributed to Joseph Dunkerly (American, active 1784–1788), about 1784, gold and watercolor on ivory.

Fig. 3. Wedding ring, Paul Revere Jr. (American, 1734–1818), 1773, gold.

Boston led the nation in developing and disseminating the aesthetic ideals of the arts and crafts movement in the late nineteenth century. Inspired by artists in Great Britain and supported by local educators such as Harvard University's Charles Eliot Norton (the first professor of fine arts in the United States), craftsmen in the city and its environs strove for harmony, balance, and simplicity in the arts, including the art of the jeweler. Norton was the catalyst for the formation of the Boston Arts and Crafts Society, a group of educators, collectors, architects, and artisans dedicated to design reform and high-quality handicraft (fig. 4).

Many of the ideals espoused by arts and crafts artists resonate with studio jewelers, artists who typically create one-of-a-kind ornaments by hand in their own studios. The Museum has an extensive collection of studio jewelry from the beginning of the movement in the 1940s to the present day. Most of the holdings in this area are the result of a generous gift (approximately 650 pieces) from Daphne Farago, a passionate collector of contemporary craft. The Farago collection of studio jewelry is the finest of its kind in the United States and includes artist-designed ornaments by Alexander Calder and Harry Bertoia, and seminal works by Art Smith, Sam Kramer, and Margaret De Patta, all early proponents of the movement. Jewelry by Margret Craver, John Paul Miller, and Mary Lee Hu (fig. 5) demonstrates extraordinary mastery of material and technique, and ornaments by conceptual artists such as Robert Ebendorf, Otto Künzli, and Lisa Gralnick are

Fig. 4 . Brooch, Josephine Hartwell Shaw (American, 1865–1941), about 1913, gold and blister pearl.

FACING PAGE

Fig. 5 . *Choker #48*, Mary Lee Hu (American, born 1943), 1979, gold, silver, and lacquered copper.

thought-provoking works that explore the themes of memory, nostalgia, and spirituality with nontraditional jewelry forms and materials.

The MFA's collection of twentieth- and twenty-first-century adornments also includes costume and haute couture jewelry by Coco Chanel, Elsa Schiaparelli, Hattie Carnegie, Miriam Haskell, Arnold Scaasi, Kenneth Jay Lane, Gucci, Butler and Wilson, and Sobral. Typically made of nonprecious materials, these ornaments are imaginative, whimsical, and playful, and often complement the designer's clothing lines. Indeed, many of the artists who design such jewelry see their work as an extension of their fashion design. Like clothing, jewelry has the capacity to communicate messages about the wearer. A socialite's luxury brand necklace, a priest's pendant cross, and a rapper's bling differ in shape and significance, but all of them signal information about the personality, social status, and beliefs of the owner.

Over the past few decades, jewelry exhibitions, galleries dedicated to jewelry, and jewelry curatorships have all contributed to the elevation of jewelry's status among the decorative arts. As part of museum collections, jewelry may be seen with other objects and understood within the cultural context in which it was created and worn. Our appreciation of portraiture, sculpture, and costume deepens in turn. Today, because jewelry created in one part of the globe may be distributed and worn in another, the medium offers insights into global consumerism and the mass appeal of specific forms and materials. Unlike some art practices whose future is uncertain, jewelry will continue to be made and worn by all strata of society.

Magical Jewels

IN THE ANCIENT WORLD, people wore adornments imbued with supernatural powers to shield themselves from potential harm, illness, and malevolent forces. Rites of passage represented particularly vulnerable points in a person's life, requiring special ornaments that could provide the wearer with magical protection. In many cultures, amuletic jewels played an important role among funerary objects accompanying the dead to the grave because they offered aid and security during the perilous journey to the afterlife.

Some of the earliest known talismanic ornaments come from ancient Egypt. Their appearance, meaning, and use are mentioned in various texts, including the *Book of the Dead,* a collection of spells, instructions, and magical formulas for the coffin or burial chamber of the deceased. Magical jewels recovered from Egyptian tombs reveal an impressive range of forms and materials. One necklace from a tomb in Sheikh Farag (Upper Egypt) gleams with an array of gold charms, including a sphinx, a falcon, several stylized *wadjet* eyes, and an image of the god Heh, all meant to ensure its owner's well-being (fig. 6). The sacred wadjet eye, one of the most common Egyptian amulets, was believed to endow its wearer with healing and restorative powers. The small Heh pendant of a kneeling man holding the hieroglyph for "year" ensured eternal life. Both the sphinx and the falcon invoked the cosmic power of the sun god and the king. The gold was believed to promote longevity, transferring its noncorrosive qualities to the wearer.

Other ancient cultures attributed different jewelry materials with magical qualities. In a pair of Mayan ear flares made of sacred jadeite, for example, the green color symbolized both the maize plant and water, key elements from which the gods created human life. The ornaments' shape added another layer of meaning, for once inserted into the earlobes, they served as conduits for spiritual energy and as portals to the supernatural. The face of each ear flare, which resembles a funnel or trumpet, is front heavy, so the wearer had to thread a counterweight composed of a long, hollow cylinder and an ovoid bead through the flare to secure the ornament.

Organic materials also provided protective powers in many cultures throughout the centuries. Amber could cure a number of somatic maladies and shield travelers, where-

FACING PAGE

Statue of a bodhisattva, Gandharan, Northwestern Pakistan, late 2nd century, gray schist.

Among this statue's many jewels is a strand of amulets worn diagonally across the torso.

Fig. 6. Beaded collar with amulets, Egyptian, 2061–1640 B.C., glazed steatite, gold, and electrum.

The ancient Egyptians wore amulets made out of materials believed to have protective powers.

as coral was particularly propitious in safeguarding children against illness. For that reason, in both Europe and North America, coral has been given as a traditional christening present—a bead or branch-coral necklace for a girl and a silver and coral rattle for a boy. Certain minerals were also invested with magical powers. Jet (a form of coal), for example, has been believed to neutralize the earth's negative energies across many different cultures.

Some cultures maintained that an animal's exceptional qualities could be transferred to a person by wearing its tooth or claw. In India tiger claws were prized for their ability to enhance the strength and fierceness of the wearer. Sometimes simply having the form of an animal gave an ornament power, as in the case of Mayan jaguar-teeth pendants fabricated from jadeite.

Medieval and Renaissance-period Europeans believed that a number of hard stones had magical capabilities. The twelfth-century bishop of Rennes declared that sapphires were virtuous stones that could act as antidotes for poisonings or the plague when worn as jewelry. Star sapphires warded off the malicious intents of others ("the evil eye"), a role played by agates in the ancient world. All varieties of ruby affected an owner's mental health in a positive way, removing unwanted thoughts and controlling physical desires. The emerald endowed the wearer with the foresight to avoid harm. The king of all gems, the diamond, has always symbolized fearlessness, invincibility, and eternity, attributes derived from the stone's hardness and transparent purity. Purity was also ascribed to rock crystal, a stone believed to come from cold mountain-cave waters. Part of crystal's allure is that it looks like water to the eye but is hard and cold to the touch.

A unique form of the magical jewel is the reliquary pendant, which typically contains potent substances such as sacred texts, the cremated ashes of a religious leader, or a bone fragment or piece of clothing belonging to a saint. The form can be a simple container or an elaborate jewel. In one medieval mandorla-shaped reliquary pendant, a crystal oval is set within a square embellished by four cabochon sapphires, with the mandorla motif repeating harmoniously to the outer edge. Under the crystal lies a foil or cloth lining for the relic, in this case a bone fragment (fig. 7).

Other religious ornaments, including pilgrim badges, rosaries, and decade rings, serve as visible symbols of faith or as devotional aids. Pilgrim badges gained popularity during the Middle Ages in Europe, and people wore them on hats, clothing, and around the neck. Mass-produced and typically made of nonprecious materials, badges attested to personal piety and indicated that the wearer had been on a pilgrimage to a saint's shrine. Decorated with emblems and saints' images, the badges also protected the owner in time of illness or danger.

Sacred rosaries have been worn and used by devotees of all major religions. Most take the form of prayer beads, with each bead representing a single prayer or sacred incantation. In Roman Catholicism, prayers recited with a rosary consist of repeated sequences of the Lord's Prayer followed by ten recitations of the Hail Mary and a single recital of the Glory Be to the Father prayer. Each sequence is known as a "decade." During the Middle Ages the faithful wore decade rings with ten knobs along the shank, each knob representing a separate rosary decade to facilitate prayer throughout the day.

Since the Enlightenment, Western cultures have paid less and less attention to jewelry's magical attributes, although people still wear birthstone rings, zodiac ornaments, and good-luck tokens such as miniature horse shoes. Several contemporary studio jewelers have created intellectually provocative and playful works that express their awareness of jewelry's historically mystical role. Unlike magical jewels of earlier times intended to safeguard and protect, these new ornaments create a dialogue between maker, wearer, and viewer about human traits.

Fig. 7. Reliquary pendant, Meuse (Germany), third quarter of the 12th century, gilt copper, vernis brun, sapphire, wood, rock crystal, and bone.

Roman Catholic reliquaries contain saints' relics, such as fragments of bone and clothing.

Pectoral

Egyptian, Dynasties 13–17, about 1783–1550 B.C.
Possibly from Thebes
Gold, silver, carnelian, and glass
11.2 × 36.5 × 0.5 cm (4 7/16 × 14 3/8 × 3/16 in.)
Egyptian Special Purchase Fund, William Francis Warden Fund, Florence E. and Horace L. Mayer Fund 1981.159

This remarkable funerary ornament depicts an Egyptian vulture with outstretched wings. In its talons it grasps two *shen* signs, symbols of the universal power of the king. The vulture represents Nekhbet, the goddess of Upper Egypt, and the rearing cobra to the left of the bird's body is associated with Wadjet, a deity of Lower Egypt. Together the emblems protected the king and represented his dominance over the northern and southern parts of the land.[1]

The ornament probably dates to the Second Intermediate period when the Hyksos, a Canaanite group in Western Asia, expanded their power base into the Egyptian delta and forced the Egyptians to remove their seat of power to Thebes in the south. In that time of turmoil, lower-ranking officials were able to adopt symbols previously reserved for royalty for their own funerary equipment. This pectoral may have belonged to a provincial governor or some other local ruler from that period.

The pectoral is constructed in three segments, each having a silver back plate to which strips of silver were soldered and later sheathed with gold foil. The back plates forming the wings curve downward, probably to accommodate the arc of the mummy or coffin lid on which it was placed when its owner was interred.

More than four hundred pieces of carnelian and colored glass inlay fill the cloisons (partitions), formed by the gold-sheathed silver strips. The carnelian inlays were cut to fit the tips of the tail feathers, the auxiliary and secondary feathers, and the centers of the shen signs. The dark purple glass was inlaid in a semimolten state and may represent early experiments in glass.[2] Both the purple and the light blue inlays have largely deteriorated. They may have been created in imitation of lapis lazuli and turquoise, thus completing the symbolic trilogy of colors (red carnelian, blue-green turquoise, and deep blue lapis) typically found in Egyptian jewelry.[3] The colors represent blood and strength, vegetation, and the revitalizing Nile.

1. Rita E. Freed, Lawrence M. Berman, and Denise M. Doxey, *MFA Highlights: Arts of Ancient Egypt* (Boston: MFA Publications, 2003), 146.

2. See Richard Newman, "Technical Examination of an Ancient Egyptian Royal Pectoral," *Journal of the Museum of Fine Arts, Boston* 2 (1990): 31–32. Glass was thought to have been introduced to Egypt from East Asia during the New Kingdom (1550–1070 B.C.), but this pectoral raises questions about glass experiments in Egypt before then, during the Second Intermediate Period.

3. Peter Lacovara, "An Ancient Egyptian Royal Pectoral," *Journal of the Museum of Fine Arts, Boston* 2 (1990): 21.

Necklace with cylindrical amulet case

Nubian, Classic Kerma, about 1770–1550 B.C.
Tomb K 1067
Silver, carnelian, rock crystal, and faience
L. of necklace: 24.5 cm (9⅝ in.), h. of pendant: 5 cm (1 15/16 in.)
Harvard University–Boston Museum of Fine Arts Expedition 13.3969

The histories of ancient Egypt and Nubia were intricately connected. Nubia, Egypt's neighbor to the south, often served as a vassal state during Egypt's golden ages and then gained ascendancy when central authority in Egypt declined. This power shift occurred during the eighteenth century B.C., when a series of weak Egyptian kings coincided with the emergence of a powerful Nubian kingdom at Kerma, a settlement located in a rich, fertile bend of the Nile south of the Third Cataract.[1]

When the Museum of Fine Arts, Boston, and Harvard University formed a joint expedition to excavate at Kerma, the team discovered many ornaments demonstrating a lively trade with Egypt. For example, this necklace, found in an intact male burial, contains blue faience stars and a cylindrical silver amulet case made in Egypt and carnelian and blue-glazed quartz beads made locally.[2] Aside from its possible magical significance, this particular amulet case may have been worn in Nubia as an exotic Egyptian import to demonstrate the elevated status of its owner.

Like the Egyptians, Kerma's ruling elite valued hard stones such as carnelian, which was readily available in the Nile Valley and was often used to create amulets and beads. Unique to Kerma was the popularity of bright blue glazed quartz beads, which are dazzling when held up to the light. The beads took considerable skill to produce, as the application of heat during the glazing process caused many of them to crack. Scholars continue to ponder why these ancient peoples invested so much time and effort creating such adornments when they had easier access to other blue materials, especially blue faience, a man-made, quartz-based ceramic that Kerma residents both imported and produced. The ancient Nubians may have believed that quartz was imbued with magical properties, possibly as a result of its mining association with gold, a substance with deep religious significance and the lifeblood of the Nubian economy. By the second millennium B.C., Egypt's southern neighbor was an important source of gold in the ancient world. The precious metal was closely tied to the land's political identity and economic prosperity.

1. Joyce L. Haynes, *Nubia: Ancient Kingdoms of Africa* (Boston: Museum of Fine Arts, 1992), 20.

2. Yvonne J. Markowitz, "Nubian Adornment," in *Ancient Nubia: African Kingdoms of the Nile*, ed. Marjorie Fisher, Peter Lacovara, Sue D'Auria, and Salima Ikram (Cairo: American University in Cairo Press, 2011), forthcoming.

Portrait mask

Olmec, early to middle Formative period, 1150–550 B.C.
Veracruz or Tabasco, Mexico
Jadeite with black inclusions (fire-grayed)
21.6 × 19.4 × 5.5 cm (8½ × 7⅔ × 2¼ in.)
Gift of Landon T. Clay 1991.968

Carved jadeite masks are unique to the ancient Olmec civilization, which once occupied the southern Gulf coast of Mexico in today's states of Veracruz and Tabasco. This outstanding example in green jadeite shows a life-size square head, triangular nose, and protruding lips, all features characteristic of Olmec art. Its bold expression is similar to those of colossal heads representing Olmec rulers found at San Lorenzo.[1] Because the mask is hollow and perforated at the eyes and mouth, some scholars believe it was worn during ceremonies or placed on a deceased person's face at the time of burial.[2]

In Olmec culture, green jadeite was a prized material associated with growth, renewal, and rejuvenation. The Olmec people traveled some three hundred miles to collect it from the Motagua River Valley in Guatemala. Jadeite is a dense, fibrous stone that is difficult to carve, particularly because Olmec craftsmen lacked metal tools and relied solely on abrasive powders to shape it.[3] Unfortunately, none of the known masks from Olmec sites have been scientifically excavated, making their use and meaning open to interpretation.

1. Michael D. Coe et al., *The Olmec World: Ritual and Rulership* (Princeton, N.J.: Art Museum, Princeton University, 1996), 156–57, no. 31.

2. Gilian Shallcross Wohlauer, with an introduction by Malcolm Rogers, *MFA: A Guide to the Collection of the Museum of Fine Arts, Boston* (Boston: Museum of Fine Arts, 1999), 278.

3. Dorie Reents-Budet and Heather Hole, "America's First Art," in *A New World Imagined: Art of the Americas*, ed. Elliot Bostwick Davis, Dennis Carr, Nonie Gadsden, Cody Hartley, Erica E. Hirshler, Heather Hole, Kelly H. L'Ecuyer, Karen E. Quinn, Dorie Reents-Budet, and Gerald W. R. Ward (Boston: MFA Publications, 2010), 10.

Pendant necklace

Egyptian, Dynasties 21–24, about 1070–712 B.C.
Gold with glass inlays
Length of loop-in-loop double chain: 60 cm (23⅔ in.)
Pendant: 7.1 × 2.5 × 0.6 cm (2 13/16 × 1 × ¼ in.)
Gift of Mrs. Horace L. Mayer 68.836

Several ancient Egyptian creation myths explain how the universe was formed. One myth associated with the middle Egyptian city of Hermopolis describes how a blue lotus emerged from Nun, the chaotic primeval waters, on the first morning. The petals of the blossom slowly unfolded to reveal the resplendent body of the young sun god. He wore a small rearing cobra on his forehead, identifying him as a king, and a sidelock of hair indicating his tender age.[1]

This pendant depicts the young god in profile enthroned on the lotus. The flower's petals once contained colored glass or stone inlays, as did the figure's elaborate broad collar, the counterpoise at the rear of his neck, and his sidelock. The now-missing inlays were probably carved out of thin slabs of semiprecious stone or colored glass, and then secured in place by organic glues. Their colors would most likely have been red-orange, blue-green, and deep blue, symbolizing blood and strength, vegetation, and the revitalizing Nile River.

Like many Egyptian adornments, the pendant is made of gold sheet, cut and shaped over a form. The facial features are finely chased, and the contours of the figure and blossom continue on the reverse of the jewel. The extension of the image to the back may represent an attempt on the part of the artist to enhance its amuletic efficacy.

The double loop-in-loop-style chain on this necklace is connected to the pendant by two tapering terminals attached by hoops on the reverse. The method of manufacture and the compactness of the weave give the chain a square shape, providing greater strength and durability than would a single-weave chain.[2] Its sturdiness suggests that the ornament was meant to be worn in life as well as in the afterlife.

1. Rita E. Freed, Lawrence M. Berman, and Denise M. Doxey, *MFA Highlights: Arts of Ancient Egypt* (Boston: MFA Publications, 2003), 174.

2. Jean Reist Stark and Josephine Reist Smith, *Classical Loop-in-Loop Chains and Their Derivatives* (New York: Chapman and Hall, 1997), 66.

Hathor-headed crystal pendant

Nubian, Napatan period, reign of King Piye (743–712 B.C.)
El-Kurru, tomb Ku 55
Gold and rock crystal
H. 5.4 cm, diam. 3.3 cm (H. 2⅛ in., diam. 1 5/16 in.)
Harvard University–Boston Museum of Fine Arts Expedition 21.321

The head of Hathor surmounts this rock-crystal jewel containing a cylindrical gold amulet case. Beloved in both Egypt and neighboring Nubia as a nurturing goddess associated with love, beauty, and music, Hathor offered protection to women throughout their adult lives. Although we do not know how or why amulet cases were worn in Nubia, where this jewel was found, we know that beginning in the Middle Kingdom (2040–1640 B.C.), cylindrical amulet cases in Egypt were worn exclusively by women, perhaps to enhance their fertility. Women may have even handed down such jewelry from mother to daughter as heirlooms.[1]

During the eighth century B.C., the kings of Nubia's Kushite Dynasty presented themselves in the manner of Egyptian pharaohs and adopted many aspects of Egyptian religion. Because the Kushite elite of this period worshiped Egyptian gods and followed Egyptian funerary practices, they sometimes included objects of Egyptian origin in their burials. This jewel was excavated from the tomb of a queen of King Piye, the ruler of the Kushite Dynasty who made his way north to the Egyptian delta, conquered all of the Nile Valley, and brought peace and stability to both Egypt and Nubia about 750 B.C. Several jewels from this burial are thought to be Egyptian in origin.

The rock-crystal orb surrounding the golden tubular element of this amulet case is rare—only one other amulet case embedded in crystal is known to exist, and it too was recovered from the same queen's tomb.[2] Rock crystal was a prized material in ancient Nubia, perhaps because gold, a substance associated with the sun god Amun, is mined from beds of quartz. Quartz crystal may therefore have been seen to embody some of his powers.

1. An Egyptian example in the Brooklyn Museum containing garnet pebbles, red stones associated with the goddess Isis, strengthens the argument that such cases were worn by women; see Hans Wolfgang Müller and Eberhard Thiem, *Gold of the Pharaohs* (Ithaca, N.Y.: Cornell University Press, 1998), 94–95.

2. The other cylindrical amulet case has a rock-crystal surround in the form of an eight-sided fluted column surmounted by a ram's head. Similar cases, minus the rock-crystal encasement, have been found at Tharros, near Sardinia, Italy; see Sabatino Moscati, *The Phoenicians* (New York: Abbeville, 1988), 692, no. 643.

Rosette

East Greek, archaic period, 660–640 B.C.
Probably from Rhodes (Kamiros)
Gold
H. 2.5 cm, diam. 4.3 cm (H. 1 in., diam. 1¹¹⁄₁₆ in.)
Henry Lillie Pierce Fund 99.279

The Greek island of Rhodes is located off the southwestern tip of Asia Minor, where the Aegean Sea meets the Mediterranean. Throughout early Rhodes's history, the island's culture, including the forms, fabrication techniques, and iconography of jewelry, was influenced by the cultures of Crete, Cyprus, Syria, Phoenicia, and Anatolia, which surround it. The head of the griffin in the center of this rosette, for example, is related to griffins depicted in the throne room of the palace of Knossos in Crete. With the body of a lion and the head and wings of an eagle, griffins were believed to be powerful, protective creatures.

Jewelry from ancient Rhodes comes in many forms, such as funerary bands with geometric patterns, diadems with rosettes, spiral earrings, necklaces with lions' heads, circular pendants with large suspension hoops (bails), rectangular pendant plaques with images of the mythical Mistress of the Animals, embossed pectorals, animal head bracelets, and decorative clothing appliqués.[1] This rosette has six larger petals decorated with raised smaller ones with granulated details. The elevation of each of these floral elements was achieved by means of a truncated hollow tube secured to both the petal and the underside of the rosette. This ornament and others like it from the nearby island of Melos may have been attached to a diadem of cloth or leather.[2]

1. Reynold Higgins, *Greek and Roman Jewellery* (Berkeley: University of California Press, 1980), 111–18.

2. Angelos Delivorrios, "Jewellery in Ancient Greek and Roman Times," in *Greek Jewellery from the Benaki Museum Collections*, ed. Alexandra Daumas (Athens: Adam Editions, 1999), 92. An example in the British Museum has a runner on the back of the rosette that would have served as the point of attachment; see Hugh Tait, *Jewellery: 7,000 Years* (New York: Harry N. Abrams, 1984), 59–60.

Earring

Achaemenid, 5th century B.C.
Western Asia (Iran)
Gold, lapis lazuli, turquoise, and carnelian
D. 3 cm, diam. 5.1 cm (d. 1³⁄₁₆ in., diam. 2 in.)
Edward J. and Mary S. Holmes Fund 1971.256

The winged figure featured on the central disk of this elaborately crafted earring may represent Ahura Mazda, a Persian creation god associated with the Zoroastrian principles of moral authority and cosmic order. Six smaller disks, three on each side of the central one, show the god rising from a crescent moon. The seventh circle at the bottom encloses a lotus blossom, also emerging from a crescent. The same design is repeated on the reverse so that the entire jewel gleams with about 250 inlays.[1]

The earring reflects the sophisticated nature of goldsmithing in ancient Iran under Achaemenid rule (also known as the Persian Empire, 550–330 B.C.). The lapis lazuli, turquoise, and carnelian inlays in Achaemenid bracelets, torques, and earrings are similar in many ways to the colorful glazed-brick decoration that embellished the Persian palace complex at Susa. For the building, the Persian craftsmen developed a cloisonné technique in which they set enamel glazes in partitions set on the surface of siliceous bricks. Jewelers soldered metal strips to gold sheets to create cloisons. They filled the shallow cavities with carved slices of semiprecious stones, some imported from Afghanistan and the Sinai.

During the sixth century B.C., Cyrus the Great, an early Achaemenid king, united the various peoples of Iran into a single national entity with an administrative center at Pasargadae in Fars (southwestern Iran). In addition to consolidating power and building a sophisticated military, Cyrus erected monumental complexes that were strongly influenced by the Ionian Greeks as well as Elamite and Mesopotamian traditions. By the time Darius I, the third king of the Achaemenids, came to power, the empire extended over three continents, bringing the entire ancient Near East under Persian rule. A uniquely Persian art evolved under Darius's leadership, as evidenced in the art and architecture of the cities he rebuilt at Persepolis and Susa.[2]

1. The mate to this earring is part of the Norbert Schimmel Collection; see Oscar White Muscarella, ed., *Ancient Art: The Norbert Schimmel Collection* (Mainz: Verlag Philipp von Zabern, 1974), no. 156.

2. Prudence O. Harper, Joan Aruz, and Françoise Tallon, *The Royal City of Susa: Ancient Near Eastern Treasures in the Louvre* (New York: Metropolitan Museum of Art, 1992), 13–15.

Earring with Nike driving a two-horse chariot

Northern Greek, 350–325 B.C.
Gold
H. 5 cm (1 15/16 in.)
Henry Lillie Pierce Fund 98.788

A masterpiece of the goldsmith's art, this earring features Nike, the goddess of victory, driving a two-horse chariot. Charioteer imagery dates back to pre-Hellenic art in Crete, which frequently depicted a chariot transporting deceased souls to the netherworld. In later Greek myths the chariot carried the gods to the heavens.

Modeled in the round, the figures form a pendant under a disk in the shape of a honeysuckle palmette. The goddess leans forward, her left hand reining in the horses so their front legs rear up with tangible force. Nike wears a belted chiton, a full skirt, and jewelry. Her elegant upraised wings add dash and verve as well as a harmonious counterbalance to the composition. The depiction of Nike's dynamism, determination, and speed is of such high workmanship that the jeweler may also have been a sculptor.[1] Given its size and quality, the earring probably adorned a royal person or a cult statue.

Similar to other jewels from antiquity, individual elements soldered together compose this one; in this case the number of parts exceeds one hundred. The figures are superbly modeled from gold sheet with further wirework embellishments and small decorative gold balls. Nike's facial features are crisp, her expression resolute. The horses appear strained and tense, while the goddess's finely chased feathery wings offset the bold and powerful interplay between the figures.

The honeysuckle palmette is a concave oval disk with curved petals and circular stamens outlined with fine twisted wires. Traces of enamel remain on several stamens, and a tear-shaped fruit encrusted with dense gold granulation and bordered by a decorative wire rests in the blossom's center.[2] A snake-head hoop on the jewel's underside most likely was attached to an ear wire that is now missing.

1. Similar motifs appear on a pair of Siren earrings and a Ganymede ornament in the Metropolitan Museum of Art; see Dyfri Williams and Jack Ogden, *Greek Gold: Jewellery of the Classical World* (New York: Harry N. Abrams and the Metropolitan Museum of Art, 1994), 44; Herbert Hoffman and Patricia F. Davidson, *Greek Gold: Jewelry from the Age of Alexander* (Brooklyn, N.Y.: Brooklyn Museum, 1965), 76–81.

2. Berta Segall, "The Earring with Winged Charioteer in the Classical Department," *Bulletin of the Museum of Fine Arts, Boston* 40 (1942): 50.

Diadem with Heracles knot

Greek, Hellenistic period, about 200–150 B.C.
Gold and garnet
H. 5.5 cm, l. 47.5 cm, d. 0.6 cm (H. 2³⁄16 in., l. 18¹¹⁄16 in., d. ¼ in.)
Edward J. and Mary S. Holmes Fund 1971.211

Large quantities of gold were available to Greek metalsmiths as a result of Alexander the Great's eastern conquests. This gold and garnet head ornament is an outstanding example of the level of sophistication those craftsmen achieved. Its Heracles-knot design was secured to the head by two eye-and-hoop fasteners attached to terminals at the ends of the straps. Similar diadems had ribbons that were fastened over a high coiffure.

The knot of Heracles originated in Middle Kingdom Egypt (2040–about 1640 B.C.), where it symbolized the unity of Upper and Lower Egypt and frequently appeared as an ornamental clasp. The Hellenistic Greeks (323–146 B.C.) rediscovered the motif and endowed it with the power to heal wounds. The Greeks also associated the knot with marriage, for a bride could secure her wedding garment with it only to allow her groom to later untie it.[1] In that case the knot embodied both male power and the binding power of marriage.

This exquisitely crafted example is flanked by capital-shaped gold plates decorated with garlands of pointed leaves surrounding a rosette originally embellished by a cabochon garnet. Both the knot and the plates are further adorned with garnet and ball-bead pendants suspended by delicate chains and capped by gold rosettes with filigree decoration.

1. See Cyril Aldred, *Jewels of the Pharaohs: Egyptian Jewelry of the Dynastic Period* (London: Thames and Hudson, 1971), 190–92, 195–96, nos. 34, 36, and 44; Anne Garside, ed., *Jewelry: Ancient to Modern* (New York: Viking Press in cooperation with the Walters Art Gallery, 1979), 87; and Dyfri Williams and Jack Ogden, *Greek Gold: Jewellery of the Classical World* (New York: Harry N. Abrams and the Metropolitan Museum of Art, 1994), 8.

Bracelet

Nubian, Meroitic period, about 100 B.C.
Gebel Barkal, Pyramid 8
Gold and enamel
H. 1.8 cm, l. 12.5 cm, d. 0.2 cm (H. 11/16 in., l. 4 15/16 in., d. 1/16 in.)
Harvard University–Boston Museum of Fine Arts Expedition 20.333

For centuries the ancient Nubian site Gebel Barkal (in Sudan, on a bend of the Nile River) served as an important religious center. The area includes the sun god Amun's sacred mountain and associated temple complex and royal cemetery. Although the cemetery was transferred to Meröe about 270 B.C., Nubia's elite continued to worship at Gebel Barkal for nearly two centuries.[1]

Despite having been plundered during ancient times, Pyramid 8 in Gebel Barkal still held this exceptional gold and enamel bracelet bearing the goddess Hathor's profile when it was excavated by the Harvard University–Boston Museum of Fine Arts Expedition in 1920.[2] The expedition team found this jewel, which may have been one of a pair, amid debris on the coffin bench in the tomb of a female member of the Meroitic royal family. Indeed, Hathor was popular among women in both ancient Nubia and Egypt. She was worshiped as a protector of women, especially during childbirth. Other artifacts recovered from Pyramid 8 include bronze and faience vessels, a bronze mirror, a bronze figure of Osiris (god of the underworld), and stone and faience beads.

The bracelet consists of three hinged segments with applied gold appliqués and colored enamels. The appliqués were made separately and soldered onto a gold-sheet substrate, thereby creating areas of raised relief. Some of the applied elements, such as the hair of the goddess, have chased ornamentation, adding texture to the overall design. Set into the negative spaces between the raised-relief gold work are enamels that reiterate the tricolor design scheme common in ancient Egypt, namely blue, green, and red-orange. The use of red enamel, which was very difficult to produce, is unique among known Meroitic jewels. Meröe had a sophisticated glass industry and experimented with glass formulas and enamels, including the application of clear enamel on gold-foil glass beads and colored enamels on glass vessels.

1. Steffen Wenig, *Africa in Antiquity II: The Arts of Ancient Nubia and the Sudan* (Brooklyn, N.Y.: Brooklyn Museum, 1978), 244.

2. Dows Dunham, *Royal Cemeteries of Kush IV: Royal Tombs at Meröe and Barkal* (Boston: Museum of Fine Arts, 1957), 59–62.

Signet ring

Nubian, Meroitic period, 185–10 B.C.
Meröe, Begarawiyah West, tomb W 333
Gold
Bezel: H. 1.2 cm, diam. 1.3 cm (H. ½ in., diam. ½ in.)
Shank: H. 2.2 cm, diam. 1.8 cm (H. ⅞ in., diam. 11⁄16 in.)
Harvard University–Boston Museum of Fine Arts Expedition 23.303

Signet ring

Nubian, Meroitic period, A.D. 90–246
Meröe, Begarawiyah West, tomb W 106
Gold
Bezel: H. 1.2 cm, diam. 1.5 cm (H. ½ in., diam. 9⁄16 in.)
Shank: H. 2.6 cm, diam. 2 cm (H. 1 in., diam. 13⁄16 in.)
Harvard University–Boston Museum of Fine Arts Expedition 24.568

In the 1830s the Italian-born military doctor and treasure hunter Giuseppe Ferlini unearthed a trove of outstanding jewels in the Meröe tomb of Queen Amanishakheto. Among the ornaments were nearly one hundred signet rings. When the archaeologist George A. Reisner excavated at Meröe in the early decades of the twentieth century with the Harvard University–Boston Museum of Fine Arts Expedition, he found several other tombs with similar rings. Both men and women of Meröe wore signet rings as powerful amuletic objects. Surviving temple reliefs in the area indicate that they could be worn seperately on several fingers or stacked on a single finger.

One example found by Reisner's team is a deeply cut intaglio bezel featuring four lions' heads arranged around a cobra holding up a sun disk. Although many Nubian deities derive from Egypt's pantheon of gods, the lion god Apetemak was indigenous to Nubia's religion. He was worshiped in many temples in and near Meröe for delivering enemies to the king and for his ties to Amun, the imperial god of ancient Meröe.[1]

Reisner's team found another signet ring in a plundered tomb containing archers' artifacts. This one shows a circular intaglio bezel with a vulture standing on a cobra. The vulture represents the Upper Egyptian goddess Nekhbet, and the cobra represents the Lower Egyptian goddess Wadjet. When shown together, these goddesses symbolized the renewable cycle of life and death.

1. Karl-Heinz Priese, *The Gold of Meröe* (New York: Metropolitan Museum of Art, 1992), 40–41.

Ring in the form of a rearing cobra

Nubian, Meroitic period, A.D. 30–175
Meröe, Begarawiyah West, tomb 179
Silver
H. 3.3 cm, diam. 1.9 cm (H. 1 5/16, diam. 3/4 in.)
Harvard University–Boston Museum of Fine Arts Expedition 24.515

The man who wore this hand-wrought silver ring to his grave was bedecked with jewels, including five other finger rings. Three of the others were three-dimensional like this one, with either a ram's head or a cobra, both royal and protective symbols. The remaining two rings were of the signet variety. This ornament was found on the deceased's right hand.[1]

Crafted from heavy silver sheet, the surface of the snake's hood has three pairs of recesses, the floors of which show tool marks. These marks suggest that the cells were carved out with a metal graver. The deep furrow outlining the cells is also consistent with the technique of engraving (removing metal) as opposed to chasing (indenting). The inlays that once filled these cells are believed to have been made by champlevé enameling. If so, they would have been among the earliest examples of champlevé enamelwork in the ancient world.[2] Meroitic craftsmen were masters of glass and enamel technology at the end of the first century B.C. Far more innovative than their Egyptian counterparts at that time, their accomplishments also included cloisonné, filigree, repoussé, en plein, and *en résille* enameling.

1. For a detailed description of this tomb and its contents, see Dows Dunham, *The West and South Cemeteries at Meröe, Royal Cemeteries of Kush* 5 (Boston: Museum of Fine Arts, 1963), 177–88.

2. Yvonne Markowitz, "A Silver Uraeus Ring from Meröe," in *Studies in Honor of William Kelly Simpson* 2, ed. Peter Der Manuelian (Boston: Museum of Fine Arts, 1996), 590–91.

Harsaphes amulet

Egyptian, Dynasty 25, 754–720 B.C.
Temple at Ehnasya el-Medina
Gold
6 × 0.7 × 1.7 cm (2⅜ × ¼ × 11/16 in.)
Egypt Exploration Fund by subscription 06.2408

Herakleopolis (today's Ehnasya el-Medina) served as the seat of ancient Egypt's government during the First Intermediate period (2250–2061 B.C.). It was also the site of later building projects, most notably a major rebuilding program undertaken during the reign of Ramesses II (1279–1213 B.C.). During the eighth century B.C., Kushites, led by King Piye, invaded Egypt from the south in a successful campaign to extend their sphere of influence. They were assisted in their efforts by Neferkare Peftjauawybast, the local king of Herakleopolis.

The base of this exquisite small statuette is incised underneath with three vertical rows of hieroglyphs designating Neferkare Peftjauawybast as "beloved of Harsaphes" and ruler of the lands east and west of the city.[1] Harsaphes was a creator and fertility god sometimes identified with the sun god Re. Cast in a two-part mold by the lost-wax process, the ram-headed deity is shown in a traditional striding posture with his arms at his sides. He wears the white crown with double plumes associated with Osiris, the god of the underworld. The pillar behind the deity has a bail, indicating that the statuette was made to be worn as an amulet. Wear on the inside of the bail points to the likelihood that the amulet was worn in life. The solid casting is unusual; most Egyptian ornaments made of gold were hollow and assembled from sheet metal or fashioned on top of a nonprecious core material.

Sir Williams Flinders Petrie, an English pioneer in applying scientific methodology to archaeology, recovered this amulet from the remains of the hypostyle hall of the temple at Herakleopolis in 1904.[2] Its location suggests that it was a votive offering.

1. Yvonne J. Markowitz, "Harsaphes Amulet," in *Art of the Ancient Mediterranean World*, ed. John Herrmann et al. (Nagoya, Japan: Nagoya/Boston Museum of Fine Arts, 1999), 99, no. 130.

2. W. M. Flinders Petrie, *Ehnasya* (London: Egypt Exploration Fund, 1905), 18–19, pl. 1.

Amulet with Demeter, Harpocrates, and Persephone

Roman, Imperial period, 3rd century A.D.
Probably from Egypt
Gold
3.1 × 2.7 × 0.4 cm (1¼ × 1$\frac{1}{16}$ × $\frac{3}{16}$ in.)
Benjamin and Lucy Rowland Fund 1997.62

This late-Roman amulet features symbols with roots in classical Greek and Egyptian cultures for prosperity in this world and the next. On the left the Greek goddess of the harvest, Demeter, appears with a tall torch and a veiled head supporting a basket of grain, two symbols also associated with her in Egyptian art during Roman rule. On the right Persephone, the queen of the underworld, holds a scepter. The two ears of corn emerging from her head indicate her connection with Demeter (her mother) and seasonal agricultural cycles. The female deities flank the youthful god Harpocrates, a later incarnation of Horus, the Egyptian symbol of the living king. He is shown wearing the crown of Upper and Lower Egypt. The style of his cloak identifies him with the Greek hero Triptolemos, who sent Demeter to teach agriculture to the world.[1]

The amulet has its origins in an earlier Egyptian type known as the Osirian triad, in which the goddesses Isis and Nephthys hold hands and frame the figure of an unclothed, youthful Horus. The use of repoussé gold work for this Roman amulet represents a departure from Osirian triads, which were typically made of faience or cast bronze.[2] The loops attached to the back of this object indicate that it was worn around the neck suspended on a chain.

1. John J. Herrmann, "Amulet with Demeter, Harpokrates/Triptolemos, and Persephone," in *Art of the Ancient Mediterranean World,* ed. John Hermann et al. (Nagoya, Japan: Nagoya/Boston Museum of Fine Arts, 1999), 237.

2. They were often placed on the lower torso of a mummy; see Carol Andrews, *Amulets of Ancient Egypt* (London: Trustees of the British Museum Press, 1994), 49.

Shaman effigy pendant

Tairona culture, 1000–1300
Sierra Nevada de Santa Marta region, Magdalena Department, Colombia
Gold alloy
16 × 12.5 × 2 cm (6 5/16 × 4 15/16 × 13/16 in.)
Gift of Landon T. Clay 2000.813

The ancient Tairona peoples inhabited centralized villages in the Sierra Nevada de Santa Marta, near the Caribbean coast of Colombia. These local goldsmiths created a variety of jewelry from gold and gold alloys. This effigy pendant is cast in a copper and gold alloy called *tumbaga* using the lost-wax method. The exquisitely crafted figure, clutching two serpents, may represent a supernatural ancestor or a shaman in a state of spiritual transformation. He wears a bat-face mask and an elaborate headdress with two forward-facing birds and zoomorphic figures in profile on each side, and several pieces of jewelry, including a diadem, necklace, earrings, belt, and anklets.

Although settlement of the Sierra Nevada de Santa Marta near the gold-rich Don Diego, Duritaca, and Guachica rivers goes back to at least the first century A.D., it was during the eleventh century that the Tairona people developed interconnected towns characterized by roads, ceremonial buildings, irrigation canals, agricultural terraces, and houses with stone foundations.[1] The wide geographic area had different climates, so some places were dedicated to farming, and others became centers of textile and metal manufacturing. In these craft centers, goldsmiths produced beads, masks, earrings, breastplates, necklaces, pendants, bracelets, lip plugs, and nose and head ornaments.

1. André Emmerich, *Sweat of the Sun and Tears of the Moon: Gold and Silver in Pre-Columbian Art* (New York: Hacker Art Books, 1984), 79.

Sutra case

Korean, Goryeo dynasty, 11th–12th century
Gilt bronze
9 × 6.1 × 2.1 cm (3 9/16 × 2 3/8 × 7/16 in.)
Charles Bain Hoyt Fund 67.1

Buddhist sutras are canonical scriptures that describe the teachings of the historical Buddha, Gautama. This portable container from Korea once held such sacred texts. It has a bail at the top for a cord that may have been tied around a person's waist, and high-relief, repoussé decoration on both the front and back. A V-shaped lid on the front and a hinge along the top edge allow the case to open and close.[1] The artist chased six mantras, Sanskrit letters intoned as sacred incantations, against a decorative background into the metal on the upper part of the case under the lid.

The repoussé decoration depicts frolicking children in a lotus pond; both children and lotuses are associated in many Asian cultures with rebirth and the Buddhist paradise.[2] In the top front panel (which is also the lid to the case), a young boy with a lotus in his right hand plays in a pond surrounded by birds, plants, and waterfowl. Below, two boys with lotus blossoms romp with similar birds. Similar dynamic motifs embellish the container's back.[3] Buddhist monks copied the scriptures for devotees to wear and carry in cases such as this one.

1. Museum of Fine Arts, Boston, *Korean Art Collection at the Museum of Fine Arts, Boston* (Korea: National Research Institute of Cultural Heritage, 2004), 317, no. 351.

2. Ann Barrott Wicks et al., *Children in Chinese Art* (Honolulu: University of Hawaii Press, 2002), 6–15.

3. A similar sutra case is part of the National Museum of Korea collection (B12822); see Kumja Paik Kim, *Goryeo Dynasty: Korea's Age of Enlightenment, 918–1392* (San Francisco: San Francisco Asian Art Museum in cooperation with the National Museum of Korea and the Nara National Museum of Japan, 2003), 205, no. 64.

Triptych pendant depicting the martyrdom of Saint Barbara, Mary Magdalen, and Saint Gereon

Cologne, Germany, 1504
Silver gilt and enamel
7.2 × 3.6 × 0.7 cm (2 13/16 × 1 3/8 × 1/4 in.) when closed; w. 6.3 cm (2 1/2 in.) when open
1941 Purchase Fund 47.1450

The kneeling figure about to be beheaded in the center of this triptych pendant is Saint Barbara, the legendary third-century daughter of a wealthy pagan who reacted violently when she converted to Christianity.[1] The father was later struck down by lightning, and Barbara became a patron saint who protected people against lightning and sudden death. Wearing this luxurious miniature altar dedicated to Saint Barbara would have established its medieval owner as devout and pious and perhaps have placed her under the saint's protection.

When opened, the triptych reveals Mary Magdalene on the left and Saint Gereon on the right. Mary Magdalene wears her characteristic blue-green tunic over a red damask gown and holds her attribute, a vessel of ointment used on Christ's feet before his burial. Saint Gereon wears a red mantle over blue armor, a plumed hat, and pointed shoes. He too carries his attributes, in this case a sword, shield, and banner. Historical accounts say that Emperor Maximian executed Gereon in the early fourth century for his refusal to make a pagan sacrifice.

The wearer of this pendant was probably associated in some way with the city of Cologne, Germany. Saint Gereon has a basilica dedicated to him there, and Saint Barbara appears as one of six female martyred saints in *The Virgin and Child with Saints*, a triptych painted in Cologne about 1510 (now in the National Gallery of Australia).

The enamel technique used to create this jewel is known as basse-taille. It entails engraving or chasing a low-relief or intaglio design in gold or silver and then filling the spaces with powdered enamels, which are then fired in a kiln. This pendant used both opaque and translucent enamels. The metal is finely hatched in places where the clear enamels were applied over gold foil. The date 1504 has been engraved on the underside of the central element, and a bail at the bottom of it suggests that it may have once supported a pearl drop.

1. Hans Swarzenski and Nancy Netzer, *Catalogue of Medieval Objects in the Museum of Fine Arts, Boston: Enamels and Glass* (Boston: Museum of Fine Arts, 1986), 128–29, no. 45.

Rosary

Southern Germany, 17th century
Gilt silver, silver, amber, painted ivory, and glass
L. 65.5 cm (25 13/16 in.)
Bequest of William Arnold Buffum 02.224

Similar to other religious ornaments, rosaries manifest religious faith. They also serve the practical purpose of aiding a worshiper's memory during prayers that require the repetition of divine names and attributes. In their simplest form they may consist of a simple string of knots or beads.[1]

Throughout Europe's Middle Ages, people both inside and outside religious orders used rosaries to assist them in the recitation of the Lord's Prayer. Known as Pater Noster beads, each strand had 150 beads, with each bead representing a Psalm. By the mid-twelfth

century, prayer beads were also used for Ave Marias, recitations associated with the joys and sorrows of the Virgin, whose status and following greatly increased during the medieval period. Aves were deemed particularly suitable for women. In 1268 the Dominican Order sanctioned the mingling of Pater Noster and Ave prayer beads on rosaries, and by the fourteenth century, a common arrangement consisted of fifty Aves broken up into groups of ten called decades, separated by a larger Gloria bead, or gaud.[2]

Rosaries come in all varieties, from plastic or bone to precious metals and gemstones. From the fourteenth to the eighteenth century, amber's supposed talismanic powers and warm, tactile quality made it particularly popular. This exquisite amber and silver rosary consists of five decades of large, faceted amber beads for the recital of Ave Marias, separated by sixty-one smaller amber beads. Five silver filigree beads mark the beginning of each decade.

Completing this rosary is a circular gilt-silver filigree medallion featuring the Coronation of the Virgin suspended from a silver wirework cross and three large, faceted amber beads. The inscription "Patrona Bavaria" (patroness of Bavaria) appears along the medal's right edge, indicating the jewel's or the wearer's place of origin. The cult of Mary was especially strong in Bavaria, the heartland of the German Counter-Reformation. A profile image of a saint holding both a lily and the Christ Child appears on the back of the medal.[3] Two silver filigree gauds adorn the middle of the second and fourth decades. The front of the larger gaud shows a nun wearing a black-and-white habit; the back shows Saint Veronica's Napkin with the face of Christ. The smaller gaud has a central, oval medallion of gilt silver with images of the seated Madonna and Child on both the front and the back.

1. Winifred S. Blackman, "The Rosary in Magic and Religion," *Folklore* 29, no. 4 (December 30, 1918): 257.

2. See Joan Evans, *A History of Jewellery, 1100–1870* (Boston: Boston Book and Art, 1970), 77–78, for a discussion of the number and arrangement of beads during this period.

3. Bridget Heal, *The Cult of the Virgin Mary in Early Modern Germany: Protestant and Catholic Piety, 1500–1648* (Cambridge: Cambridge University Press, 2007), 189–91.

Pendant depicting the avatars of Vishnu

Rajasthani, early 18th century
North India, probably Jaipur
Gold, enamel, yellow sapphire, diamond, emerald, and ruby
4.9 × 4.8 × 0.4 cm (1 15/16 × 1 7/8 × 1 9/16 in.)
Otis Norcross Fund 39.764

The sacred Hindu text Bhagavad Gita describes the avatars (incarnations) of Vishnu, the Supreme God, as protectors of law and order and as being capable of destroying negative forces. On the reverse of this complex champlevé enamelwork pendant, one of the avatars, Krishna, is shown in the center giving advice to the warrior hero Arjuna. Surrounding this scene, starting in the upper register from the left, are other avatars: Narasimha appeased by Prahalada; Rama, his wife, Sita, and brother Lakshmana addressed by the monkey Hanuman; and the Jagannatha trio. From the top of the right edge

and proceeding clockwise are Matsya the fish and Kurma the tortoise, and then Bali and his wife and Kalki offering a pledge to Vamana, and then Kalki depicted with his white horse. Along the left edge are Parashurama with his ax at the bottom and the boar-headed avatar Varaha standing on the body of the demon Hiranyaksha at the top. A devotee of Krishna may have worn the pendant with the hope that it would place him under Krishna's protection.[1]

Europeans introduced decorative enameling to India during the sixteenth century. It became a specialty of northern India, where it gained popularity after the Mughal emperor Jalaluddin Muhammad Akbar sent an art delegation to Goa from 1575 to 1577 to learn from European masters. The earliest Indian enamels were opaque; translucent enamels were produced by the mid-seventeenth century.[2] Both types appear in this early-eighteenth-century pendant. The figures in the central panel are executed in opaque champlevé enamels, whereas their backdrop consists of transparent green enamel. The same technique was used in the border design, although the background there is an opaque white with transparent red, green, blue, and clear enamel highlights on the costumes of the sacred figures and the devotees.[3] Like many adornments from the Rajasthan region, the front of this jewel is set with precious gems in the *kundan* style. Floral shapes of diamond and emerald surround a faceted octagonal yellow sapphire against a ruby background.

1. Joan Cummins, ed., "Pendant Depicting the Avatars of Vishnu," in *Vishnu: Hinduism's Blue-Skinned Savior* (Nashville: Frist Center for the Visual Arts; Ahmedabad, India: Mapin Publishers, 2011), 122.

2. For a discussion of the European sources of north Indian enameling, see Manuel Keene, "The Enamel Road, from Siena, Paris, London and Lisbon, Leads to Lucknow," *Jewellery Studies* 10 (2004): 99–100; Michael Spink, *Islamic and Hindu Jewellery* (London: Spink & Son, 1998), 6.

3. Oppi Untracht, *Traditional Jewelry of India* (New York: Harry N. Abrams, 1997), 358–62, no. 786.

Necklace

Possibly northwest India, 19th century
Gold, resin, and cord
28 × 17 × 1.5 cm (11 × 6 11/16 × 9/16 in.)
Denman Waldo Ross Collection 19.350

According to a Hindu creation myth, the universe originated in a golden womb or egg. When it split in two, one half made of gold became the heavens, and the other half made of silver formed the earth. Hinduism therefore associates gold with the gods and the creation of the world. According to its traditions, gold has medicinal properties and the miraculous power to purify water, as well as the power to repel evil spirits when worn on the body.[1]

The amulet case is a popular form of gold jewelry in India. The earliest examples date to the first century B.C., but there are similar ornaments from the ancient Near East dating from Egypt's Middle Kingdom (2040–1640 B.C.). In India the shape, number of cases worn at one time, and nature of magical contents vary by region. Most common are containers enclosing religious texts and spells written on palm leaves or paper. In the past, even the illiterate were in awe of such written charms because they believed the words had the power to protect the wearer and control outside forces such as natural disasters and epidemics.

The four amulet cases on this necklace, two on each side of the central leaf-shaped element, are made of thin gold sheet, with repoussé decoration over a natural shellac core. The hollow forms are empty. Perhaps over the centuries the unique shapes of these pendants were imbued with amuletic powers without having to hold any written charms. The central element, composed of the same materials as the four cases, may be a stylized version of a leaf from the sacred fig tree (*Ficus religiosa*). According to tradition, Siddhartha Gautama was sitting underneath such a tree when he attained enlightenment.[2]

1. Oppi Untracht, *Traditional Jewelry of India* (New York: Harry N. Abrams, 1997), 278.
2. Ibid., 102–4.

Armlet (*Nava-ratna*)

India, 19th century

Gold, enamel, ruby, emerald, sapphire, pearl, aquamarine, grossular garnet, amethyst, coral, citrine, turquoise, rose quartz, and cord

3 × 40 × 1 cm (1³⁄16 × 15¾ × ⅜ in.)

Bequest of Mrs. Thomas O. Richardson 25.224

According to Hindu cosmology, the universe consists of seven planets and the ascending and descending nodes of the moon. Each one of these is personified by an astral deity (*navagraha*) and associated with a gemstone, and the combination of the nine associated stones is considered auspicious.[1] As a group, the gems protect the wearer from harm, especially against the deleterious effects of certain planets, such as Mars and Saturn, which can undermine the cosmic order. The traditional arrangement of the stones and the planets they represent form a spatial mandala that serves as a metaphor for the universe.[2] By the late nineteenth century, jewelers no longer closely followed the rules for positioning the stones in relation to one another, as this nineteenth-century armlet demonstrates.

The gemstones associated with the navagraha reflect the range of colors in the spectrum. The one associated with the all-powerful deity, most often a red stone such as a ruby or spinel, usually appears in the center of the nine-gem arrangement. Other stones paired with heavenly bodies include pearl for the moon, emerald for Mercury, diamond for Venus, sapphire for Saturn, garnet for Mars, topaz for Jupiter, zircon (or hyacinth) for the ascending node, and cat's eye chrysoberyl for the descending node. The color of the stone is more important than its mineralogical composition, so substitutions can occur, such as white sapphire or clear quartz for diamond.

1. The complex association of astral deities with gemstones is explained in the *Ratnaparīka*, a sixth-century text by Buddha Bhatta.

2. According to the jewelry historian Oppi Untracht, the collective gems' power polarizes "all space in relation to the Sun, the ultimate source of life, and man in relation to the Universe. In so doing, the nava-ratna jewel becomes a manifestation of the Divine plan for every living creature"; see Untracht, *Islamic and Hindu Jewellery* (London: Spink & Son, 1998), 17, 24.

Pendant charm

American colonies, about 1776
Silver
5.4 × 4.8 × 0.5 cm (2⅛ × 1⅞ × 3⁄16 in.)
Gift of Robert T. Moffatt 40.751

Protective charms played a role in Revolutionary America, but amulets containing human body parts were exceedingly rare. One highly unusual example is said to contain the caul of Samuel R. C. Moffatt, a New England naval captain. According to family tradition, Captain Moffatt was born in 1776 with his fetal membrane intact, a condition presumed to confer lifetime protection from drowning. Wearing the encased, desiccated caul further guaranteed this safeguard.[1]

The charm consists of two heart-shaped concave plaques of silver joined together by a narrow metal strip soldered along the perimeter. An engraved bird surmounting a quartered shield with other birds decorates the front. The name Moffatt appears in the scroll below. The reverse of the charm bears the following inscription: “Samuel R C Moffatt / of Portsmouth New / Hampshire New / England in North / America.”[2] Captain Moffatt died in New Orleans in 1816 at the age of forty.

1. Martha Gandy Fales, *Jewelry in America, 1600–1900* (Woodbridge, Suffolk, UK: Antique Collectors’ Club, 1995), 59–60; Yvonne J. Markowitz, “Jewelry as Biography,” *Adornment: The Newsletter of Jewelry and Related Arts* 3, no. 3 (Fall 2001): 2.

2. Kathryn C. Buhler, *American Silver, 1655–1825, in the Museum of Fine Arts, Boston*, vol. 2 (Boston: Museum of Fine Arts, 1972), 492.

Luck

Kiff Slemmons (American, born 1944)
1994
Silver, ebony, dice, mirror, and typewriter keys
45.7 × 17.8 × 1.3 cm (18 × 7 × ½ in.)
The Daphne Farago Collection 2006.523

Studio jeweler Kiff Slemmons demonstrates an awareness of jewelry's potential amuletic role in her mixed-media necklace *Luck*. By incorporating words and images that reflect popular notions of chance both good and bad, she pays homage—playfully and intellectually—to the power of superstitions. The broken mirror, ladder, black cat, sidewalk cracks, spilled salt, "snakes' eyes" dice, and number thirteen all refer to encounters that result in bad luck. To neutralize such dangers, the artist includes a horse shoe and several four-leaf clovers for good luck.[1]

1. Signe Mayfield, *The Thought of Things: Jewelry by Kiff Slemmons* (Palo Alto: Palo Alto Art Center, 2000), 10.

Emblems of Wealth & Power

JEWELRY HAS THE CAPACITY to establish the wearer as a person of wealth, position, or influence, particularly when the materials used to make it are rare, come from distant sources, or require the skills of trained artisans. Its importance as an emblem of wealth and power is evident in antiquity. For example, in the Roman city of Palmyra (in what is now Syria) during the first to third centuries A.D., funerary portrait reliefs carved out of limestone depicted the region's elites lavishly coiffed, dressed, and bejeweled. Located in an oasis along the caravan route that carried goods from the Mediterranean Sea across the Syrian Desert, Palmyra and its citizens profited from the constant flow of travelers and the access to quality luxury goods that trade along the route offered. The portrait bust of one woman, Aththaia, daughter of Malchos, includes an engraved diadem on the forehead, garlands of jewels in the hair, earrings with double pendants, two necklaces, an elaborate circular brooch with three gem-set pendants, matched bangles, and three finger rings, indicating the quantity, quality, and range of ornaments owned by a Palmyrene lady (fig. 8).

Some of the most lavish and resplendent jewelry known to exist was created and worn by the leading citizens of the Renaissance in sixteenth-century Italy. The discovery of sea routes to Asia and the Americas brought untold wealth to Europe in the form of gold, diamonds, emeralds, sapphires, rubies, and pearls. Most important was the discovery in the late 1490s of a direct route to India by the Portugese explorer Vasco da Gama, making it possible for European merchants to acquire large quantities of diamond. Diamond was desirable for several reasons: it is the hardest known substance on earth; it is mined in remote regions of the world; it requires skilled lapidary artists to cut the material; it has a dazzling appearance when faceted; and few can afford it. The stones were cut in Antwerp at first, but by 1585 Amsterdam surpassed Antwerp as the center for European diamond cutting.

Renaissance jewelers acquired pearls primarily from the Persian Gulf, and gold, silver, and emeralds from South America. Sri Lanka's vast corundum deposits produced both rubies and sapphires, which were exploited by the Portuguese. In addition to having

FACING PAGE

Portrait of a Woman in a Pearl Necklace, Lorenzo Costa (Italian, 1460–1535), about 1485–1495, oil on panel.

This early Renaissance portrait conveys the sitter's social status in the delicate depiction her costly necklace and fine clothes.

ΘΘΑΙΑ
ΧΑΙΡΕ

sumptuous jewelry made out of these precious materials, the European aristocracy often used them as a medium of foreign exchange when they needed to finance wars.

Italian painters and sculptors frequently demonstrated an in-depth knowledge of jeweled adornment in this period because they apprenticed with goldsmiths. Surviving ornaments and portraits indicate that the most common jewelry forms were hat jewels, pendants, finger rings, and long, decorative chains (p. 48). The pendants, which often artfully incorporated large baroque pearls, were highly sculptural and enlivened by colorful enamels and gems. In subject matter there was an emphasis on classical, quatrefoil, and secular motifs.

Gem materials were so highly prized during the Renaissance that substitutes, including glass, white sapphire, and colorless zircon, were used in lieu of precious diamonds. These less costly materials could be further enhanced through the use of colored foils set behind the clear proxies. Jewelers created imitation emeralds, rubies, and blue sapphires in this manner or used lesser-colored stones, such as spinel, in the place of ruby.

Many societies throughout the world and throughout history have enacted sumptuary laws limiting the ownership and use of specific luxury goods. Such rulings reinforced social hierarchies by identifying what could, or could not, be worn by certain groups. In Japan during the Tokugawa period (1603–1868), for example, when aristocratic warriors sought to distinguish themselves from increasingly affluent merchants, the samurai government issued edicts prohibiting the use of certain types of clothing and accessories by anyone outside of the ruling class.

A less visible aspect of the power inherent in jewelry is its ability to persuade or influence the opinions of others. Some ornaments, designed to express sympathy for or affiliation with political positions, are forms of wearable propaganda. Jewelry reflecting the passions of the abolitionist, temperance, and suffrage movements in the United States, as well as the intense feelings associated with the First and Second World Wars, are relatively recent examples. These were often in the form of pins or brooches and were worn by both men and women.

The ornaments made and worn during the war years, known as "sweetheart" jewelry, first appeared during World War I and became fashionable during World War II when mobilizing the civilians on the home front was a vital component of the war effort. The jewelry, which was worn by the sweethearts, sisters, wives, and mothers of those serving in the armed forces, testified to their loved one's patriotism and sacrifice. Much of this sweetheart jewelry was commercially mass-produced and sold not only in military post exchanges but also in small shops, department stores, and mail-order houses (fig. 9). Many of the ornaments spell out a branch of military service (U.S. Army, U.S. Navy, and U.S. Marine Corps), whereas others display military emblems associated with the differ-

FACING PAGE

Fig. 8. Funerary monument of Aththaia, daughter of Malchos, Palmyrene, A.D. 150–200, limestone.

This ancient Syrian funerary monument presents a richly bejeweled daughter of an illustrious and wealthy family of the city of Palmyrene.

Fig. 9. Charm bracelet, United States, about 1945, silver.

During World War II, women on the American home front wore mass-produced "sweetheart jewelry" to show their support for loved ones fighting abroad.

ent services. In addition, enameled pins with one or more five-pointed stars (called "in-service stars") were worn to indicate the number of family members on active duty. "V" for victory brooches, "Remember Pearl Harbor" adornments, and patriotic lockets incorporating photos of servicemen were also popular. Materials usually included base metal, silver or gold plate, silver, wood, aluminum, shell, mother-of-pearl, and plastic, but several high-style firms, such as Tiffany and Company, Trabert & Hoeffer-Mauboussin, and J. E. Caldwell, made sweetheart jewelry using precious materials. These ornaments, both precious and high-style, created a sense of solidarity and common cause.

Wreath of oak leaves and acorns

Greek, late classical or early Hellenistic period, 4th century B.C.
Gold
D. 3.1 cm, diam. 3.5 cm (D. 1¼ in., diam. 1⅜ in.)
Centennial Gift of Landon T. Clay 69.1076

The ancient Greeks created gold wreaths composed of leaves, blossoms, acorns, and occasionally insects to confer status on individuals of merit or to adorn sculptural representations of deities. Some golden wreaths, such as this one, are so paper-thin that they would have been difficult to wear in life. Scholars have suggested that such fragile ornaments were intended for funerary use, and indeed several examples have been found in the tombs of important citizens in northern Greece.[1]

Two tubular gold branches form the base of this naturalistically rendered wreath. Their two looped ends fasten in front when the wreath is worn on the head. The appearance of abundant foliage was achieved by attaching almost-sheer gold acorns and veined oak leaves to the branches by tiny gold-wire stems. Oak leaves were associated with the underworld and the cult of the dead. They were also sacred to Zeus. Temple inventories contain records of both wreaths and sprays of oak as common offerings.[2]

1. Cornelius C. Vermeule III, "Greek, Etruscan and Silver I: Archaic to Hellenistic Gold," *Burlington Magazine* 112, no. 813 (December 1970): 822.

2. Dyfri Williams and Jack Ogden, eds., *Greek Gold: Jewelry of the Classical World* (New York: Harry N. Abrams and the Metropolitan Museum of Art, 1994), 41.

Penannular armlet

Irish, late Bronze Age, 800–750 B.C.
Ballycotton, County Cork, Ireland
Gold
1.5 × 7 × 5.8 cm (9⁄16 × 2¾ × 25⁄16 in.)
Gift of the Eire Society and Harriet Otis Cruft Fund 50.8

This penannular ornament with trumpet-shaped terminals was a popular jewelry form in Bronze Age Ireland. It was used for torques, earrings, bracelets, rings, and dress fasteners, and most examples, including this one, were cast in high-karat gold without decoration.[1] Research suggests the gold came from County Wicklow in northeastern Ireland, dubbed the El Dorado of western Europe.[2] Scholars hypothesize that these ornaments served as emblems of wealth, rank, and authority, and that they may have been deposited in caches as part of a community ritual or ceremony.[3]

Augustus Henry Pitt Rivers, an ethnologist and archaeologist who served in the British army at Cork between 1862 and 1864, discovered this armlet while excavating in Ireland. The artifacts he acquired during his overseas postings formed the basis of the Pitt Rivers Museum at the University of Oxford. In 1882 Pitt Rivers became Britain's first inspector of ancient monuments.

1. An examination by Richard Newman and Michele Derrick, of the Scientific Research Laboratory, Museum of Fine Arts, Boston, revealed the following composition for the armlet: gold (79.7+/-2.0), silver (13.8+/-0.8), and copper (6.5+/-1.2). For analyses of other penannular bracelets, see C. Mortimer, "Bronze Age Gold Analyses," in *The Laboratories of the National Museum of Scotland*, vol. 2, ed. T. Bruce and J. Tate (Edinburgh: National Museum of Antiquities of Scotland, 1999), 62–67.

2. E. C. R. Armstrong, *Guide to the Collection of Irish Antiquities: Catalogue of Irish Gold Ornaments in the Collection of the Royal Irish Academy* (Dublin: Browne and Nolan, 1920), 3–4.

3. Mary Cahill, "Before the Celts: Treasures in Gold and Bronze," in *Treasures of the National Museum of Ireland: Irish Antiquities*, ed. Patrick F. Wallace and Raghnall O. Floinn (Dublin: Gill and Macmillan, 2002), 88–89.

Bracelets

Greek or Roman, late Hellenistic or early Roman Imperial period, about 40–20 B.C.

Possibly from Egypt

Gold, emerald, and pearl (modern replacement)

H. 6.4 cm, diam. 6.2 cm (H. 2¾ in., diam. 2½ in.)

Classical Department Exchange Fund 1981.287–8

These elaborate bracelets illustrate the transition from the highly decorative gold surfaces characteristic of Hellenistic jewelry to the gem-set ornaments with plain, polished metal surfaces popular during the Roman period. During this change in style, the use of color also evolved. Whereas the Greeks used opaque enamels and an occasional gem highlight to add color, Roman jewelers often created ornaments as vehicles to display gemstones, typically cabochons set in gold-backed bezels. Fashionable gems for wealthy Romans included pearl, garnet, emerald, amethyst, blue sapphire, and banded agate. The Romans sourced their emeralds from Egypt, where this pair of bracelets may have originated.

The bracelets were worn on separate wrists as a matched pair. Each one consists of a pearl-studded gold band with a central urn-shaped element (*kalathos*) made of cast gold. Two heavy gold wires flank the vessel and coil around the base and lateral bosses, and the top of each wire terminates in a cast snake's head with a pearl crown. Emeralds of varying shapes are mounted in the center of the urn as well as below and above it; the one above forms a finial with a smaller urn-shaped element surmounted by a pearl. Similar shapes are found on bezel-set emeralds flanking the circular bosses. Pinned hinges, a common fastener in ancient jewelry, secure the front of the bracelet to the band.

In the classical imagination, snakes were associated with the cult of Asklepios, god of health, and the activities of Dionysus, god of wine and nature. In Egypt they were associated with the goddess Isis as a symbol of fertility and the afterlife. Similar bracelets are known from jeweled representations on mummy shrouds from Egypt's early Roman period.[1]

1. Christine Kondoleon, Richard A. Grossman, and Jennifer Ledig, *MFA Highlights: Classical Art* (Boston: MFA Publications, 2008), 143.

Necklace with a solidus of Roman emperor Valens

Roman, late Imperial period, about A.D. 364–78

Gold

Pendant: 3.7 × 3.3 × 0.6 cm (1 7/16 × 1 5/16 × 1/4 in.)

Length of chain: 21.5 cm (8 7/16 in.)

Theodora Wilbour Fund in memory of Zoë Wilbour 65.1

The gold solidus (coin) on this ancient necklace shows a portrait bust of the Roman emperor Flavius Julius Valens (A.D. 328–78). The solidus bears an inscription that means "Our lord Valens, forever the fortunate Augustus," an imperial title with both religious and political connotations.[1] A gold frame bordered by an openwork lotus design conceals the coin's reverse, which probably has another inscription, most likely "Restorer of the Republic," and a standing Valens holding a small image of Victory. In the late Roman Empire, it was common to mount coins in jewelry, not only because they symbolized wealth but also because they served as a safeguard against inflation.

Valens's rule was far from illustrious. As coemperor with his older brother, Flavius Valentinian, Valens controlled the eastern portion of the empire, with Constantinople as its capital. He sparred with the Persians and waged an unsuccessful war against the Goths, diminishing the empire. His personal tent and considerable store of treasures plundered, Valens died in battle at Hadrianopolis. Some scholars have suggested that "some lucky barbarian may have received this necklace as his share of the loot."[2]

Numismatic ornaments continued to be popular during the Middle Ages and late-Victorian era, when silver currency was partly effaced and embellished with engraved designs. More recently, in the 1970s, the Italian jewelry company Bulgari reintroduced gold jewelry with ancient coins and heavy modernist chains.

1. Translated by Richard Grossmann, Mary Bryce Comstock Assistant Curator of Greek and Roman Art, Museum of Fine Arts, Boston, by personal communication, July 1, 2010.

2. Museum of Fine Arts, Boston, Department of Classical Art, "Necklace Made from a Solidus of Valens," in *Romans and Barbarians* (Boston: Museum of Fine Arts, 1976), 117.

Bracelet with a cameo of Medusa

Byzantine, early Byzantine period, 5th century A.D.
Gold, chalcedony, garnet, and green glass paste (modern)
Bezel: H. 4.1 cm, diam. 7.3 cm (H. 1⅝ in., diam. 2⅞ in.)
Promised gift of George D. and Margo Behrakis in memory of Erene Koukias

The bezel on this bold Byzantine ornament features a carved stone cameo of Medusa, one of the three Gorgon sisters from Greek mythology. In the myth, Athena punished Medusa for her sexual transgression by turning her into a monster with writhing serpents in the place of hair. Medusa was so terrifying to behold that people turned to stone when they looked at her. The hero Perseus later beheaded her, and her hideous face and hair became a powerful talisman to ward off evil.

In antiquity, hard-stone intaglios and cameos were worn with pride, given as gifts, handed down as heirlooms, and sometimes traded. Occasionally artisans remounted them as jewelry or objets d'art, as exemplified by this bracelet. Here, a Roman cameo has been set into a gold mount with an elaborate, interlocking scroll design composed of circular garnet inlays and at one time enamel, now replaced with glass paste. The bracelet's band of three twisted gold tubes latches on to the bezel by removable pins that also allow attachment to the wrist.

The bracelet's materials, workmanship, and chased and repoussé design on the bezel's reverse suggest that it was created by tribes living on the periphery of the Byzantine Empire, possibly the Vandals, Huns, or Alans.[1] A pendant from the Olbia Treasure unearthed in the Crimea in 1891 and now in the Dumbarton Oaks collection has a similar decorative design composed of four palm branches enclosing a quadrangle with a central rosette.[2]

1. Christine Kondoleon, George D. and Margo Behrakis Senior Curator of Greek and Roman Art, Art of the Ancient World, Museum of Fine Arts, Boston, personal communication, October 4, 2010.

2. Marvin C. Ross, *Catalogue of the Byzantine and Early Medieval Antiquities in the Dumbarton Oaks Collection: Jewelry, Enamels, and Art of the Migration Period*, vol. 2 (Washington, D.C.: Dumbarton Oaks, Trustees of Harvard University, 2005), 117–19, no. 166A, pl. 80.

Necklace

East Java, Indonesia, 12th century
Gold
19 × 19 × 1.8 cm (7½ × 7½ × 11⁄16 in.)
Frederick L. Jack Fund 1981.44

This Javanese necklace traces its origins to the tiger-claw amulets donned by women and young boys in India. Tiger claws were worn as trophies, usually as single or double pendants, and symbolized the animal's strength and might.[1] Over time, the form evolved, and the claws were transformed into gold pendants with abstract, stylized vegetal decoration.

This exquisitely crafted necklace consists of twelve graduated stylized claw pendants and a central tortoise-shaped pendant made of hammered gold sheet raised by working the metal from behind (repoussé) and then adding chased detail. The artist used a sharp tool in select areas during the repoussé process, creating small, ball-like protrusions that resemble granulation. The pendants are soldered to cylindrical beads that are threaded on a thick gold wire. A similar ornament dating from the early tenth century was found inside a jar in the vast Wonoboyo hoard excavated in Central Java in 1990.[2]

1. Anne Richter, *The Jewelry of Southeast Asia* (New York: Harry N. Abrams, 2000), 176–77.

2. Cecelia Levin, "*Hiranyasraj*: Classical Javanese Gold and the South Indian Jewellery Tradition," in *Icons in Gold: Jewelry of India from the Collection of the Musée Barbier-Mueller*, ed. Usha R. Bala Krishnan et al., trans. John Tittensor (Aosta, Italy: Musumeci, 2005), 75–91.

Death of Meleager

Probably Italy, 16th century
Gold and shell (*Cypraea tigris*)
2.3 × 3.4 × 0.6 cm (7⁄8 × 1 5⁄16 × 1⁄4 in.)
Henry Lillie Pierce Fund 99.119

This finely carved Renaissance cameo depicts the myth of Meleager, son of King Oeneus of Calydon and his wife, Althaea. It was prophesied that Meleager would die when a certain log caught fire and burned. Althaea hid the log, and Meleager grew up to become a handsome and strong Argonaut. When Oeneus neglected to make proper sacrifices to Artemis, the goddess turned a wild boar loose to ravage the land. Meleager set out to kill the beast with other heroes and the virgin huntress Atalanta. Atalanta wounded the boar, and Meleager dealt the final blow. He graciously awarded the head and skin to Atalanta, which angered his uncles. A fight ensued, and the uncles were killed. Althaea was so enraged over the death of her brothers that she threw the ill-omened log into the fire, causing Meleager's death.[1]

Moving clockwise from the lower left, the cameo depicts four scenes from the Meleager myth: an amorous couple; Artemis in her chariot pointing a finger at Meleager; Zeus astride an eagle and surrounded by gods; and the death of the hero amid a lamenting crowd. The boar appears along the right edge.[2] The cameo is a tour de force of shell carving, with twenty-seven figures arranged in a dynamic composition that is both harmonious and balanced. The elongated bodies in exaggerated poses help to date the jewel to the mid-sixteenth century, a period when artists often looked to classical art and literature for inspiration. Depictions of Meleager's story had forerunners in several Roman sarcophagi in Milan and Rome, which may have served as source material for later artists.[3]

The cameo was once owned by Thomas Howard, Earl of Arundel (1585–1646), an avid collector of paintings, sculpture, and antique jewelry. This treasure passed through several generations of family before being acquired by the fourth Duke of Marlborough, whose legendary collection of cameos and intaglios was eventually auctioned off in 1899.

1. Edmund Fuller, *Bullfinch's Mythology* (New York: Dell Publishing, 1959), 113–16.

2. John Boardman et al., *The Marlborough Gems Formerly at Blenheim Palace, Oxfordshire* (Oxford: Oxford University Press, 2009), 52, no. 49.

3. Phyllis Pray Bober and Ruth Rubinstein, *Renaissance Artists and Antique Sculpture: A Handbook of Sources* (Oxford: Harvey Muller Publishers in conjunction with Oxford University Press, 1986), 144–47.

Casket

Probably Kotte, Ceylon (present-day Sri Lanka), mid-sixteenth century
Gold, gilt bronze, ivory, ruby, turquoise, and glass
10.9 × 16.5 × 10.2 cm (4 5/16 × 6 1/2 × 4 in.)
Bequest of William A. Coolidge 1993.29

During the sixteenth through the eighteenth centuries, rulers of Ceylon presented ivory caskets from the Sinhalese city of Kotte as diplomatic gifts to the court of Portugal. The earliest examples have Sinhalese decoration; later ones have a mixture of European and Sinhalese motifs.[1] The first such gift to be recorded, from ambassador Sri Radaraksa Pandita during his 1541–42 visit to Lisbon on behalf of Emperor Bhuvaneka Bahu, appears in an inventory of Queen Catherine (1507–1578), wife of King John III and an avid collector of Asian luxury goods.[2]

This sumptuous and delicate box is similar to another one presented to Queen Catherine.[3] Like all such presentation caskets, this one has multiple interlocking ivory panels on the sides and a pitched lid supported by a gold framework inlaid with precious materials, in this case red glass, rubies, and cabochon turquoises. The glass and gold corners are in the form of square pillars; the openwork ivory panels are deeply carved with images of people and animals within spiraling lotus vines. The right end panel features two Sinhalese dancers, whereas the left shows a goddess holding two lotuses. Pairs of *gandharvas*, male spirits known for making beautiful music for the gods, decorate the central panels of the lid. Other areas of the box have been carved with *sardulas* (mythical leonine beasts), ganders, a variety of birds, rabbits, monkeys, bulls, deer, antelope, and small heads on lotus pedestals.

1. Amin Jaffer and Melanie Anne Schwabe, "A Group of Sixteenth-Century Ivory Caskets from Ceylon," *Apollo* (March 1999): 3.

2. Annemarie Jordan Gschwend, "The Marvels of the East: Renaissance Curiosity Collections in Portugal," in *The Heritage of Rauluchantim*, ed. Antonio Manuel Hespanha (Lisbon: Museu de São Roque, 1996), 103–5.

3. The casket is now in the Munich Schatzkammer Residenz; see Jaffer and Schwabe, "Sixteenth-Century Ivory Caskets," 12.

Armband

India (Mughal Empire), 18th century
Gold and emerald
13.7 × 3.6 × 0.6 cm (5⅜ × 1⁷⁄₁₆ × ¼ in.)
Gift of Miss Louise M. Nathurst 19.799

The emperors of India's Mughal Dynasty (1526–1707) once ruled over most of the Indian subcontinent. They were renowned for their opulent lifestyle and the influence they exerted on art, architecture, and the decorative arts. Detailed watercolor miniatures document court life and illustrate the Mughal passion for jewelry, which included head and turban jewels, earrings, bracelets, armlets, necklaces, and finger rings that combine Hindustani, Iranian, and European design traditions.

The Mughals prized gems and avidly acquired them by purchase, conquest, and trade. Diamonds, rubies, sapphires, and emeralds were highly regarded and were simply polished and pierced for stringing or set *kundan* style (a bezel-free method) into metal settings.[1] Pearls, another favorite, were worn in long strands or combined with precious stones. By the end of the sixteenth century, Indian jewelers were masters in the arts of stone carving, wirework, granulation, and inlaying.[2]

An elite Mughal gentleman may have worn this ornate emerald armband on his upper arm. Made of five hinged segments set with foil-backed gemstones, it would have been secured to the body by fabric cords attached to decorative bails on each end of the jewel. As was typical of Mughal ornaments, the back is decorated with white, red, and green enamels set into small cells created by carving into the gold (*champlevé* enameling). This tricolor scheme has roots in Indian architecture designed with white stone inlaid with flower patterns of red and green. The floral and bird motifs complementing the rosette and leaf designs also reflect that tradition.[3]

1. The kundan style was especially suitable for irregularly shaped gems. For a discussion of the kundan style of stone setting, see Oppi Untracht, *Traditional Jewelry of India* (New York: Harry N. Abrams, 1997), 364–65.

2. Susan Stronge, "Mughal Jewellery," *Jewellery Studies* 1 (1983–84): 51.

3. Susan Stronge, Nina Smith, and J. C. Harle, *A Golden Treasury: Jewellery from the Indian Subcontinent* (London: Victoria and Albert Museum, 1988), 37.

FACING PAGE

Fig. 10. *Bhim Singh of Jodphur*, Northwest India (Rajasthan), early 19th century, opaque watercolor and gold on paper. This maharaja wears an elaborate array of jewels, including a gem-set armband.

Bracelet

Probably England, about 1783
Gold and mother-of-pearl (*coque de perle*)
H. 2.2 cm, l. 17 cm, d. 0.3 cm (H. ⅞ in., l. 6¹¹⁄₁₆ in., d. ⅛ in.)
Gift of Miss Annie Jewett 13.586e

Pearl and pearlescent jewelry enjoyed considerable popularity in eighteenth-century America. The wealthy could adorn themselves with genuine freshwater pearls from American rivers or imported sea pearls from the Indian Ocean and Persian Gulf. Faux substitutes from France made of hollow glass spheres lined with a pearly mixture of ammonia, lacquer, and fish scales could be purchased by those with somewhat lesser means. We know that even a first lady of the United States might fall into the latter category, for there is a portrait of Abigail Smith Adams wearing a strand of such faux pearls wrapped several times around her neck.[1]

Coque de perle jewelry made from the inner, pearly nautilus shell (*Nautilus Pompilius*), such as the example here, was also fashionable during that period.[2] Known in the trade as *osmena* pearls, the cut shells were usually mounted as cabochons in simple precious-metal settings. This lovely bracelet composed of eight graduated shell ovals mounted in gold was worn by Sarah Hill Huse of Boston, Massachusetts, on her wedding day, November 12, 1783. Her father, Alexander Hill, was one of the city's leading merchants during the Revolutionary War.

1. For a discussion of imitation pearls in France, see Marie-José Opper and Howard Opper, "Imitation Pearls in France," *Beads: Journal of the Society of Bead Researchers* 8–9 (1996–97): 23–24. The 1766 pastel portrait on paper of Adams by Benjamin Blyth is in the collection of the Massachusetts Historical Society. Adams's necklace is now in the collection of the Smithsonian Institution.

2. Ginny Redington Dawes, with Olivia Collings, *Georgian Jewellery, 1714–1830* (Woodbridge, Suffolk, UK: Antique Collectors' Club, 2007), 49.

“Slave in Chains” medallion

Wedgwood Manufactory (English, founded 1758)
1787
Gold and ceramic (jasperware)
3 × 2.8 × 0.3 cm ($1\frac{3}{16} \times 1\frac{1}{8} \times \frac{1}{8}$ in.)
Bequest of Mrs. Richard Baker 96.779

During the late-eighteenth-century abolitionist movement in England, the seal for the Society for the Abolition of the Slave Trade showed a manacled slave on bended knee above the words “Am I Not a Man and Brother?” Josiah Wedgwood, a member of the society and a ceramics manufacturer, used the image to mass-produce hundreds of cameos in black-and-white jasperware with raised text and rim. One of his company artists, William Hackwood, made the prototype. Wedgwood distributed the badges widely in both England and the United States, where abolitionists set them so that they could be worn as hat pins, brooches, pendants, and watch fobs. The noted abolitionist Thomas Clarkson commented in his writings of the period that these Wedgwood ornaments were powerful tools in “promoting the cause of justice, humanity, and freedom.”[1]

In 1788 Wedgwood sent a batch of the badges to Benjamin Franklin, who was president of the Pennsylvania Society for the Abolition of Slavery, as well as a Quaker.[2] In a letter accompanying the cameos, Wedgwood stated, “I embrace the opportunity . . . to enclose for the use of Your Excellency and friends, a few Cameos on a subject which I am happy to acquaint you is daily more and more taking possession of men’s minds on this side of the Atlantic as well as with you. / It gives me great pleasure to be embarked on this occasion in the same great and good cause with you, Sir, and I ardently hope for the final completion of our wishes.”[3]

It is not known if this jasperware medallion was one of the ones sent to Franklin, but it does come from Wedgwood’s first run of the product. Subsequent issues are larger and of different colors.

1. Thomas Clarkson, *History of the Rise, Progress and Accomplishment of the Abolition of the African Slave Trade*, vol. 2 (London: Longman, Hurst, Rees, and Orme, 1808), 191–92.

2. Robin Reilly, *Wedgwood: The New Illustrated Dictionary* (Woodbridge, Suffolk, UK: Antique Collectors’ Club, 1995), 396–97.

3. Josiah Wedgwood to Benjamin Franklin, February 29, 1788, Wedgwood Museum archives.

Cut-steel jewelry suite

Probably Birmingham, England, about 1820
Steel
Necklace: 9.5 × 39.5 × 0.5 cm (3¾ × 15⁹⁄₁₆ × ³⁄₁₆ in.)
Bracelet: 2.1 × 20.1 × 0.7 cm (¹³⁄₁₆ × 7¹⁵⁄₁₆ × ¼ in.)
Each earring: 6.7 × 3 × 0.5 cm (2⅝ × 1³⁄₁₆ × ³⁄₁₆ in.)
Largest brooch: 4.2 × 0.6 cm (1⅝ × ¼ in.)
The Elizabeth Day McCormick Collection 43.2110a–h

An outgrowth of the burgeoning steel industry in Woodstock and Birmingham, England, cut-steel jewelry enjoyed a heyday throughout Europe, spanning the mid-eighteenth century through the early nineteenth century. Birmingham produced a wide variety of wearable cut-steel goods including chatelaines, buttons, buckles, necklaces, earrings, bracelets, and hair accessories. Elaborate suites that included multiple matched adornments represent some of the finest ornaments of this genre.[1]

The designs used in cut-steel jewelry, including this suite, mirror the styles of gem-set jewelry from the same period. Densely packed, faceted steel studs served as faux gems, with minute rivets secured to base plates usually composed of a silver alloy. A rosette motif characterizes this suite's necklace, bracelet, brooches, pendant cross, and girandole-style earrings. The set may have been made at Matthew Boulton's Soho Manufactory, an industrial complex near Birmingham that specialized in cut-steel goods as well as silver, Sheffield plate, and decorative ormolu (gilded) objects.

The creation of such ornaments was a time-consuming process, as each stud had to be chip-carved in order to replicate popular diamond cuts. The result, especially in a candlelit room, was a splendid adornment with glittering surfaces.[2] A suite that includes a tiara, once worn to the Lafayette Ball of 1824, is evidence of cut-steel jewelry's presence at high-society events.[3]

1. Shena Mason, *Jewellery Making in Birmingham, 1750–1995* (Chichester, West Sussex, UK: Phillimore, 1998), 9–10. Cut-steel jewelry was popular to a lesser degree in North America during that period. It continued to be manufactured well into the twentieth century.

2. Anne Clifford, *Cut-Steel and Berlin Iron Jewellery* (South Brunswick, UK: A. S. Barnes, 1971), 18–19.

3. The tiara is now in the collection of the New York Historical Society; see Martha Gandy Fales, *Jewelry in America, 1600–1900* (Woodbridge, Suffolk, UK: Antique Collectors' Club, 1995), 119.

Bust of George IV

Rundell, Bridge, and Rundell (English, 1797–1843)

1830

Gilt bronze, enamel, gold, diamond, emerald, and ruby

49.5 × 30 × 26 cm (19½ × 11¹³⁄₁₆ × 10¼ in.)

William Francis Warden Fund and Gift of Martin Levy in honor of Horace W. Brock 2005.93

George IV was king of Hanover and the United Kingdom of Great Britain and Ireland for only ten years, from 1820 to 1830. During his reign he was known for his extravagant lifestyle, unpredictability, controversial relationships with women, and political conservatism. He also was an avid and astute collector and patron of the arts, commissioning architect John Nash to design Regent's Park, build the Royal Pavilion in Brighton, and remodel both Buckingham Palace and Windsor Castle. As a connoisseur, the king's discerning style contributed to the elegance and glamour of the Regency era (1795–1837).

This jeweled bust of King George IV portrays him in the classical pose and tunic of Imperial Rome's emperors. Elaborate jewelry adorning the king—a diamond-studded tunic with a graduated, channel-set ruby neckline and an emerald fibula and pendant—testifies to the opulence of his reign.[1] The bust was made by the London jewelry firm Rundell, Bridge, and Rundell, which served Britain's royalty and the nobility, and was based on a marble bust by Sir Francis Leggatt Chantrey, a sculptor of international renown.[2] The royal family presented this bust to Sir Henry Halford, physician to George III, George IV, William IV, and the young, future queen Victoria.[3]

The bust sits on a hexagonal plinth decorated in the Gothic style and features an enameled coat of arms from the House of Hanover. A gold medallion mounted on the back by Benedetto Pistrucci commemorates George IV's coronation on July 19, 1821.

1. Ginny Redington Dawes, with Olivia Collings, *Georgian Jewellery, 1714–1830* (Woodbridge, Suffolk, UK: Antique Collectors' Club, 2007), 16.

2. Robert W. Lovett, "Rundell, Bridge & Rundell: An Early Company History," *Bulletin of the Business Historical Society* 23, no. 3 (September 1949): 152–62.

3. Christopher Hartop et al., *Royal Goldsmith: The Art of Rundell and Bridge* (Cambridge: John Adamson for Koopman Rare Art, 2005), 82–83.

Necklace with matching bracelets

France or England, about 1830

Gilt metal and amethyst

Necklace: H. 2.3 cm, l. 47 cm, d. 0.6 cm (H. 7/8 in., l. 18 1/2 in., d. 1/4 in.)

Each bracelet: H. 2.5 cm, l. 16 cm, d. 0.7 cm (H. 1 in., l. 6 5/16 in., d. 1/4 in.)

Gift of Miss Martha C. Codman 23.283–285

Delicate *cannetille* jewelry was the height of fashion in Europe during the 1820s and 1830s. Closely related to filigree, its name derives from the coiled gold-thread embroideries on eighteenth-century military uniforms.[1] The cannetille decoration in this set of jewelry is in the form of coiled-wire circles topped with alternating gold spheres and flat beads. These are soldered to an oval openwork plate composed of fine-textured wires arranged to create a lacelike effect. In the center of each bracelet and in the five graduated ovals on the necklace are pale faceted amethysts from Brazil.[2] The handmade chains are wrought of lightweight strips of metal that are textured to allow for a play of light on the golden surface. The use of multiple chains on bracelets and necklaces during this period was common. In the case of neck ornaments, where typically three chains were used, the chains served as festoons when worn.

The necklace and bracelets were donated to the Museum of Fine Arts, Boston, in 1923 by Martha Catharine Codman, a descendant of a wealthy Boston family, who married the opera singer Maxim Karolik. Together the couple amassed an important collection of early American art, which they also donated to the Museum.

1. Jack Ogden, *Jewellery* (London: Intelligent Layman Publishers, 2006), 201.

2. Other stones frequently used in cannetille jewelry are pink topazes, aquamarines, and chrysoberyls; see Ginny Redington Dawes, with Olivia Collings, *Georgian Jewellery, 1714–1830* (Woodbridge, Suffolk, UK: Antique Collectors' Club, 2007), 24.

Colt family necklace with matching earrings

Probably retailed by Tiffany and Company (American, founded 1837)

1856

Gold, enamel, and diamond

Necklace: 15.5 × 14 × 1 cm (6 1/16 × 5 1/2 × 3/8 in.)

Each earring: D. 1.8 cm, diam. 1.6 cm (D. 11/16 in., diam. 5/8 in.)

Frank B. Bemis Fund, William Francis Warden Fund, and funds donated anonymously 2010.221.1–3

In the mid-nineteenth century, Americans exhibited an unbridled taste for luxurious, costly, and exotic adornments. Charles Lewis Tiffany, one of the founders of Tiffany and Company, helped cultivate and define those inclinations. After acquiring outstanding gems and diamond jewelry in France from aristocrats displaced by the economic and political crisis of 1848, Tiffany found ready buyers among America's growing entrepreneurial class. This influx of diamonds into the country caused quite a stir in the press, which dubbed Tiffany the "King of Diamonds."[1]

By the 1850s, Tiffany and other leading jewelry retailers in the United States were working with firms in Newark, New Jersey, to design and fabricate gem-set ornaments in an attempt to avoid the high U.S. tariffs (enacted in 1828 and 1841) on mounted gems from Europe. Stylistically, these domestic adornments were similar to their European counterparts, especially those made in England. The diamonds used in both places initially came from India, but when rich deposits were discovered in Bahia, Brazil, in 1850, exceptional Brazilian diamonds with outstanding clarity and color found their way to the United States. The stones used in this suite, especially the large, round mine cuts, most likely came from that source.

Among Tiffany and Company's clients were America's leading industrialists and financiers—individuals eager to display their newfound wealth and status in society. One such person was "Colonel" Samuel Colt, a Hartford, Connecticut, native who revolutionized the arms industry through his invention of the revolving, breach-loading pistol with machine-made, interchangeable parts. By the time he married Elizabeth Hart Jarvis of Middletown, Connecticut, he was one of the wealthiest men in America. By all accounts, the Colt wedding, which took place on June 5, 1856, was a lavish affair, with the bride wearing a Tiffany diamond necklace with matching earrings, a present from her husband rumored to have cost $8,000.[2] Unfortunately, Sam Colt died six years after the marriage, leaving one heir, Caldwell Colt. This necklace-and-earrings set descended in the family.

1. Yvonne J. Markowitz, "The Power and Allure of Gems," in *American Luxury: Jewels from the House of Tiffany*, ed. Jeannine Falino and Yvonne J. Markowitz (Woodbridge, Suffolk, UK: Antique Collectors' Club, 2006), 38–39.

2. "Marriage of Col. Sam Colt—a Gala Day among His Friends," *Hartford Daily Courant*, June 7, 1856. See also John Loring, "The Glamour of Tiffany," in *Bejewelled by Tiffany, 1837–1987*, ed. Clare Phillips (New Haven, Conn.: Yale University Press, 2006), 102.

Hand ornament (*hathphul*)

Northwest India (Rajasthan), 19th century
Gold, ruby, emerald, white sapphire, and glass (replacement ruby)
15.5 × 11 × 0.7 cm (6⅛ × 4$\frac{5}{16}$ × ¼ in.)
Gift of Denman Waldo Ross 19.326

In India jewelry is an important component of a bride's dowry. The quantity and quality of the adornments depend on the economic circumstances and social standing of the bride's family, and in many instances the jewelry later constitutes the wife's only personal asset.[1] The types of jewelry used for this purpose vary according to regional customs. In Rajasthan a hand and wrist ornament called a *hathphul* (literally, "a flower for the hand") is one of several elaborate ornaments worn by women, sometimes in matched pairs.[2] The hathphul customarily joins decorations on the backs and palms of the hands colored with henna, a red-orange dye derived from the leaves of the flowering plant *Lawsonia inermis*.[3]

This example of a hathphul consists of a central stylized blossom that rests on the back of the hand. Two rows of tear-shaped emeralds and rubies surround the flower's central ruby cabochon. Ruby-studded metal links connect the rosette to an inflexible wrist plate. Two gem-set finger rings (*mudri*), also part of the ornament, would have been worn on the first and fourth fingers of the hand.[4] Additional gold and ruby links attached to the inflexible band fasten the bracelet to the hand. All stones are set in the *kundan* style.

1. For a discussion of dowry jewelry, see Oppi Untracht, *Traditional Jewelry of India* (New York: Harry N. Abrams, 1997), 162.

2. For a listing of the forms of ornament worn by Rajasthani women, see Vandana Bhandari, *Costume, Textiles and Jewellery of India: Traditions in Rajasthan* (London: Mercury Books, 2004), 130–52.

3. Emma Pressmar, *Indian Rings* (Frankfurt: Insel Verlag, 1982), 20–21.

4. Other rings are also associated with the hathphul—the *arsi,* or mirrored thumb ring, and the *damma*, a set of two interlinked rings worn on the central fingers of the hand.

Headband with forehead ornament (*tikka*)

South India, 19th century
Gold, silver, ruby, emerald, white sapphire, and pearl
Length of band: 37.9 cm (14 15/16 in.)
Pendant: 3.2 × 4.3 × 0.3 cm (1 1/4 × 1 11/16 × 1/8 in.)
Bequest of Miss Ellen Starkey Bates 28.128

Following centuries of tradition, young women of social standing in India's southern state Tamil Nadu wear luxurious headbands with forehead pendants on their wedding day. This gem-studded example has a pattern of crescents, an auspicious shape associated with the moon. The abundant rubies are associated with the Hindu sun god Surya, who, as the center of the universe, nourishes and revitalizes all of life.

The flexible band of this headpiece was formed by stringing the ruby-filled crescents through the sides, along with small pearl and gold-bead accents on the perimeter. When worn, the oval pendant rests in the middle of the forehead, just below the hairline. Similar to other headband pendants, this one is embellished with delicate and freely moving pearl drops on the bottom edge.[1] All of the jewels—cabochon rubies, rose-cut diamonds, and a single cabochon emerald—are set in the *kundan* style.

Tamil Nadu's brides complement such an adornment by wearing floral arrangements, especially jasmine garlands, in their hair.[2] The glittering gems and fragrant blossoms heighten the bride's femininity and sensual appeal.

1. Oppi Untracht, *Traditional Jewelry of India* (New York: Harry N. Abrams, 1997), 215.

2. Usha R. Bala Krishnan and Meera Sushil Kumar, *Indian Jewellery: Dance of the Peacock* (Mumbai: India Book House, 2001), 178.

Cameo suite

France, about 1840

Gold and shell

Necklace: 4 × 0.4 × 43 cm (1 9/16 × 3/16 × 16 15/16 in.)

Brooches: H. 3.5–4.5 cm, w. 5.6–6.6 cm, d. 0.6–1.8 cm (H. 1 3/8–1 3/4 in., w. 2 3/16–2 5/8 in., d. 1/4–11/16 in.)

Gift of the Misses Cornelia and Susan Dehon in memory of Mrs. Sidney Brooks 93.147–152

During the nineteenth century, several spectacular archaeological discoveries of ancient Greek and Roman artifacts profoundly influenced jewelry making in Western Europe and the United States. Troves of hard-stone cameos with classical themes and portraits particularly captured the public imagination. They especially appealed to the newly rich, industrial class which saw in them an illustrious ancient lineage with which they wanted to be associated.

In response to this phenomenon, Italian carvers, many of whom worked in Rome, produced large quantities of cameos from both hard stones and less expensive and more easily worked shell. Both types of cameos were sold all over Europe. Wealthy Americans traveling there on Grand Tours, which included archaeological sites such as Pompeii and the Colosseum, acquired such wearable art as keepsakes.[1] Some American artists, including Augustus Saint-Gaudens, also began to study and produce cameos at home.

This versatile cameo suite could be worn in its entirety, but its owner probably wore select pieces separately. It includes two brooches with idealized profiles of Minerva, Roman goddess of wisdom and the arts, set in elaborate gold settings. Three other brooches with similar mounts illustrate scenes from classical mythology. The necklace that accompanies the brooches is composed of six large cameo medallions alternating with six smaller oval carvings, all of which also depict ancient themes and gods. The cameo carving is Italian, whereas the design of the suite and goldwork is French. The scroll pattern and pendant balls were worked in repoussé with chased and engraved detail; graduated granulated balls decorate the cameo's frames.

1. Charlotte Gere and Judy Rudoe, *Jewellery in the Age of Queen Victoria: A Mirror to the World* (London: British Museum Press, 2010), 466. See also Martha Gandy Fales, *Jewelry in America, 1600–1900* (Woodbridge, Suffolk, UK: Antique Collectors' Club, 1995), 229.

Coral revivalist suite

Italy (Naples), about 1840–60

Gold and coral

Necklace: 47 × 6 × 1 cm (18 1/2 × 2 3/8 × 3/8 in.)

Brooch: 5.5 × 6 × 1.5 cm (2 3/16 × 2 3/8 × 9/16 in.)

Each earring: 7.5 × 2.8 × 1 cm (2 15/16 × 1 1/8 × 3/8 in.)

The Elizabeth Day McCormick Collection 43.2114a–d

During the eighteenth and nineteen centuries, European and North American craftsmen sought out coral as a material for the decorative arts because of its beautiful color, ready availability, and relative softness for carving.[1] Popular motifs for coral adornments included floral sprays, good-luck tokens, and classical themes revived by well-publicized archaeological finds in popular magazines and newspapers such as the *Illustrated London News* and the *Illustrated Times Weekly*.

The brooch in this elaborate, revivalist suite features a detailed carving of the head of Bacchus, the Roman god of wine and revelry, who wears grape clusters in his hair and circles of delicate gold grape vines wrapped around his head. He is flanked on either side by hybrid images of female heads and rams. Below them are three pendant amphorae, vessels often used to store wine.

The god-grape-amphora motif continues on the necklace, but in this ornament, representations of Bacchus alternate with the heads of maenads, raucous female spirits who animate nature. Each head is separated by a stylized ram in profile. The rams represent an unusual choice because the animal was rarely associated with Bacchus in classical art.[2] Revivalist jewelers often created pastiches incorporating motifs from a variety of ancient cultures, and such mixing of iconography would not have seemed incongruous to the jewelry's owner.

1. George Frederick Kunz, *The Curious Lore of Precious Stones* (Philadelphia: J. B. Lippincott, 1913), 68–69.

2. An exception can be found in Kratinos's fifth-century-B.C. play *Dionysalexandros*, in which Dionysus (the Roman Bacchus) turns into a ram. See Thomas H. Carpenter, *Dionysian Imagery in Fifth-Century Athens* (Oxford: Clarendon Press, 1997), 106.

Cameo bracelet

William Morris Hunt (American, 1824–1879)
About 1840
Gold and shell
18.7 × 3.7 × 0.6 cm (7⅜ × 1 7/16 × ¼ in.)
Bequest of Miss Jane Hunt 08.211

Before devoting himself to painting, the American artist William Morris Hunt mastered cameo cutting, probably learning the craft from John C. King or Peter Stephenson, both of whom were known for their cameo portraits.[1] Hunt carved this bracelet of shell cameos around 1840. The portraits are of Hunt and his three brothers: Richard Morris Hunt, a preeminent architect; Leavitt Hunt, a well-known photographer and attorney; and Jonathan Hunt, a physician in Paris. The cameos are bezel-set in gold, each joined by figure-eight links; the bracelet closes with a box clasp.

Hunt's importance as an artist extended beyond his output of paintings or sculptural work, for he profoundly influenced other Americans by introducing them to the French Barbizon school of painting, which emphasized a realistic approach to portraiture and landscapes. Hunt figured prominently in Boston society and counted among his friends Henry Wadsworth Longfellow, William James (who briefly studied painting with him), and Erastus Brigham Bigelow, one of the founders of the Massachusetts Institute of Technology. Hunt gave lectures on art, taught painting, and encouraged collectors to buy works by European artists.

1 .Gertrude S. Cole, "Some American Cameo Portraitists," *Antiques* (September 1946): 170–71.

Berlin iron jewelry suite

Berlin, Germany, about 1850

Cast iron

Bracelet: 5.7 × 1.5 × 18.8 cm (2¼ × 9⁄16 × 7⅜ in.)

Brooch: 9 × 5 × 1 cm (3 9⁄16 × 1 15⁄16 × ⅜ in.)

Gift of Miss Alice M. Longfellow and Mrs. Joseph G. Thorp 17.201, 17.203

To raise money during the Napoleonic Wars, the Prussian state asked its female citizens to trade their precious-metal jewelry for ornaments made of cast iron. At first just decorative emblems of patriotism, the adornments eventually sparked a fashion for black–lacquered iron jewelry that continued for decades. Many of the original pieces bore the inscription "Gold gab ich für Eisen" (I gave gold for iron) and featured a portrait medallion of Frederick William III (1770–1840) on the back. Other early examples followed neoclassical trends.[1] By the 1830s, openwork designs reminiscent of Gothic architecture became fashionable, as did filigree patterns that resembled wrought-iron gates or grilles. A decade later, advertisements for Berlin iron jewelry and decorative objects appeared in the United States, where cosmopolitan individuals eager to have the latest that Europe had to offer eagerly sought them out.[2]

In the winter of 1851, Countess Pulasky of Hungary gave Frances Appleton Longfellow, the poet Henry Wadsworth Longfellow's wife, a gift of two black-lacquered Berlin cast-iron bracelets with a matching filigree brooch while visiting the couple as part of a broader trip to the United States. She was accompanied by her husband and the noted Hungarian patriot Louis Kossuth, who greatly admired Henry Longfellow's poetry; the admiration was mutual, for Longfellow knew all about Kossuth's prodemocracy efforts in Hungary and welcomed him enthusiastically. Most likely this jewelry suite was made in the Berlin foundry of Devaranne and Son, for similar ornaments by this firm were displayed at the Crystal Palace Exhibition in London in 1851.[3]

1. Anne Clifford, *Cut-Steel and Berlin Iron Jewellery* (New York: A. S. Barnes, 1971), 26–27.

2. Martha Gandy Fales, *Jewelry in America, 1600–1900* (Woodbridge, Suffolk, UK: Antique Collectors' Club, 1995), 256–57.

3. Charlotte Gere and Judy Rudoe, *Jewellery in the Age of Queen Victoria: A Mirror to the World* (London: British Museum Press, 2010), 257–58.

Brooch

Jones, Ball and Poor (American, 1846–1853)
About 1850
Gold, diamond, and pink topaz
5.2 x 2.8 × 0.7 cm (2 1/16 × 1 1/8 × 1/4 in.)
Textile Curator's Fund and Helen and Alice Colburn Fund 2011.30

Jewelry incorporating topaz gemstones from the Brazilian mines of Minas Gerais were the height of fashion in Europe during the early decades of the nineteenth century. Lapidary artists often heat-treated the naturally yellow- or orange-colored stones to obtain a soft, pink hue, and set them in delicate gold mounts.[1] Few ornaments designed with this type of topaz were made in the United States during this period.[2] This brooch is an elegant and rare exception. It was once owned by Rosamond Warren Gibson (1846–1934), a prominent Bostonian whose home is now the Gibson House Museum.

The brooch is set with an oval-shaped, faceted pink topaz and old mine-cut diamond accents within a scrolling, foliate 18kt gold mount. A teardrop-shaped pendant also set with a faceted pink topaz and diamonds hangs down from it. The pin catch is a simple, curved wire. The ornament, which retains its original custom-fitted leather box, was made and retailed by Jones, Ball and Poor, a prominent Boston manufacturer of jewelry and silverware frequented by high-society families during the late 1840s and early 1850s. Its elaborate showroom with frescoed ceilings and walls on the ground floor and an extensive workshop for metalsmithing, repair, and stone-setting below street level were located on the corner of Washington and Summer Streets, Boston.[3] Also specializing in imported watches and other luxury goods from Europe, it was considered the best equipped and fashionable jewelry establishment in the United States.

1. Ginny Redington Dawes, with Olivia Collings, *Georgian Jewellery, 1714–1830* (Woodbridge, Suffolk, UK: Antique Collectors' Club, 2007), 111.

2. Tiffany and Co. would later design an elaborate pink topaz suite for the 1893 World Columbian Exposition in Chicago.

3. Martha Gandy Fales, *Jewelry in America, 1600–1900* (Woodbridge, Suffolk, UK: Antique Collectors' Club, 1995), 278.

Brooch with matching earrings

United States, about 1860

Gold, enamel, and diamond

Brooch: D. 1.3 cm, diam. 3 cm (D. ½ in., diam. 1³⁄₁₆)

Each earring: D. 2.4 cm, diam. 2.1 cm (D. ¹⁵⁄₁₆ in., diam. ¹³⁄₁₆)

Museum purchase with funds donated by Susan B. Kaplan and by exchange from a Bequest of Maxim Karolik, The Elizabeth Day McCormick Collection, Gift of Mrs. William Reynolds, Gift of Mrs. Alfred Redfield, Gift of Mrs. Samuel Cabot, Gift of Mrs. Oric Bates, Gift of Miss Eleanor Randall, Gift of Miss Eleanor E. Barry, Gift of Mrs. Lorenz E. Ernst, Gift of Miss Penelope B. Noyes from the Estate of Mrs. Winthrop H. Wade, Gift of Mrs. Charles H. Pease, Gift from the Estate of Mary Babcock Alward, Gift of Mrs. George E. Bates, Gift of Miss Helen R. Humpage in memory of William and Winifred Humpage, and Gift in memory of Mary Wade White from her children 2008.313, 2008.314.1–2

This suite once belonged to Mary Todd Lincoln, wife of President Abraham Lincoln. Following the president's assassination, Mrs. Lincoln fell into dire financial circumstances and was forced to sell many of her possessions. An avid shopper with an eye for fashion and quality, Mrs. Lincoln expected the sale of her clothes and jewelry to offset her debts, estimated at $6,000. The sale took place at Brady and Company in New York City and drew much presale publicity, most of it negative. One West Virginia newspaper article described the sale as "low . . . sordid . . . disgraceful."[1] As a result, the items sold for less than expected.[2] An article describing many of the sale objects appeared in *Frank Lesley's Illustrated Newspaper* of October 26, 1867. It presented this suite with a sale price of $350, which would have been its going price when new.[3] Its final selling price was not published.

Mrs. Lincoln probably purchased these jewels at Galt and Brothers in Washington, D.C. The brooch and earrings are gold with prong-set, mine-cut diamonds, all under a karat. The decoration of black tracery enamel made the set appropriate to wear for late mourning. Considering that the Lincolns' beloved son Willie died in 1862 and that Mrs. Lincoln purchased $3,200 worth of jewelry during a buying spree at Galt's in late 1864,[4] it may be that the suite was purchased at that time.

Although Congress granted Mrs. Lincoln the remainder of her husband's salary for the year in which he died and an annual stipend for life, her troubles continued. Her youngest son, Tad, passed away in 1871 at the age of eighteen, and then her oldest and only surviving son, Robert, had her committed briefly to a private sanatorium in Batavia, Illinois, in 1875. Mrs. Lincoln had apparently been acting erratically, and Robert feared for her safety. Sadly, mother and son were estranged for the remainder of Mrs. Lincoln's life.[5]

1. "Disgraceful," *Clarksburg (WV) Conservative*, November 9, 1867, 6.

2. For an account of Mrs. Lincoln's financial situation, see Mark E. Neeley Jr. and R. Gerald McMurtry, *The Insanity File: The Case of Mary Todd Lincoln* (Carbondale: Southern Illinois University Press, 1986), 15, 127. For the scandal surrounding the sale of Mrs. Lincoln's clothing, see Donna McCreary, *Fashionable First Lady: The Victorian Wardrobe of Mary Lincoln* (Charlestown, Ind.: Lincoln Presentations, 2007), 127–35.

3. The cost today would be approximately $5,000.

4. Neely and McMurtry, *Insanity File*, 15.

5. During the 1980s, a trove of letters written by Mrs. Lincoln was discovered in a steamer trunk once owned by Robert Lincoln's children. Dating from 1871 to 1876, the letters provide considerable insights into her predicament after the death of Tad and through her insanity trial of 1875.

Necklace

Antonio Civilotti (Italian, 1798–1870)
About 1870
Gold and glass tesserae
0.8 × 41 × 6 cm (5⁄16 × 16⅛ × 2⅜ in.)
Bequest of Caroline Louise Williams French 15.231

Micromosaic artists of the late eighteenth and nineteenth centuries drew their inspiration from Roman and Byzantine mosaic floors, walls, and ceilings. Their intricate form, which incorporates glass fragments known as tesserae in miniature designs, developed in Italy, where archaeologists discovered outstanding examples of ancient mosaics such as the *Doves of Pliny* at Hadrian's Villa in Tivoli. By 1866 Rome had eighteen mosaic workshops employing 172 artisans, many of whom were creating designs for jewelry. Like painters of the period, these artists favored Roman ruins and romantic naturalistic landscapes as subject matter for adornments and objets d'art. The skill and time required to produce a single scene made such items the preserve of the well-to-do. The most sophisticated examples were produced in the 1830s, after which their quality declined.[1]

Instrumental in spurring the popularity of micromosiac jewelry was the Castellani firm in Rome. Its early designs in the 1850s were inspired by Etruscan and Greek metalwork and the images, symbols, monograms, and religious inscriptions of Greek, Roman, and early-Christian art. Later, in the 1860s, as supporters of Italian unification, the Castellanis created micromosaic brooches, pendants, and bracelets with the letters *ROMA* made of glass tesserae to arouse nationalistic sentiments. Wealthy Americans touring Italy in this period purchased various forms of the Roma ornaments, in part as souvenirs but also as marks of their status as international travelers.

Antonio Civilotti, the goldsmith who crafted this exquisite necklace, incorporated micromosaic ornaments symbolizing Rome's imperial past. The central portrait is of Julius Caesar, Rome's dictator during the mid-first century B.C., and includes a Latin inscription that means "I am the leader." The necklace's other allusions to Rome's glorious past include the eagle, the initials *SPQR* (Senate and Roman people), and the *fasces,* a bundle of sticks with a double ax that symbolized power and jurisdiction.

1. Judy Rudoe, "Micromosaics and Their Sources," in *Castellani and Italian Archaeological Jewelry*, ed. Susan Weber and Stephanie Walker (New Haven, Conn.: Yale University Press, 2004), 153–54, 168.

Tiger-claw necklace

Northern India, 1870s

Silver and tiger claw

20.3 × 38.1 × 1 cm (8 × 15 × 3/8 in.)

Gift of Mindy Markowitz Setzen in honor of Dr. Joseph Sataloff 2009.336

When the British government assumed direct control of India in the mid-nineteenth century, it created a demand at home for Indian luxury goods. This nineteenth-century necklace was made in India for that Western export market. Brooches were also popular.[1] Other tiger-claw adornments from the period, especially those with elaborate gold mounts, were made in England with trophy claws acquired in India.[2]

The Prince of Wales (later King Edward VII) inadvertently set off a fashion for tiger-claw ornaments in the United States after a trip to India in 1876. He participated in several tiger hunts during his visit, and then returned to England with a collection of claws that jewelers mounted as pendants and brooches. When these novelties came to the attention of luxury-goods mogul Charles Lewis Tiffany, he promptly had his jewelers design several gold-mounted claw brooches and promoted them at Tiffany and Company's New York store.[3] By the 1890s, however, American and European interest in jewelry made with exotic materials waned, and tiger-claw ornaments fell out of fashion.

1. For an example of a brooch made in the high-Victorian style, see Oppi Untracht, *India: A Jewelry Spectrum* (New York: Bard Graduate Center for Studies in the Decorative Arts, 1998), 56, no. 315.

2. Margaret Flower, *Victorian Jewellery* (New York: Duell, Sloan and Pearce, 1951), 151, fig. 53.

3. "Tiffany & Co.," *New York Times*, December 16, 1877, 7.

Brooch

Castellani (Italian, 1814–1927)
About 1870
Gold
D. 0.6 cm, diam. 5 cm (D. ¼ in., diam. 1 15/16 in.)
Bequest of Mrs. Arthur Croft–The Gardner Brewer Collection 01.6505

When the Etruscan Regolini-Galassi tomb (named for its excavators) in Cerveteri, Italy, was excavated in 1836, the papal government invited noted jeweler Fortunato Pio Castellani and his thirteen-year-old son, Alessandro, to examine, and later restore, the extraordinary gold adornments found in the burial. Young Alessandro was particularly fascinated by the golden granulation on several ornaments. After many years of experimentation, he eventually mastered the art of embellishing gold sheet with minute gold balls based on the Etruscan examples, making the technique a hallmark of the Castellani firm.[1] This circular, lobed brooch decorated with thousands of such spheres represents one of Castellani's hand-fabricated designs.

From the 1850s to the 1880s, the Castellanis enjoyed high demand for their jewelry in the "archaeological style" among wealthy Europeans and Americans visiting the family shops in Rome, Paris, and Naples. The firm also won resounding praise at the great international expositions, inspiring other jewelers to explore the art of ancient goldsmithing. Tiffany and Company, for example, produced replicas of the ancient Cypriot jewelry excavated by Luigi di Palma Cesnola in Cyprus during the early 1870s. For its efforts, Tiffany's received the grand prize for goldsmithing at the 1878 Paris Exposition, which led to even greater demand by Americans for jewelry in the ancient style.

With the change in ladies' fashions at the close of the nineteenth century and a shift in interest from the relics of the past to the challenges of the new era, revivalist jewelry fell out of style, to be rekindled briefly by a passion for all things Egyptian following the discovery of Tutankhamen's tomb in 1922.

1. See Jack Ogden, "Revivers of the Lost Art: Alessandro Castellani; The Quest for Classical Precision," in *Castellani and Italian Archaeological Jewelry*, ed. Susan Weber and Stephanie Walker (New Haven, Conn.: Yale University Press, 2004), 180–98. See also Shirley Bury, "Alessandro Castellani and the Revival of Granulation," *Burlington Magazine* 117, no. 871 (October 1975): 664–68.

Bracelet with matching belt buckle

Vilhelm Christesen (Danish, 1822–1899)

About 1870

Gold

Belt buckle: D. 0.7 cm, diam. 5 cm
(D. ¼ in., diam. 1¹⁵⁄₁₆ in.)

Bracelet: 3.2 × 6.4 × 5.7 cm (1¼ × 2½ × 2¼ in.)

Gift of Mrs. Francis C. Foster 16.228–9

Danish citizens experienced a surge of nationalism after winning the Three Years' War with Prussia (1848–51). Jewelers were no exception, and following the publication of J. J. A. Worsaae's *Nordic Antiquities: The Royal Museum in Copenhagen* (1854), they had access to detailed engraved plates of historic adornments dating to the Bronze and Iron Ages, the Migration Period, and the Middle Ages.[1] Goldsmiths used these illustrations to make exact copies of earlier jewelry as well as ornaments in the spirit of the antique.

This hinged bangle and belt buckle were designed by the Copenhagen jewelry firm of Vilhelm Christesen, who earned a reputation for creating ornaments in the Old Nordic style. After Christesen and two other Danish firms, E. F. Dahl and Anton Michelsen, exhibited at the international expositions of the second half of the nineteenth century, those styles became popular beyond Scandinavia, particularly in England.[2]

These matching ornaments are made of heavy gold sheet decorated with twisted wires, gold balls, and thick gold appliqués in the form of snakes, masks, and Nordic crosses. A row of alternating diamond-shaped appliqués and small gold balls border both objects. The background of textured matte provides a contrast to the polished decorative elements.

1. Charlotte Gere and Judy Rudoe, *Jewellery in the Age of Queen Victoria: A Mirror to the World* (London: British Museum Press, 2010), 437.

2. Jacob Thage, *Danske Smykker / Danish Jewelry* (Copenhagen: Komma & Clausen, 1990), 53–55; Charles Boutell, *The Arts and the Artistic Manufactures of Denmark* (London: A. Borgen, 1874), 79–81.

Bracelet

Tiffany and Company (American, founded 1837)
1870–85
Gold and chalcedony
5.8 × 6.1 × 1.5 cm (2 5/16 × 2 3/8 × 9/16 in.)
Gift of Susan B. Kaplan in memory of Dr. Joseph Sataloff 2008.1043

During the second half of the nineteenth century, Tiffany and Company retailed and made jewelry in the popular archaeological revival style. At first, during the 1850s, the firm purchased complete cameo and micromosaic suites made in Europe and sold them in custom-fitted Tiffany boxes in the company's Paris and New York City stores. By the 1870s, however, Tiffany's own jewelers were making the mounts for necklaces, earrings, brooches, and bracelets directly in the Tiffany workshop.

This bracelet falls into the latter category. Tiffany and Company purchased the central *nicolo*, a carved-gem form based on examples from the Roman world. The Italian lapidary artist carved the white layer at varying depths, and then stained the chalcedony background black for dramatic contrast. This process created a range of tonalities: some areas have a blue-white translucence, whereas others appear opaque white.[1] The result is a painterly sculpture in miniature with bold, opaque carving in the foreground and soft transparency in the background.

The scene's central putto holds a horn as two of his companions dangle birds and another restrains a dog. Similar cameos were used by Tiffany and Company in brooches with diamond surrounds, one of which was owned by Jane Stanford, who founded Stanford University with her husband, Leland Stanford.[2] The goldwork surrounding the cameo complements the classical theme of the centerpiece by incorporating two decorative palmettes, which have their origin in ancient Greece. These ornaments are riveted to the pierced, openwork band on each side of the cameo. Engraved decoration on both the palmettes and band enrich the yellow gold surface. A flush hinge with square-gap flaps and a box clasp operates the bracelet.

1. Oppi Untracht, *Jewelry Concepts and Technology* (New York: Doubleday, 1982), 592.

2. Claire Phillips, ed., *Bejewelled by Tiffany, 1837–1987* (New Haven, Conn.: Yale University Press, 2006), 51, fig. 29.

Amber suite in the archaeological revival style

Possibly by the firm of Castellani (Italian, 1814–1927)
About 1880–90
Gold and amber
Necklace: L. 51.5 cm (20 1/4 in.)
Brooch: W. 4.8 cm (1 7/8 in.)
Each earring: H. 6.5 cm (2 9/16 in.)
Bequest of William Arnold Buffum 02.91–94

Amber, a fossilized tree resin, was a passion of William Arnold Buffum (1821–1901), a New Englander who pursued archaeological studies in Italy and at one time served as U.S. consul to Trieste, the Austro-Hungarian Empire's leading port. While assisting at an

excavation in Palestrina, Italy, Buffum was struck by the beauty of the delicate amber ornaments unearthed at the site. He decided on the spot to build a collection that would document the use of this extraordinary material in the decorative arts.

Buffum eventually donated his collection of 164 amber works to the Museum of Fine Arts, Boston, in 1902. The objects were of the highest caliber and included reliquaries, chess sets, statuettes, jewelry caskets (see p. 86–87), and personal adornments. Among the jewels, the most significant is this suite in the archaeological revival style. Buffum was closely involved in its design, having based it on a multihued amber necklace worn by a young woman he met while vacationing in Sicily. He noted that the gems in the necklace ranged in color from "faint blue to deepest azure, from pale rose to intense, pigeon blood, ruby red."[1] By the time Buffum acquired the amber for this necklace, however, the availability of Sicilian specimens in a range of hues had greatly diminished.[2]

There is some question over the suite's maker. At the time of Buffum's bequest, a Museum staff member noted that the gift included "two necklaces of Sicilian amber mounted in gold after Greek and Etruscan patterns—under the supervision of Castellani and Pieret [*sic*] of Rome."[3] Both Alessandro Castellani and Ernesto Pierret were renowned for their revivalist designs, and well-to-do Americans were frequent customers at their shops. Further research suggests that the suite was most likely fabricated by the Castellani firm.

1. W. Arnold Buffum, *The Tears of the Heliades, or Amber as a Gem* (New York: G. P. Putnam's Sons, 1896), xvii.

2. See Patty C. Rice, *Amber: Golden Gem of the Ages* (Bloomington, Ind.: Authorhouse, 2006), 289.

3. Ledger notes of Miss Charlotte Irissman, Art of Europe Archives, Museum of Fine Arts, Boston, 1902. Irissman refers to the firm of Alessandro Castellani in Italy and Ernesto Pierret, a Paris-born jeweler working in Rome.

Necklace with a cameo of Elizabeth I

Charlotte Newman (English, active 1870–1910)
Georges Bissinger (French, active 1860s–1890s)
Gold, silver, diamond, emerald, pearl, and agate
3.8 × 3.1 × 1 × 36.5 cm (1½ × 1¼ × ⅜ × 14⅜ in.)
Museum purchase with funds provided by Susan B. Kaplan 2011.7

The late nineteenth century was a glorious age for England. Because Queen Victoria greatly expanded the British Empire, she was often compared to her illustrious predecessor Elizabeth I, the powerful Tudor monarch who ruled England in the sixteenth century during a period that was later regarded as a golden age.[1] Inspired by this comparison and influenced by the fashion for revivalist jewelry, contemporary jewelers and gem carvers made profile bust cameos of the earlier queen in the Elizabethan revival style, setting them in gem-encrusted mounts.[2]

This Elizabethan revival necklace has an agate cameo pendant of Elizabeth I. As the focal point of the jewel, the cameo shows the queen in profile wearing an elaborate coiffure, a deep ruff, and an oval pendant necklace. Georges Bissinger, a noted French lapidary artist who worked in Paris during the last quarter of the nineteenth century, cut the portrait. He supplied carved, figural gems to the leading jewelers of Europe, including Boucheron and the Italian revivalist jeweler Carlo Giuliano.

Charlotte Newman, a talented jeweler who apprenticed with the British archaeological revivalist jeweler John Brogden, made the neck chain and cameo mount. She exhibited with Brogden at the Paris Exposition Universelle in 1867, and when Brogden was awarded the Légion d'honneur in 1878, she received a *médaille d'honneur* as a *collaboratrice*.[3] After Brogden's death in 1885, Newman established her own workshop in London, employing several of his skilled workers as well as apprentices.

The choker-length chain of this ornament is made up of graduated links composed of alternating pearls and diamonds (mine cuts) set in silver-on-gold mounts. The cameo has an oval surround with ten emeralds carved in the form of a laurel wreath separated by ribbons of diamonds (rose cuts) set in silver. The design for the mount that frames the cameo is based on a clasp of a bracelet that was once owned by Elizabeth I.

1. Charlotte Gere and Judy Rudoe, *Jewellery in the Age of Queen Victoria* (London: British Museum Press, 2010), 348.

2. Roy Strong, *Gloriana: The Portraits of Queen Elizabeth I* (London: Thames and Hudson, 1987), 120–122.

3. Charlotte Gere, *American and European Jewelry* (New York: Crown Publishers, 1975), 212.

Amber jewel casket

Fritz von Miller (German, 1840–1921)
1880–85
Ebony, ivory, gilt metal, silver, lapis lazuli, and amber
46 × 44 × 30.8 cm (18⅛ × 17 5/16 × 12⅛ in.)
Bequest of William Arnold Buffum 02.86

William Arnold Buffum commissioned this extraordinary casket to showcase his collection of Sicilian amber cameos, intaglios, and cabochons acquired in Italy during his extensive European travels, including the years he served as U.S. consul in Trieste.[1] The translucent carvings depicting the heads of Olympian gods and goddesses, theater masks, gorgons, stylized plants, insects, and abstract designs are based largely on ancient hard-stone gems. The box is in the Renaissance revival style, a design movement based on the art and architecture of sixteenth-century Italy.

To design the casket, Buffum chose Fritz von Miller, a noted German metalsmith who was professor and later director of the Kunstgewerbeschule (School of Arts and Crafts) in Munich. Von Miller was a leading figure in the movement to incorporate historicism in

the decorative arts. He is best known for his elaborate centerpieces, light fixtures, and sculptures.[2] This casket, remarkable for its ample size, is made of ebony with ivory panels overlaid by gilt-metal scrollwork. Male and female silver caryatids support the corners. The amber carvings are bezel-set and secured to the scrollwork along the sides and top, and the lid's carvings attach by rivets to the ebony. Four rectangles of lapis lazuli further embellish the box, which rests on four decorative feet.

1. Kristina Preussner, "*Tears of the Heliades*: The William Arnold Buffum Collection of Amber" (master's thesis, Bard Graduate Center, 2009), 35–37.

2. Joseph von Schmaedel, "Professor Fritz von Miller," *Kunst und Handwerk* 61 (1910–11): 37–71.

Painted miniature pendant/brooch

Delhi, India, second half of the 19th century
Gold, watercolor on ivory, and glass
4.7 × 5.8 × 0.6 cm (1⅞ × 2⁵⁄₁₆ × ¼ in.)
Gift of Mrs. Henry P. Sturgis 92.2734

India has a long tradition of miniature painting that began around the tenth century. Early examples were part of religious manuscripts, which were often painted on palm leaves. Six centuries later, after the Mughal conquest of most of the subcontinent, miniaturists working at the emperor's court recorded royal likenesses, dynastic ceremonies, hunting ventures, military expeditions, and noteworthy events in a style strongly influenced by Persian painting, as well as realistic European miniatures brought to India by merchants and royal emissaries.[1] After 1650, Mughal artists who painted miniatures to be worn as jewelry shifted from using paper as a ground to thin sheets of ivory, a practice that was subsequently adopted by the West.

Delhi emerged as a center for the production of limned miniatures on ivory during the nineteenth century. The subjects were typically Mughal luminaries or historical events, and the form took the oval shape common in European miniatures. This Delhi miniature from that period depicts a procession of one of the last Mughal emperors, either Akbar Shah II (reigned 1807–1837) or his son, Bahadur Shah II (reigned 1837–1858). Although it was probably made for the Western market, its subject matter is unusual; most miniatures in that category were bust-length portraits or scenes of famous buildings.[2]

The gold mount for the tiny painting represents an Indian jeweler's interpretation of European *cannetille* work, a labor-intensive form of filigree popular in England and France in the early nineteenth century. In this case, however, the decorative surround is composed of double cone-shaped protrusions rather than twisted wires.

1. Oppi Untracht, *Traditional Jewelry of India* (New York: Harry N. Abrams, 1997), 375; Joan Cummins, *Indian Painting from Cave Temples to the Colonial Period* (Boston: MFA Publications, 2006), 42.

2. Joan Cummins, Lisa and Bernard Selz Curator of Asian Art, Brooklyn Museum, personal correspondence, July 29, 2010.

Bicycle brooch

England, mid-1890s
Gold, enamel, diamond, and ruby
4 × 6.5 × 1 cm (1⁹⁄₁₆ × 2⁹⁄₁₆ × ⅜ in.)
Museum purchase with funds donated by Mona Sadler 2009.2419

The 1890s witnessed a cycling craze in England, Europe, and the United States. Millions of people bought bicycles, and hundreds of organizations sprouted to promote bicycling for pleasure, work, and exercise. For women coming out of the Victorian age eager to assert a new sense of independence, the bicycle was a welcome invention.[1] In an interview with the *New York Sunday World* in 1896, suffragist Susan B. Anthony commented that bicycling had "done more to emancipate women than anything else in the world."[2] The bicycle not only offered transport to activities outside the home but also contributed to dress reform. Trousers were eminently suitable for cycling and were championed by Amelia Jenks Bloomer, an American social reformer who wore loose, Turkish-style pants gathered at the ankles and topped by a short dress or skirt.[3]

This jeweled bicycle was probably made during the English bicycle boom of 1894 to 1897. Its diamond-studded frame includes two mudguards to reduce splatter and a coiled brake part on the front tube, features found on English bikes of the period. Its design resembles a "cob" model, a short-reach bicycle made for women dressed in garments that afforded safety and comfort.[4] The vehicle's gold wheels, which rotate when spun, are set with brilliant-cut diamonds. The pedals also work, turning the ultrafine chain that spins the rear wheel. A small ruby is set in the oil lamp, and the brown enamel seat mimics leather. Perhaps a well-to-do "New Woman" on the cutting edge of female cycling fashion wore the brooch to express her feeling of empowerment.

1. The bicycle was invented in 1817 by Karl von Drais (1785–1851) but did not gain popularity until the second half of the nineteenth century.

2. Nellie Bly, "Champion of Her Sex," *New York Sunday World*, February 2, 1896, 10.

3. Elizabeth Ewing, *Dress and Undress: A History of Women's Underwear* (New York: Drama Book Specialists, 1978), 63–65. See also Patricia A. Cunningham, *Politics, Health, and Art: Reforming Women's Fashion, 1850–1920* (Kent, Ohio: Kent State University Press, 2003), 60–61.

4. I am grateful for the assistance of Nicholas Oddy, Department of Historical and Critical Studies, Glasgow School of Art, Scotland, in determining the date and design of the bicycle, by personal communication, May 7, 2009.

Renaissance revival neck ornament

Designed by G. Paulding Farnham (American, 1859–1927)

Tiffany and Company (American, founded 1837)

1900–1904

Platinum, gold, enamel, diamond, ruby, emerald, cat's eye chrysoberyl, sapphire, and pearl

L. 147.3 cm, d. 0.7 cm (L. 58 in., d. ¼ in.)

Promised gift of Susan B. Kaplan

Tiffany and Company has long been regarded as America's premier maker and retailer of fine luxury goods, particularly jewelry. Charles Lewis Tiffany, one of the company's founders, capitalized on the industrial era's wealthy class and its desire for high-style jewels that would rival those owned by European aristocrats. An astute entrepreneur, Tiffany promoted the brand through the firm's award-winning displays at international expositions. He also sought and encouraged outstanding artists, including G. Paulding Farnham.

Farnham led Tiffany's jewelry department from 1891 to 1907, creating many jewels in the Renaissance revival style, among others.[1] It was during that time that Farnham designed this necklace, a long, gem-studded, and enameled chain meant to be worn wrapped around the neck. Its scrolls and soft color palette are related to a Farnham pendant based on a design by Hans Holbein the Younger.[2] Both ornaments incorporate a variety of precious and semiprecious stones that evoke the Renaissance passion for gem-set jewelry.

As a Tiffany client, railroad magnate Henry Walters, an avid patron of the arts and later the founder of Baltimore's Walters Art Museum, visited the firm's displays at international expositions.[3] He purchased this necklace around the turn of the twentieth century for his sister, Jennie Walters Delano.

1. Farnham's revivalist jewelry was made in the Renaissance, Louis XIV, Louis XV, and Louis XVI styles. For an understanding of his ability to interpret the past, see John Loring, *Paulding Farnham: Tiffany's Lost Genius* (New York: Harry N. Abrams, 2000), 98–147.

2. Ibid., 145.

3. For detailed information on the collecting habits of Henry Walters, see William R. Johnston, *William and Henry Walters: The Reticent Collectors* (Baltimore: Johns Hopkins University Press, 1999).

Japanesque brooch

Lacloche Frères (Spanish, founded 1875)
About 1925
Platinum, gold, enamel, diamond, ruby, and onyx
3.6 × 5.2 × 0.6 cm (1 7/16 × 2 1/16 × 1/4 in.)
William Francis Warden Fund 2009.2533

This art deco brooch of delicate Japanesque design was once owned by Great Britain's Queen Mary (1867–1953), wife of George V (1865–1936), who most likely gave the jewel to the Honorable Mrs. Angela Lascelles (née Dowding) as a wedding present in 1952, when she married the Honorable Gerald Lascelles, the second son of Princess Mary, the Princess Royal and Countess of Harewood.

The international art deco style emerged in all the decorative arts following the First World War and flourished throughout the 1920s and early 1930s.[1] Its designers relied on simple geometric shapes, linear stylization, and saturated colors to express their fascination with change, speed, and technology. Many art deco artists took inspiration from the arts of Asia, as is evident in this jewel's asymmetrical flowering branches.[2] The brooch also heralds the return to platinum and diamond, materials largely avoided by arts and crafts and art nouveau jewelers of the previous era.

The Spanish firm Lacloche Frères, founded by the brothers Fernand, Jacques, Jules, and Leopold Lacloche in 1875, made this brooch. During the 1920s and 1930s, the brothers created outstanding ornaments and accessories in the art deco style, many of which were inspired by the arts of Japan, China, and India. In addition to its flagship store in Madrid, the firm had shops in Paris; San Sebastián, Spain; and Biarritz, France.[3]

1. For an explanation of the evolution of the style, see Alistair Duncan, *Art Deco* (London: Thames and Hudson, 1988), 7–10.

2. Many art nouveau artists also took inspiration from Asia; for examples, see Yvonne J. Markowitz and Elyse Zorn Karlin, *Imperishable Beauty: Art Nouveau Jewelry* (Boston: MFA Publications, 2008), 55, 61.

3. Much of the Lacloche jewelry during this period was made in Paris and bears French assay marks. For information on the firm, see Sylvie Raulet, *Jewelry of the 1940s and 1950s* (New York: Rizzoli, 1988), 320.

Bulldog

Peter Carl Fabergé (Russian, 1846–1920)
About 1910
Gold, silver, agate, diamond, and ruby
8.9 × 2.7 × 11.6 cm (3½ × 1¹⁄₁₆ × 4⁹⁄₁₆ in.)
Gift of Sidney A. Levine 1980.649

Lapidary artists in the Fabergé workshops created exquisitely carved animal sculptures from a wide range of semiprecious stones, matching the natural color and inclusions of particular gems with their designs.[1] Some of the sculptures were portraits of prized pets. This highly naturalistic carved agate bulldog has his name and address—"Cody, Av. Bosquet 9"—engraved on a plaque soldered to his jeweled collar. The neck ornament also features a diamond-studded buckle, a polished gold bell, and a ring at the back for a leash. The dog's arresting eyes are cabochon rubies set in gold.[2]

Cody was one of several Fabergé and Cartier gifts given to the actress Elizabeth Balletta by Grand Duke Alexei Alexandrovich, son of Alexander II and a high admiral in the Russian Imperial Fleet. Balletta, who performed for many years at the Imperial Theater in Saint Petersburg, was a favorite of the duke, who showed his admiration through lavish gifts. After twenty-five years of acting, Balletta settled in Paris at Avenue Bosquet 9.

Fabergé's earliest carved animals were made by a workshop in Idar-Oberstein, Germany, or by the Imperial Peterhof Lapidary Works in Saint Petersburg. However, the firm was able to produce its own works in hard stones after it hired noted lapidary artists Pepijn Kremlev and P. Derbyshev in 1908.[3]

Fig. 11. The actress Elizabeth Balletta's beloved canines pose in front of her Paris residence.

1. For examples of the ingenious use of banded and included stones in Fabergé animals, see Peter L. Schaffer, *Fabergé: A Loan Exhibition for the Benefit of the Cooper-Hewitt Museum* (New York: A La Vieille Russie, 1983), 111–23.

2. For a similar dog from Queen Alexandra's collection, see Henry Charles Bainbridge, *Peter Carl Fabergé: Goldsmith and Jeweller to the Russian Imperial Court* (London: Spring Books, 1972), pl. 80.

3. Dr. Géza von Habsburg, *Fabergé: Imperial Craftsman and His World* (London: Booth-Clibborn, 2000), 298–99.

Brooch

Probably by Oscar Heyman and Brothers (American, founded 1912)

Made for Marcus and Company (American, 1892–1941)

About 1928

Platinum, diamond, and emerald

5.3 × 5.4 × 1.1 cm (2 1/16 × 2 1/8 × 7/16 in.)

William Francis Warden Fund, Marshall H. Gould Fund, Frank B. Bemis Fund, Mary S. and Edward J. Holmes Fund, John H. and Ernestine A. Payne Fund, Otis Norcross Fund, Helen and Alice Colburn Fund, William E. Nickerson Fund, Arthur Tracy Cabot Fund, Edwin E. Jack Fund, Frederick Brown Fund, Elizabeth Marie Paramino Fund in memory of John F. Paramino, Boston Sculptor, Morris and Louise Rosenthal Fund, Harriet Otis Cruft Fund, H.E. Bolles Fund, Seth K. Sweetser Fund, Helen B. Sweeney Fund, Ernest Kahn Fund, Arthur Mason Knapp Fund, John Wheelock Elliot and John Morse Elliot Fund, Susan Cornelia Warren Fund, Mary L. Smith Fund, Samuel Putnam Avery Fund, Alice M. Bartlett Fund, Benjamin Pierce Cheney Donation, Frank M. and Mary T.B. Ferrin Fund, and Joyce Arnold Rusoff Fund 2008.179

This stunning platinum, diamond, and emerald brooch was a favorite of the heiress and art collector Marjorie Merriweather Post.[1] A renowned jewelry collector by the time of her third husband's ambassadorship to Moscow in the late 1930s, Mrs. Post first began acquiring pieces in her twenties, favoring leading American and European jewelers such as Harry Winston and Cartier. She had a special affection for emeralds. Before her presentation at the British court in 1929, she purchased several outstanding emerald ornaments, including this brooch set with a seventeenth-century carved Mughal stone.

Mughal emperors and provincial maharajas in India also prized the emerald, ranking it among the five *maharatnani* (great gems). Their stones came from the Muzo and Chivor mines of Colombia and arrived in India through trade with Spain and Portugal. Indian lapidary artists carved the crystals into a variety of shapes for use in turban ornaments, necklaces, armlets, belt buckles, and other forms of traditional jewelry.[2]

During the 1920s, American and French jewelers incorporated antique stones from India into their designs to add an exotic flair. A jeweler with the American firm Oscar Heyman and Brothers of New York fabricated the Post brooch with an antique carved emerald, suspending it by wire from a platinum and diamond mount. The emerald was then framed with a diamond swag, a design remnant from the Edwardian era. The swag in this jewel is flexible and further ornamented by thirteen tear-shaped emerald drops. Two additional emeralds, both table-cut squares, abut the horizontal bar.

Oscar Heyman and Brothers created the brooch for retail by Marcus and Company, an important high-style jewelry firm in New York City from the end of the nineteenth century through the first half of the twentieth. Founded in 1892 by Herman Marcus and his sons William Elder and George Elder, Marcus and Company had a reputation for exceptional design and superior craftsmanship. Stylistically, its earliest pieces followed prevailing trends in Europe such as the revivalist mode. By the turn of the twentieth century, the company was creating jewelry and hollowware in the arts and crafts and art nouveau styles. Similar to its competitor Tiffany and Company, Marcus and Company sometimes combined different styles in a uniquely American tradition.[3]

Fig. 12. *Portrait of Marjorie Merriweather Post*, Douglas Chandor (English, 1897–1953), 1952, oil on canvas.

1. For an insightful biography of Mrs. Post, see Nancy Rubin, *American Empress: The Life and Times of Marjorie Merriweather Post* (Lincoln, Neb.: Universe Star, 1995). The most spectacular of Mrs. Post's jewels are now in the National Museum of Natural History, Smithsonian Institution. Additional jewels are in the Hillwood Museum and Gardens, Mrs. Post's former Washington, D.C., estate.

2. Oppi Untracht, *Traditional Jewelry of India* (New York: Harry N. Abrams, 1997), 327–32.

3. Janet Zapata, "The Legacy of Herman Marcus and Marcus & Co.," pt. 1, "The Early Years, 1850–1892," *Magazine Antiques* (August 2007): 68–77.

Gem-set necklace

Bulgari (Italian, founded 1884)
About 1986
18kt gold, pearl, tourmaline, citrine, and peridot
16.5 × 13 × 1 cm (6½ × 5⅛ × ⅜ in.)
Gift of Bulgari 2010.597

The Italian jewelry house of Bulgari has an international celebrity clientele that includes Sophia Loren, Elizabeth Taylor, and Sharon Stone, as well as European royalty. Its jewelry from the 1980s incorporates colorful stones that one Bulgari designer described as a "harmony" resulting from a careful study of color combinations.[1] Often favoring bold pairings from opposite ends of the color spectrum as a complement for fashions of the period, Bulgari's aesthetic in the 1980s aimed for "volume, striking colors, clean shapes, stylized decorative motifs and awareness of antiquity."[2] This stunning necklace made in Italy with pearls, citrines, peridots, and pink and green tourmalines for the American licensee Danaos is an outstanding example of that style.

Bulgari's roots go back to the Greek town of Kallarrytes, located near the Albanian border in an area known for metalwork. Political upheavals in the Balkan Peninsula caused the family of jewelry designer and fabricator Sotirios Boulgaris to relocate to Italy in 1880. He started the firm several years later in Rome.

1. Amanda Triossi, *Bvlgari: Between Eternity and History, from 1884 to 2009* (Milan: Skira, 2009), 217.

2. Daniela Mascetti and Amanda Triossi, *Bvlgari* (New York: Abbeville Press, 1996), 96.

Fish Lunching on a Pearl

Marilyn Cooperman (born in Canada, 1936, active in the United States)

1999

18kt gold, patinated silver, diamond, emerald, sapphire, pearl, tsavorite, and spinel

6.2 × 4.8 × 1.5 cm (2 7/16 × 1 7/8 × 9/16 in.)

Anonymous gift in honor of Susan B. Kaplan 2007.964

During the last quarter of the twentieth century, a small coterie of North American high-style jewelers created limited editions of precious ornaments that could be worn with both day and evening wear. Working closely with clients, they often modified their designs to achieve customer preferences, especially when it came to the ornament's motifs or gemstones. The training of these boutique jewelers varied considerably. Some worked as apprentices in the ateliers of noted jewelers, whereas others learned through coursework, private instruction, or self-study. This jewel's designer, Marilyn Cooperman, followed a typical route of seeking advanced training when needed but gaining her exceptional skills for the most part through experimentation.

Today Cooperman's jewels arrest the eye with their bold, imaginative, and innovative style. The artist draws inspiration from the natural world, the historic past, and a variety of cultures. Her works are highly sculptural and demonstrate a sophisticated understanding of gem materials and metals, which she exploits to great advantage. This particular brooch is sixth in a series of ten, each having a different arrangement of gemstones, and in some cases gold fins rather than emeralds.[1]

1. The first was made in 1996. For another fish in the series, see Suzanne Tannenbaum and Janet Zapata, *The Jeweled Menagerie: A World of Animals in Gems* (London: Thames and Hudson, 2001), 176, 199.

SACRED
to the Memory
of Nathaniel Austin
OB 11 May 1807
Æ 43 YRS

Tokens of Affection & Remembrance

FACING PAGE

Mourning embroidery, American, about 1807, ink and pigment on silk plain weave embroidered with silk.

This embroidery mourning thirteen-year-old Nathaniel Austen is akin in subject matter and sentiment to a brooch depicting a mother grieving for her young children (see p. 113).

JEWELRY CAN HELP A PERSON express feelings of friendship, love, or loss. Some tokens of affection or remembrance have highly personal elements hidden from view, whereas others have imagery or text that communicates messages to a broader community. Often called sentimental jewelry, adornments that represent our most intimate relationships are typically made from precious materials and incorporate mementos such as painted miniature portraits, photographs, and clippings of hair.

Personal adornments from antiquity often express the longings of the heart with imagery taken from literary sources such as the ancient love poetry of Egypt's Eighteenth Dynasty (1550 B.C.–1295 B.C.), the lyric poems of the Greek poet Sappho (about 630 B.C.–570 B.C.), and the erotic verses of the Roman poet Gaius Valerius Catullus (about 84 B.C.–54 B.C.). These writers sought the intervention of deities associated with love and sexuality. By wearing jewelry that incorporated images of these gods and goddesses, or just their attributes and emblems, they might attract and beguile the object of their desire.

Renaissance jewelry shows a renewed interest in the classical cult of Aphrodite, as well as in allegorical subjects such as the Judgment of Paris, the birth of Venus, the rising Phoenix (a symbol of love revived), and Cupid stung by bees (a warning of the pain that accompanies true love). Also popular were romantic expressions on finger rings, brooches, lockets, and pendants. Such amatory phrases remained fashionable throughout the nineteenth century. One early-seventeenth-century English locket bears the inscription "In thy sight is my delight," but the text under the bezel of a late-eighteenth-century French ring reads "Je cache mes amours" (I hide my loves).[1] Other phrases on jewelry include "Forget Me Not," "Je ne m'attache qu'a vous" (I belong only to you), "Dear Love of Mine / My Heart is Thine," and "Love is Enough."

The portrait miniature, a portable likeness that served as a concrete reminder of a dear friend or loved one, was an important expression of sentiment in Europe during the eighteenth and nineteenth centuries. The miniature was typically mounted as a pendant or as the clasp of a bracelet. A matched pair of bracelet clasps owned by Martha Custis Washington is an outstanding example of the genre in colonial America. The clasps are set

Fig. 13. Lover's eye brooch, England, about 1820, gold, ruby, watercolor on ivory, and crystal.

with miniatures of two of Martha's children by her first husband, Daniel Parke Custis. The portraits were painted by Charles Willson Peale, and each bracelet would have been worn with the miniature in the center and nine strands of either pearls or chains around the wrist.[2]

Some painted miniature jewelry was allegorical. In 1778, the year he set sail for France to advance the cause of the colonies during the American Revolution, John Adams gave his wife, Abigail, a navette-shaped pendant with a miniature scene painted on ivory and set in a gold frame. The central element in the painting is a solitary woman dressed in a neoclassical gown. Seated on the shoreline beneath a tree, the woman gazes at a ship sailing into the distance as she rests her right arm on a tablet. The inscription reads "I yield / whatever / is . . . is / right." In the foreground, an anchor, a symbol of hope and steadfastness, rests on the ground. Abigail spent many months away from her husband during the Revolutionary era, a sacrifice she bore because she believed the patriot cause was "right." Offering further consolation, the ornament contained a compartment on its reverse with a lock of the future president's hair and his wife's initials, "AA."[3]

Miniatures of a sitter's eye, known as "lover's eyes," were fashionable in England during the late eighteenth century to about 1830 and in America during the early decades of the nineteenth century. At first they were exchanged between lovers who wanted to keep their identities a secret, but over time they were readily and openly exchanged between close platonic friends. Such eyes were usually set in decorative frames and mounted as brooches, rings, and stickpins (fig. 13). Occasionally, a tiny tear in the form of a diamond was set in the corner of the eye as a symbol of the anguish experienced in the absence of one's beloved.

In Europe and North America during the eighteenth and nineteenth centuries, a person could express his or feelings through a shared language of flowers and gemstones. Certain plant and mineral forms were believed to symbolize affection, love, or passion. To send a message, one could select specific flowers for a gift bouquet or have gems arranged on a

Fig. 14. Heart-shaped earrings, England, about 1880, gold, silver, diamond, emerald, amethyst, ruby, sapphire, and topaz.

The first letter of the name of each gemstone on this pair of heart-shaped earrings spells "Dearest."

piece of jewelry so that the first letter of each stone's name spelled out a word or phrase such as "Dearest," "Regard," or "I love you" (fig. 14).

Death occasioned its own jewelry. Portrait and allegorical miniatures were also worn after the death of a close friend or family member. These trace their origins to medieval memento mori ("remember, thou must die") jewelry, ornaments that contained frightening images or symbols such as skulls and skeletons to remind the living of the precariousness of life and the imminence of death. By the eighteenth century, jewelry with romanticized

Fig. 15. Mourning band for George Washington, United States, 1799, ink on silk plain weave (ribbon and crepe).

mourning scenes depicting sorrowful women in white dresses adjacent to funerary monuments became the standard convention for the personal and public expression of grief. Some included inscriptions, such as "Gone to bliss," "In silent sorrow o'er thy tomb I'll mourn," and "Heaven has in store what thou has lost." Such miniatures were mounted in oval and marquise-shaped mounts and worn as pendants, brooches, and rings. The frames often had an enameled border in black if the deceased was an adult, white if a child. In addition, the initials and life dates of the departed were often engraved in the metalwork. Many items also contained a receptacle for the person's hair, an intimate, physical, and durable artifact. Simple enameled finger rings with the name and life dates of the deceased were also made and distributed to family and friends at funerals.

During the nineteenth century, mourning rituals became highly formalized in England and to a lesser degree in the United States. Dress and jewelry appropriate to the various stages of mourning became de rigueur, and various dark-colored materials, such as jet, vulcanite, and bog oak, were commonly used to fabricate adornments worn during the protracted period of bereavement. A similar phenomenon occurred following the death of beloved public figures, such as George Washington and Abraham Lincoln. After their demise, there was a period of national mourning when men, women, and children wore rings, brooches, pendants, stickpins, and armbands memorializing the deceased (fig. 15).

By the twentieth century, jeweled tokens of affection largely fell out of style, although heart-shaped ornaments, charm bracelets with amorous motifs, and wedding jewelry remain fashionable even today. By midcentury mourning jewelry was seen as maudlin and old-fashioned. Since the early twenty-first century, several companies have promoted lab-grown diamonds made from the cremated remains of a loved one—a permanent memorial to the deceased because diamond is said to be the most durable substance on earth. Contemporary studio jewelers have also addressed the subjects of loss and grief as a way of exploring jewelry's capacity to evoke powerful emotions. These works, as exemplified in Dan Jocz's *American Requiem 3047.9.11.2001* (p. 118), are more personal and abstract expressions of remembrance.

1. The locket is in the collection of the Museum of London (Mol.A10488). The ring is in the Museum of Fine Arts, Boston (43.2291b).

2. The clasps are part of the collection of the Mount Vernon Ladies' Association, Mount Vernon, Virginia.

3. The pendant is located at the Adams National Historical Park, Quincy, Massachusetts (Adam 11).

Pair of earrings with pendant doves

Greek, Hellenistic period, 150 B.C.–100 B.C.
Gold, garnet, and enamel
5.2 × 1.2 × 2.6 cm (2 1/16 × 1/2 × 1 in.)
Harriet Otis Cruft Fund 68.5a–b

The ancient Greeks associated the dove with Aphrodite, the goddess of love. Popular myths and cults of Aphrodite focused on sexuality and marriage in the Hellenistic as well as in the later Roman period.[1] Doves were frequently depicted in Greek earrings in the third and second centuries B.C. and this pair of gold dove pendant earrings embellished with gold granulation, gems, and enamel is an outstanding example. The birds are suspended from loops and tapered hooks, a linking system found in other Hellenistic earrings. Here that arrangement connects the doves to gold discs with central cabochon garnets surrounded by rows of granulation.[2] This pendant-dove pair also incorporates stylized Egyptian crowns composed of small bezel-set garnets that mirror the larger gem setting below. This element demonstrates Egypt's continuing cultural influence on the Greek world, especially in Alexandria. Located on the coast of the Mediterranean Sea in north-central Egypt, Alexandria was a significant artistic center from the death of Alexander the Great in 323 B.C. until the Romans conquered the Greeks in 146 B.C.

Dove earrings fabricated from gold remained fashionable until the first century B.C. In other examples from the same period, the doves stand on top of a plain gold box instead of the garlanded altars in this pair.[3] These doves are also more elaborately decorated with gems, placing the jewelry closer to a Roman style, which incorporated more stones.

1. Christine Kondoleon, ed., *Aphrodite and the Gods of Love* (Boston: Museum of Fine Arts, 2011).

2. For a discussion of Hellenistic gold earrings with hanging doves, see Tony Hackens, *Catalogue of the Classical Collection: Classical Jewelry* (Providence: Museum of Art, Rhode Island School of Design, 1976), 87.

3. Ibid., 87.

Cameo featuring the wedding of Cupid and Psyche

Signed by Tryphon
Roman, late Republican or early Imperial period, mid- to late 1st century B.C.
Sardonyx
3.7 × 4.5 × 0.6 cm (1 7/16 × 1 3/4 × 1/4 in.)
Henry Lillie Pierce Fund 99.101

In the myth of Cupid and Psyche, Venus (Aphrodite) became so jealous of Psyche that she concocted a scheme against her, sending her son Cupid (Eros) to strike the beautiful young woman with a golden arrow that would make her fall in love with the first face she saw. Venus wanted Psyche to be smitten with a hideous creature, but instead Cupid was captivated by her beauty and woke her by mistake. In the confusing moment that followed, Cupid scratched himself with his own arrow and fell deeply in love. Eventually the gods granted Cupid and Psyche permission to marry.

In this finely carved cameo, a winged boy leads blindfolded Cupid and veiled Psyche in a procession toward a conjugal bed. The figure carries a torch on his left shoulder, an allusion to nighttime Roman wedding processions. Cupid carries a bird, perhaps a dove, and another winged boy follows with a ritual basket of pomegranates, a symbol of fertility.[1] The last figure on the right lifts the covers of the bed with a welcoming gesture. This cameo has no known parallel, but some scholars suggest that the scene could represent a Dionysian initiation for the couple rather than a wedding.[2]

The jewel is signed in Greek letters by Tryphon, a master gem carver who provided cameos to Roman elites. Here he crafted the sardonyx's tints with such skill that some of the figures, rendered in a translucent, dusky layer of the stone, appear to reflect the torch's imagined light. The Italian Renaissance architect and painter Pirro Ligorio allegedly admired this cameo and made a drawing of it. Later, the Flemish painter Peter Paul Rubens acquired it for his art collection. The cameo was subsequently purchased by Thomas Howard, Earl of Arundel, in the seventeenth century and was later owned by George Spencer, the 4th Duke of Marlborough. The scene proved popular with eighteenth- and nineteenth-century artists, for in 1779 it appeared in a Wedgwood catalogue where it was advertised as being available in jasperware of varying sizes.

1. Christine Kondoleon, Richard A. Grossmann, and Jennifer Ledig, *MFA Highlights: Classical Art* (Boston: MFA Publications, 2008), 91.

2. John Boardman with Diana Scarisbrick, Claudia Wagner, and Erika Zwierlein-Diehl, *The Marlborough Gems Formerly at Blenheim Palace, Oxfordshire* (Oxford: Oxford University Press, 2009), 30–34.

Ring with clasped hands

Roman, Imperial period, 3rd century A.D.
Gold and sardonyx
1 × 2.3 × 1.9 cm (3/8 × 7/8 × 3/4 in.)
Gift in memory of R. E. and Julia K. Hecht 63.1555

The ancient Romans frequently gave inscribed cameos set as pendants, earrings, and rings as engagement or New Year's gifts. Symbols of protection, remembrance, or accord enhanced the written messages, which most often appeared in raised relief in Greek, the language used by the upper classes in Rome's eastern Mediterranean provinces.[1] This ancient Roman betrothal or marriage ring features a central oval cameo with clasped right hands. A bracelet on one wrist indicates that it belongs to a woman; presumably the unadorned one belongs to a man. Below a garland, the joined hands symbolize not only friendship but also the legally sanctioned contractual agreement between an engaged or married couple. The inscribed word "OMONIA" (harmony) stands for Harmonia (the Roman Concordia), a Greek goddess who appears on coins commemorating the marriages of imperial couples by the second and third centuries A.D. The octagonal shape of the ring, also common to late-Roman and Byzantine rings inscribed with magical invocations, further strengthened the marital bond.[2]

1. Christine Kondoleon, Richard A. Grossmann, and Jennifer Ledig, *MFA Highlights: Classical Art* (Boston: MFA Publications, 2008), 94. The carvers themselves may also have been Greek; see Martin Henig, "Ancient Cameos in the Content Family Collection," in *Cameos in Context: The Benjamin Zucker Lectures, 1990*, ed. Martin Henig and Michael Vickers (Oxford: Derek J. Content in association with the Ashmolean Museum, 1993), 28.

2. Ibid., 94. Annewies van den Hoek, Denis Feissel, and John L. Herrmann, "Lucky Wearers: A Ring in Boston and a Greek Epigraphic Tradition of Late Roman and Byzantine Times," *Journal of the Museum of Fine Arts, Boston* 6 (1994): 41–62.

Earrings

Roman, late Imperial period, 4th century A.D.
Gold and sardonyx
3.2 × 1 × 0.7 cm (1¼ × 3/8 × ¼ in.)
Helen and Alice Colburn Fund 66.318a–b

These imperial Roman earrings were probably a betrothal or wedding present. The rectangular component on top bears an inscription that means "to the beautiful one." The teardrop intaglio pendant features red-banded sardonyx, bezel-set in a gold mount and decorated with open wreaths, possibly an allusion to the crowning-of-wreaths ritual in the Roman marriage ceremony.[1] Many of ancient Rome's wedding and marriage customs resonate with contemporary Western culture. The betrothal ring, the marriage contract, and the presence of witnesses at the event all have their origins in the Roman world.[2]

1. Alicia Walker, "Marriage," in *Byzantine Women and Their World*, ed. Ioli Kalavrezou et al. (Cambridge, Mass.: Harvard University Art Museums and Yale University Press, 2003), 215. Other cameos of the period bear similar inscriptions, such as "a gift to the beautiful one"; see Martin Henig, *The Content Family Collection of Ancient Cameos* (Oxford: Derek Content in association with the Ashmolean Museum, 1990), 8.

2. Walker, "Marriage," 215.

Marriage pendant

Italy (Florence), about 1455–65
Silver-gilt and niello
D. 1.2 cm, diam. 4.1 cm (D. ½ in., diam. 1⅝ in.)
H.E. Bolles Fund 69.74

Italian Renaissance jewelers from the mid-fifteenth to the sixteenth century produced large numbers of double-sided niello pendants. This one consists of back-to-back niello plaques set in a silver-gilt frame with a twisted-cord motif. The front features engraved facing portraits of a finely dressed young couple against a background of a fruited vine. The bountiful foliage represents the tree of life and suggests that the ornament was intended for an engaged or married woman.[1] Similar representations appear on rings, majolica pottery, and glass objects from the same period.[2]

The medallion's reverse illustrates the Lamb of God (Agnus Dei), with the haloed lamb resting on a book and looking back at a cross. Niello containers with similar imagery are believed to have originated in the fourteenth century, when popes gave them out as protective, talismanic ornaments. Wax renderings of the lamb or relics of a saint or other religious artifacts were placed inside these adornments.[3] The Agnus Dei on the reverse of this marriage pendant may have served to protect its wearer during pregnancy, childbirth, and illness.

1. Hugh Tait, ed., *7000 Years of Jewelry: An International History and Illustrated Survey from the Collections of the British Museum* (New York: Harry N. Abrams, 1984), 144.

2. Andrea Bayer, ed., *Art and Love in Renaissance Italy* (New York: Metropolitan Museum of Art, 2008), 103–4.

3. Jacqueline Marie Musacchio, *Art, Marriage, and Family in the Florentine Renaissance Palace* (New Haven, Conn.: Yale University Press, 2008), 177.

Pair of cuff links

England or American colonies, 18th century
Silver, quartz, gold, and textile
1.2 × 1.2 × 0.9 cm (½ × ½ × ⅜ in.)
Gift of Miss Amy M. Sacker 53.2118a–b

Stuart crystals, crystal jewelry memorializing a specific individual, take their name from England's House of Stuart, which included King Charles I. When the king was executed under Cromwellian rule in 1649, royal followers adopted the fashion of wearing crystal mourning ornaments with painted miniatures of the king or his initials fabricated from thin, twisted gold wire under a carved quartz stone.[1] Similar crystals continued to be worn during the eighteenth century to memorialize loved ones, but by then jewelers were also adopting the format for pure decoration. Shapes varied from round, oval, and octagonal to heart-shaped crystals, typically cut with flat tables and faceted sides. Some ornaments from the period have backgrounds of hair or black silk and memento mori imagery in lieu of portraits and ciphers.

The lack of initials or other emblems of death on this pair of eighteenth-century crystal cuff links suggests that they were worn purely as ornament. They were made in either England or the American colonies entirely, or the crystal was fashioned in England first and then exported to the colonies for setting. Silver prong mounts with closed backs hold the crystals, and a thick silver figure-eight element connects the two button parts of each link. Like other crystals, these examples are cut flat on top and beveled along the perimeter. Under each one lies a colorful rose foil, further adorned by a trefoil motif of twisted gold wire in place of the more common cipher. A looped border surrounds this design, which sits on a small square of what may be brown woven cloth. The cuff links may have belonged to Benjamin Swan of Boston, who died in 1813.[2]

1. Joan Evans, *A History of Jewellery, 1100–1870* (Boston: Boston Book and Art, 1970), 143.

2. Martha Gandy Fales, *Jewelry in America, 1600–1900* (Woodbridge, Suffolk, UK: Antique Collectors' Club, 1995), 29.

Ring

France, about 1770
Gold, ivory, pigment, and glass
3.2 × 2.1 × 2.4 cm (1¼ × 13/16 × 15/16 in.)
The Elizabeth Day McCormick Collection 43.2191

The beautifully carved ivory column rising from a plinth in the center of the dark, octagonal bezel of this ring may allude to Venus's columned temple on the Velian Hill in Rome. At the top is an amorous pair of doves, which symbolize passionate love.[1] Flanking the column are sprays of roses, a flower sacred to Venus and perhaps an allusion to the passion shared by the ring's giver and wearer. The inscription on the column and plinth is an abbreviated form for *un soupir vient souvent d'un souvenir*, "a sigh often comes from a remembrance."[2] The oval shield at the bottom right, opposite the dog (a symbol of fidelity), bears another inscription that means "sacred to friendship." Affectionate mottos and emblems often adorned eighteenth-century French and English jewelry, as well as textiles, costume accessories, and small decorative boxes. Such items were typically given as gifts to loved ones.

1. Geoffrey C. Munn, *The Triumph of Love* (London: Thames and Hudson, 1993), 50.

2. James Hogg, *Titan: Conjoined Series; Hogg's Instructor 23* (Edinburgh: James Hogg and R. Groombridge and Sons, 1856), 492.

Patch box

France, about 1775
Glass, thread, and wood
D. 2 cm, diam. 4 cm (D. 13/16 in., diam. 1 9/16 in.)
The Elizabeth Day McCormick Collection 43.2286a–b

Throughout eighteenth-century Europe it was the height of fashion for women and some men to wear small dark patches of gummed taffeta on their face. The designs varied from simple spots, stars, and crescents to highly detailed representations of birds, insects, and flowers. Although patches could cover blemishes and heighten the whiteness of the skin, they could also communicate tacit messages. Their placement could indicate a person's political sympathies, marital status, or sexual availability.

Patches were kept in small oval, round, or rectangular boxes similar to this one. Like snuff boxes, they could be made of various materials, including precious metal, ivory, tortoiseshell, and enameled copper. This box, however, is covered with *sablé* beadwork (*sablé* means "covered with sand"). This decorative art form, popular in late-eighteenth-century France, used silk threads to string tiny beads of opaque and translucent glass on a framework. In this patch box, simple looping stitches joined many rows of beads, which were then removed from the framework and applied to the wooden box's lid and bottom. The beads are remarkable for their minuscule size—there are nearly one thousand beads per square inch of the artwork. Fewer than one thousand sablé beadwork objects are known to exist, and scholars believe that they were created in only one or two Parisian workshops.[1] Amatory motifs and mottos decorated many patch boxes, including this example. A crown surmounts two flaming hearts—a symbol for passionate love—with exotic, fanciful flowers spreading to each side.[2] The beaded text along the box's rim means "They are united / in spite of envy."

1. Larry Salmon, "Ballooning: Accessories after the Fact," *Dress: The Journal of the Costume Society of America* (1976): 3.

2. Geoffrey Munn, *The Triumph of Love* (London: Thames and Hudson, 1993), 56.

Miniature of Judge John Lowell

Charles Willson Peale (American, 1741–1827)
About 1782
Watercolor on ivory with hair (on reverse) and gold
3.8 × 3.2 cm (1½ × 1¼ in.)
A. Shuman Collection–Abraham Shuman Fund 51.9

Renowned American artist Charles Willson Peale painted this miniature of Judge John Lowell during the Continental Congress in Philadelphia. Born in Newburyport, Massachusetts, "the Old Judge" (as he was fondly called later in life) had been a member of the Massachusetts Assembly and a participant in the Massachusetts Constitutional Convention of 1779–80 before joining the Philadelphia convention. The portrait shows an amicable middle-aged man with powdered hair and pale blue eyes, dressed in a white ruffled shirt and a green, patterned banyan (jacket) lined with pink silk. The reverse of the pendant features two angels holding a wedding wreath

and the marriage god Hymen's torch above two entwined trees, the larger probably representing Judge Lowell and the smaller his third wife, Rebecca Russell Tyng. In the background, on the right, is the Temple of Love, and on the left is a row of six trees representing the judge's children at the time.[1] The use of the family's hair, which Peale worked into the tree's foliage, is a feature that is also seen in mourning brooches and rings.

As a young Maryland native, Peale apprenticed to a local saddle maker before turning his attention to painting, studying briefly under John Singleton Copley and later with Allan Ramsay and Benjamin West in London. Peale made many miniatures of leading citizens of the day, such as Benjamin Franklin, George Washington, and Thomas Jefferson, capturing the character of the sitter with penetrating realism. The portrait miniatures typically were mounted in simple gold or gilt-metal frames and were worn or carried as personal mementos. Occasionally, the reverse contained the sitter's hair, a monogram, an emblematic device, or a miniature scene, as in this piece. Formal portraits of the period frequently show the sitters wearing these treasured keepsakes of loved ones. Artists like Peale painted on commission, usually to commemorate special occasions such as engagements, marriages, or deaths.[2]

1. Martha Gandy Fales, *Jewelry in America, 1600–1900* (Woodbridge, Suffolk, UK: Antique Collectors' Club, 1995), 86.

2. Susan E. Strickler, *American Portrait Miniatures: The Worcester Art Museum Collection* (Worcester, Mass.: Worcester Art Museum, 1989), 14.

Mourning ring

United States, 1791
Gold, hair, and glass
Diam. 1.9 cm (¾ in.)
Bequest of Maxim Karolik 64.870

The joint monogram and two loose plaits of different-colored hair of this mourning ring graphically and physically commemorate a couple's shared life. The gold letters "LCW" stand for Levi and Catherine Willard, who lived and died in Massachusetts in the late eighteenth century. Both the hair and the initials are mounted under glass over the ring's curved, elliptical bezel. Inscriptions on the ring's shoulders and below the bezel provide the Willards' dates of death and their ages at the time: *Levi Willard, died July 11. 1795 . aged 48* (an engraving error; he died in 1775), and *Catherine / Willard, / died Jany 10, 1791. / aged 56.*

The ring was made when Catherine Willard died in 1791.[1] Levi Willard was a great-grandson of Major Simon Willard, the commander-in-chief of Massachusetts' forces during King Philip's War (1675–76). A resident of Lancaster, Massachusetts, Levi Willard served as county collector of taxes and as a justice of the peace. He held the military rank of lieutenant colonel and with his brother-in-law owned the largest mercantile business in Worcester County. He married Catherine Chandler, daughter of Judge John Chandler of Worcester, and together they had five children. The Willards were known for their loyalist sympathies, and several family members, including their eldest son, went to England shortly before the American Revolution.[2]

Figs. 16–17. *Levi Willard* and *Mrs. Levi Willard (Catherine Chandler)*, Winthrop Chandler (American, 1747–1790), about 1770–75, oil on canvas.

1. Kathryn C. Buhler, *American Silver, 1655–1825, in the Museum of Fine Arts, Boston* (Boston: Museum of Fine Arts, 1972), 321.

2. John N. McClintock, *The Bay State Monthly* 1, no. 6 (June 1884): 379.

Mourning brooch/pendant

Rowland Parry (American, active about 1790–1796)
James Musgrave (American, active about 1792–1813)
Jeremiah Boone (American, active about 1790–1796)
1792
Gold, watercolor on ivory, hair, and glass
5.7 × 4.8 × 1.3 cm (2¼ × 1⅞ × ½ in.)
The Daphne Farago Collection 2006.418

This brooch or pendant conveys a mother's sorrow over the loss of her young children. Ruth McConnell, represented as the grieving female figure in neoclassical dress, stands next to two funerary urns bearing the initials of Thomas R. and William H. McConnell. The urns stand on a plinth with the inscription "Not lost; / but gone / *before*." As Mrs. McConnell supplicates cherub angels in the clouds with one hand raised and a finger pointed in the direction of heaven, her other hand clutches her breast. A weeping willow behind the urns expresses her distraught state and profound grief. The scene was painted in watercolors and incorporates the hair of the deceased children in certain areas. An inscription within a guilloché on the reverse of the jewel provides the tender ages of the children when they passed away: "In Memory of / T.R.Mc.C. / Aged six years & three months / and / W.H.Mc.C. / aged 2 years & 10 months." All of the symbols—the neoclassical figure, urns, willow, angels, and hair—were part of a shared language of grief that frequently appeared on eighteenth- and early-nineteenth-century mourning jewelry and embroidered artworks.

The inclusion of the artist's signature and date inside the back cover of this piece is a rare occurrence: "Parry & Musgrave / Philadelphia / Sept. 13, 1792." The metalsmith James Musgrave worked primarily in silver in the 1790s with his partner, Rowland Parry.[1] A partial label backing the ivory panel also provides the name of the hair worker, J. Boone of 33 South Street, Philadelphia.

1. Martha Gandy Fales, *Jewelry in America, 1600–1900* (Woodbridge, Suffolk, UK: Antique Collectors' Club, 1995), 149.

Suite featuring *amorini* on doves

Attributed to Giacinto Melillo (Italian, 1846–1915)
About 1870–80
Gold
Brooch: 2.7 × 3.8 × 2.7 cm (1 1/16 × 1 1/2 × 1 1/16 in.)
Gift of Susan B. Kaplan 2009.2195
Earrings: 2.7 × 2.7 × 1.1 cm (1 1/16 × 1 1/16 × 7/16 in.)
Gift of Edward Jackson Holmes 41.917a–b

These finely crafted repoussé ornaments in the archaeological revival style feature *amorini* (cupids) subduing Venus's doves with silken cords. Their maker, probably the master goldsmith Giacinto Melillo, most likely drew inspiration for the subject from the collection of antiquities owned by the Campana family of Rome. Giovanni Pietro Campana was an archaeologist who added many excavated works from his expeditions in Etruria to his father and grandfather's collection of ancient Etruscan, Greek, and Roman jewelry. Like other nineteenth-century jewelers, Melillo shared the Campanas' interest in the classical subjects and forms depicted by such artifacts from the Mediterranean world.

As a jeweler for the firm of Castellani, the heads of which were friends and restorers for the Campagnas, Melillo had extensive access to this vast and important collection. Melillo apprenticed in Rome in the early 1860s with Alessandro Castellani, a son of Fortunato Pio Castellani, the company's founder. By then the firm of Castellani had gained renown for its reinvention of Etruscan and Greek methods of working in gold, especially as it related to fine granulation and filigree work. Alessandro opened a workshop in Naples in 1863 to further his research in the ancient art of granulation and to take advantage of the Neapolitan jewelers' metalsmithing skills. In 1865 he hired Melillo as the shop's manager. When Alessandro returned to Rome in 1870, Melillo took over the business.[1] The two men probably worked closely together when they were together in Naples, with two or more other jewelers in the firm fabricating different components of the same piece.[2]

1. Geoffrey C. Munn, *Castellani and Giuliano: Revivalist Jewellers of the 19th Century* (New York: Rizzoli, 1984), 35, 159.

2. Susan Weber Soros and Stephanie Walker, eds., *Castellani and Italian Archaeological Jewelry* (New Haven, Conn.: Yale University Press for the Bard Graduate Center, 2005), 195.

Bangle with pendant charm

United States, 1864
Gold, hair, and glass
2.1 × 7.5 × 8.3 cm (13⁄16 × 2 15⁄16 × 3 1⁄4 in.)
Gift of Mrs. Joseph A. Cushman 64.735

A popular form of expressing affection and remembrance in the eighteenth and nineteenth centuries, hair jewelry provided the wearer with a lasting and intimate means of keeping a physical part of loved ones close. Early hair ornaments were made of plaited or woven hair arranged in attractive designs and placed under glass on the reverse of painted miniatures set in pendant, brooch, and bracelet mounts. This style gave rise to a specialized category of artisan, the hair worker.[1] By the mid-nineteenth century, the hair itself became the ornament's focal point, and watch chains, bracelets, earrings, and rings made primarily of hair became fashionable. Schools for young girls in New England and the southern states began to teach hairworking techniques about this time, and kits and instruction books available by mail order made it possible for women to create hair jewelry at home.[2]

This hollow gold bangle with a spherical pendant locket memorializes four members of one New England family. The locket opens to disclose an inner ball, which swivels to show four crystal compartments containing plaited hair of various shades. Cursive script engraved on the metal frame of each compartment identifies the hair samples as "Father," "Mother," "Robert," and "George." The bottom of the moving ball has another inscription: "RCB to HMW / 1894." The use of an outer cover to hide and protect a more delicate and valuable interior was a common practice in nineteenth-century jewelry. In this example, the outside orb is suspended from a rotating band that allows the pendant to move with the wearer without hitting the bangle. The oval bracelet opens by means of a concealed hinge and closes with a tongue-and-groove clasp.

1. Martha Gandy Fales, *Jewelry in America, 1600-1900* (Woodbridge, Suffolk, UK: Antique Collectors' Club, 1995), 98.

2. One such book was Mark Campbell's 1875 book entitled *The Art of Hairwork, Hair Braiding, and Jewelry of Sentiment*. See Maureen DeLorme, *Mourning Art and Jewelry* (Atglen, Penn.: Schiffer Publishing, 2004), 66–67.

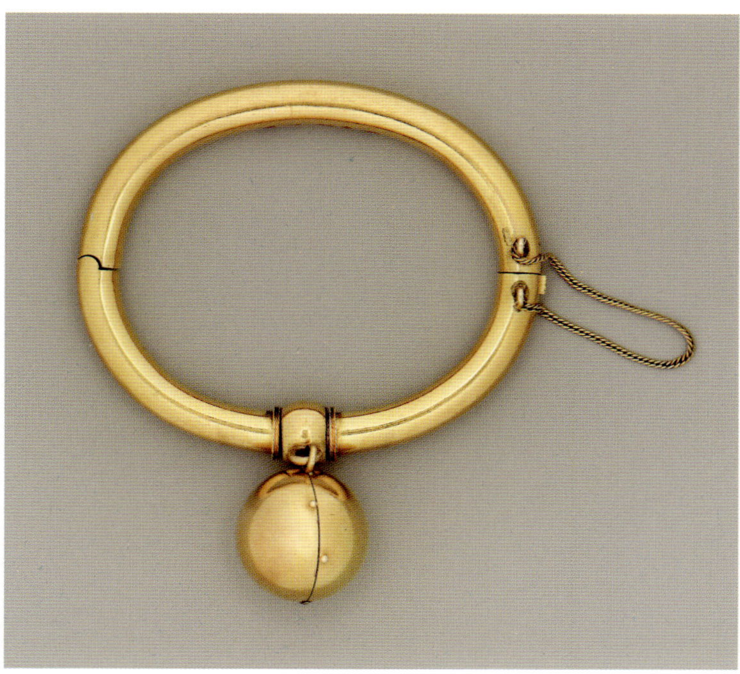

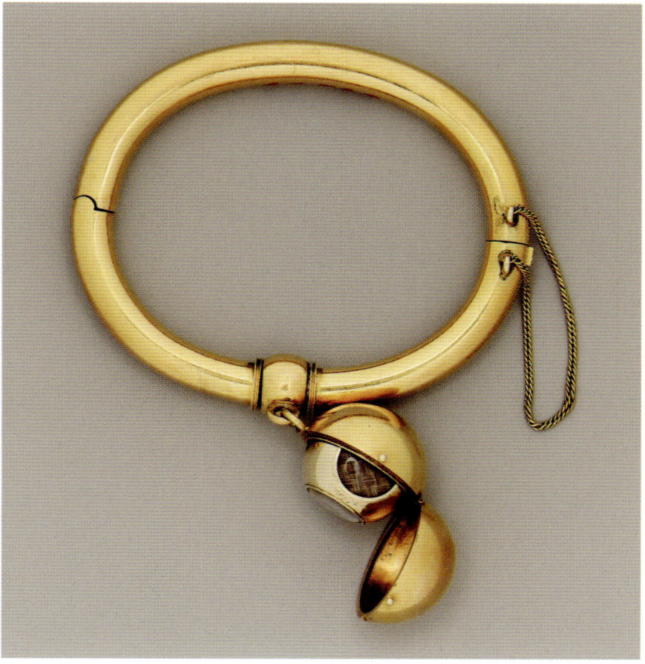

The Tragedy of Great Love (size 6)

Lisa Gralnick (American, born 1956)
1994
Gold, silver, glass, salt, sugar
Pendant: 4.5 × 5.4 × 1.9 cm (1¾ × 2⅛ × ¾)
Length of chain: 86.4 cm (34 in.)
The Daphne Farago Collection 2006.217

For all its contemporary minimalism, this hinged locket with a negative, circular recess on the polished silver front is a traditional adornment bearing a public exterior and a secret interior known only to the wearer. When opened, the locket reveals another circular recess, but this one holds a gold ring, the archetypal wedding band and symbol of eternity. Below the removable ring and behind a glass window are two granular substances labeled "sugar" and "salt," metaphors for the sweet and bitter aspects of love. Over time, the salt corroded the silver interior, an effect that was part of the jewel's concept. According to the artist, "Although the sugar and salt looked the same when the piece was made . . . over time one would remain stable and one would be corrosive."[1] The jewel thereby symbolizes the public-private aspect of love relationships and poetically addresses the complex and often contradictory nature of "great love."[2] Gralnick's personalization of the necklace by adding "(size 6)" to the title points to a specific individual and love history, and her inclusion of one eighteen-karat gold link in the jewel's silver chain suggest that love is precious and difficult to find.

1. Personal communication of the artist to MFA research fellow Michelle Finamore, November 8, 2007, object folder 2006.217, Department of the Art of the Americas, Museum of Fine Arts, Boston.

2. Yvonne J. Markowitz, "Tradition and Innovation: The Cultural Functions of Studio Jewelry," in *Jewelry by Artists: In the Studio, 1940–2000* (Boston: MFA Publications, 2010), 191; see also *American Craft*, exhibition review of artists' work at Jewelerswerk Galerie, Washington, D.C. (December 1994/January 1995): 68.

American Requiem 3047.9.11.2001

Daniel Jocz (American, born 1943)

2002

Sterling silver, fine silver, 18kt gold, 14kt gold, 22kt gold granulation, 23kt gold leaf, sapphire, glass, and pigment

Width of each brooch: 6.8–8.2 cm (2 11/16–3 1/4 in.)

Promised gift of The Daphne Farago Collection

Studio jeweler Daniel Jocz created these six brooches in response to the September 11, 2001, terrorist attack on New York City's World Trade Center. Although they express grief much like traditional mourning jewelry, they represent an abstracted, highly personal response to a collective loss rather than a memorial to a specific individual using a culturally shared language of symbols. Jocz invented his own imagery with materials that express his private thoughts and feelings. Like other conceptual artists, he helps the viewer understand his work by accompanying it with a written text about his intentions.

Jocz mounted the brooches in a frame in two rows of three so that they may be viewed as one composition. Each brooch can also be removed and worn individually to evoke a specific emotion or thought.[1] The artist envisioned these parts as a series of musical movements, taking inspiration from the structure of the Catholic Church's Requiem Mass for the dead. The individual titles of the brooches refer to other requiems, including Berlioz's *Grande messe des morts*, Verdi's *Messe de requiem*, and Mozart's *Requiem*.

Jocz's brochure on this work describes how distraught he was after the attack and how his "emotions finally manifested themselves in a creative way. What I saw in my mind's eye was a small piece of paper bleeding. This notion, of a sheet of paper emitting a singular emotion, eventually became a series of silver tablets on which I could interpret my feelings."[2] The first of his tablets is a sheet of burned metal with tattered edges; it depicts toppling girders, two of which suggest a Christian cross, an allusion to death and sacrifice. The second, a distorted citylike grid of burned silver with gold flecks, recalls the immediate impact of the planes on the buildings. The third consists of a dull silver rectangle with crimson glass droplets that appear to ooze out of the metal, a representation of both pain and loss. The fourth, which features darkened fragments of silver highlighted by granulated gold *Xs*, symbolizes the souls of the deceased rising from a damaged earth. The fifth pin, a shimmering sheet of blackened silver with applied ghostlike wires of gold, signifies remembrance and a glimmer of hope. The final brooch, a restored grid with multiple five-pointed gold stars representing rising souls, completes the cycle.[3]

1. Yvonne J. Markowitz, "Messages and Meanings: The Cultural Functions of Studio Jewelry," in *Jewelry by Artists*. Kelly H. L'Ecuyer, with contributions by Michelle Tolini Finamore, Yvonne J. Markowitz, and Gerald W. R. Ward (Boston: MFA Publications, 2010), 204–5.

2. Daniel Jocz, *American Requiem 3047.9.11.2001* (Boston: Daniel Jocz, 2002).

3. For a more detailed analysis of the meaning of the work, see Paul Massari, "Daniel Jocz: Eternal Rest, Perpetual Light," *Ornament* 26, no. 3 (Spring 2003): 40–45.

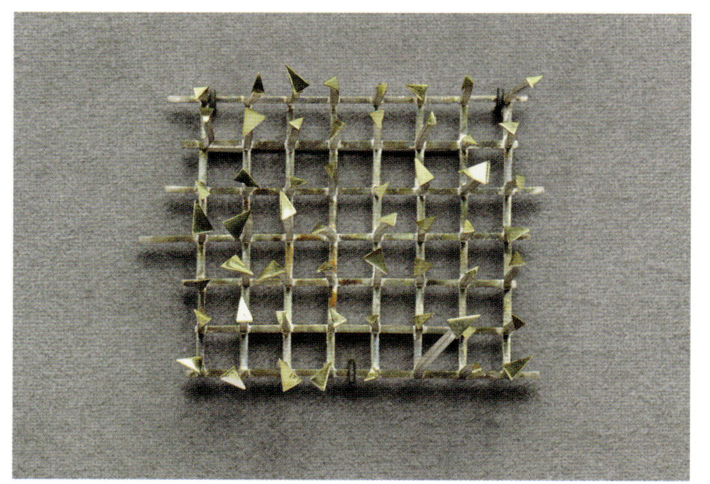

Dress & Adornment

JEWELRY OFTEN SERVES both a functional and an ornamental purpose. Pins, brooches, cloak clasps, belt buckles, buttons, and cuff links all secure garments in place. Hair accessories such as combs, sticks, pins, and barrettes can support an elaborate hair arrangement and beautify it at the same time. One of the most utilitarian adornments is the portable watch. The earliest examples featured decorative cases made of precious materials and were worn on chains or ribbons. By the twentieth century, however, the pendant watch was supplanted by the even more practical wristwatch.

Dress and jewelry have a reciprocal relationship: sometimes the specific form of one influences the form or appearance of the other. For example, before pockets were widely added to Western clothing, hooks called chatelaines were hung at the waist to keep necessities at hand (fig. 18). The term comes from medieval France, where a chatelaine referred to the mistress of a castle, who wore a large key ring at her waist. By the early nineteenth century, the chatelaine and its hanging accessories were worn mostly for personal decoration. In Japan, before Western-style clothing was widely adopted, men wore small containers at the waist to carry personal items such as medicines or seals. The most popular type of container was the multitiered stacked box, which hung from a carved toggle called a netsuke on a cord. Tucked under a man's sash, the netsuke kept the ensemble from slipping away.

Dress and jewelry can also share precious materials. Fine gold threads can be woven with silk to create shimmering, luxurious fabrics, or the precious material may be embroidered on or attached to a finished garment (fig. 19). Portraits of Queen Elizabeth I of England, for example, show pearls sewn copiously onto her dresses. The fashion for wearing pearls sewn onto clothing appears in later centuries as well. The French artist François-Hubert Drouais painted an elegant woman of the mid-eighteenth century wearing swags of pearls in her hair and rows of gems around her neck, wrists, and upper arms. Probably the sleeves' pearls were sewn onto the opulent Turkish costume of the sitter, purportedly the mistress of Louis XV, Mademoiselle de Romans. Glamorous dresses and accessories glittering with applied ornamentation were also popular during the 1920s, and again in

FACING PAGE

Indoor Party Scenes, Japan, about 1661–73, panel with ink, color and gold on paper.

The man in the lower left corner of this section of painted panel wears his personal effects hanging from his sash by a *netsuke*, a miniature carved toggle (see p. 135).

Fig. 18. *Infanta Maria Theresa*, studio of Diego Rodríguez de Silva y Velázquez (Spanish, 1599–1660), 1653, oil on canvas.

The Infanta wears a waist-hung pocket watch and a vinagrette on ribbons

Fig. 19. Woman's jacket, England, about 1610 with later alterations, linen plain weave, embroidered with silk and metallic threads and spangles, metallic bobbin lace.

The fabric of this jacket is lavishly embroidered with costly gold and silver threads

the 1980s. When the boundaries between dress and adornment are so fluid and interconnected, it can be difficult to determine where one begins and the other ends.

One of the most significant developments in fashion-bound adornments occurred from the late nineteenth century through the early decades of the twentieth century, when costume jewelry was invented. Originally the term may have been coined to describe jewelry designed for the stage. By the late 1930s, costume jewelry was the height of fashion in the United States, and nearly three hundred firms were producing it, mainly in Providence, Rhode Island; New York City; Newark, New Jersey; and southern Massachusetts. The popular appeal of these ornaments was no doubt fueled by the economics of the Great Depression and the scarcity of precious metals and fine gemstones during the Second World War.

Some costume-jewelry manufacturers produced imitations of high-style jewelry from leading European jewelry houses, but others felt free to create their own whimsical designs using innovative, low-cost materials such as base-metal alloys, colorful enamels, faux

Fig. 20. Necklace, Elsa Schiaparelli (Italian, active in France, 1890–1973), silver-colored metal and colored glass.

Elsa Schiaparelli created some of the most sumptuous Parisian couture and costume jewelry of the mid-twentieth century.

stones, simulated pearls, and a variety of plastics. Dozens of companies, including Coro, Trifari, and Marcel Boucher, patented signature designs. *Vogue America* and other women's magazines promoted the wares of such manufacturers, encouraging consumers to purchase items that augmented the haute-couture and ready-to-wear fashions of the day. The larger firms created two collections per year (spring-summer and fall-winter) to complement the fashion industry's seasonal lines. Bright, enameled ornaments were appropriate for day wear, and rhodium-plated rhinestone jewelry was reserved for evening wear.

The finest mid-twentieth-century American costume jewelry retailed in leading department stores, such as Lord and Taylor, Bloomingdale's, Bonwit Teller, and Saks Fifth Avenue. Couture houses, including Coco Chanel and Elsa Schiaparelli in Paris (fig. 20), and Nettie Rosenstein and Hattie Carnegie in New York City, also created and sold costume jewelry. In the case of the Parisian designers, the jewelry was made by *paruriers,* craftsmen working in small jewelry workshops. Costume jewelry for haute couture remains popular today, with new designs appearing every season.

Comb

Egyptian, Naqada I, 3850–3650 B.C.
From Naga el-Hai (Qena), tomb K 495
Ivory
14 × 3.7 × 1.2 cm (5½ × 1 7/16 × ½ in.)
Harvard University–Boston Museum of Fine Arts Expedition 13.3509

A prehistoric skull discovered with preserved hair adorned with a long-tined comb at Abadiyeh in Upper Egypt suggests that the earliest Egyptians used such combs as both grooming tools and ornaments.[1] This example in the shape of a stylized ibex comes from Naga el-Hai, a settlement approximately forty miles north of Luxor. The ibex and other animal motifs, including wild sheep, dogs, ruminants, birds, giraffes, gazelles, and various quadrupeds, can also be found on early cosmetic implements and other types of hair accoutrements.[2] Such attention to the natural world endured in the visual arts throughout the course of Egyptian dynastic history.[3]

1. Sir William Flinders Petrie, *Diospolis Parva: The Cemeteries of Abadiyeh and Hu* (London: Egypt Exploration Fund, 1901), pl. VI, B 378.

2. Rita E. Freed, Lawrence M. Berman, and Denise M. Doxey, *MFA Highlights: Arts of Ancient Egypt* (Boston: Museum of Fine Arts, 2003), 44.

3. Helene J. Kantor, "Prehistoric Pottery in the Art Museum," *Record of the Art Museum, Princeton University* 12, no. 2 (1953): 76–78.

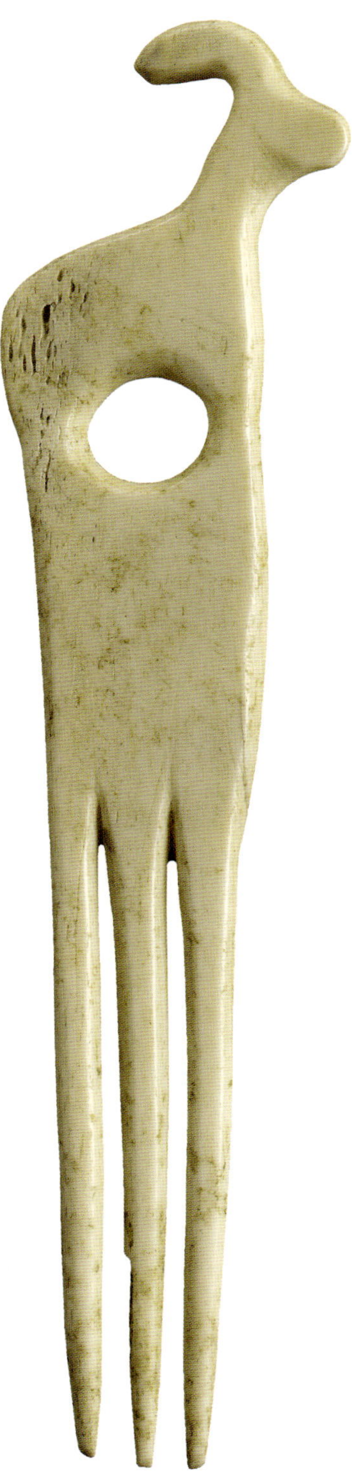

Bead-Net dress

Egyptian, Dynasty 4, reign of Khufu, 2551–2528 B.C.
Giza, tomb G 7440Z
Faience and gold
Reconstructed by Millicent Jick
113 × 44 cm (44½ × 17⁵⁄₁₆ in.)
Harvard University–Boston Museum of Fine Arts Expedition 27.1548.1–2

Although standard dress for women in ancient Egypt consisted of a plain linen sheath, depictions in sculpture, painting, and relief occasionally feature women wearing garment sheaths decorated with a lozenge pattern.[1] Egyptologists believe that the designs represent beadwork either sewn onto the dress or worked into a separate net worn over the linen. Such a net dress was found in Giza on the female occupant of tomb G 7740Z, which was erected during the reign of King Khufu, builder of the Great Pyramid. The dress' stringing material had largely deteriorated by the time the tomb was excavated, but a few swatches of woven beads survived. They indicated that the garment was once a separate net dress with an open, lozenge pattern for the main body, a striped V-shaped halter top, and a fringed hemline. The lady also wore a separate broad collar composed of faience cylinders, floral pendants, and small ring beads. Detailed excavation records and extensive photographic documentation of the tomb's contents made it possible for scholars to reconstruct both the dress and the neck ornament.[2] Although only the front part of the dress could be restrung, a sufficient number of beads were recovered to indicate that the back would have been covered as well.[3] The garment is the earliest known bead-net dress in the world and one of only three reconstructed dresses dating to the Old Kingdom.[4]

1. For Old Kingdom examples of women wearing patterned dresses, see Millicent Jick, "Bead-Net Dress from Giza, Tomb G7740 Z, Old Kingdom Dynasty IV, Reign of Khufu," *Ornament* 14, no. 1 (1990): 52.

2. Sue D'Aria, Peter Lacovara, and Catharine H. Roehrig, *Mummies and Magic: The Funerary Arts of Ancient Egypt* (Boston: Museum of Fine Arts, 1988), 78–79.

3. When the dress was reconstructed in the late 1980s, it was decided to preserve, and not use, swatches with original stringing. Keeping such bead groups intact is crucial to further beadwork research.

4. The second dress was re-created at the Petrie Museum in London, and the third dress was recently reconstructed at the Museum of Fine Arts, Boston. See Yvonne J. Markowitz, Joyce L. Haynes, and Rita E. Freed, *Egypt in the Age of the Pyramids: Highlights from the Harvard University–Museum of Fine Arts, Boston Expedition* (Boston: Museum of Fine Arts, 2002), 115.

Head of a pin

Greek, classical period, about 420–400 B.C.

Possibly from a tomb in the northwestern coast of the Peloponnese, near Aigion or Patras

Gold

7.7 × 4.9 × 5.1 cm (3 1/16 × 1 15/16 × 2 in.)

Catharine Page Perkins Fund 96.717

This golden bouquet of blossoms, fruits, leaves, and bees guarded by rampant lions is a four-sided pinhead that once secured a draped tunic (chiton) at the shoulder. A pinecone capped by a flower forms the bouquet's core, while large bees drink nectar just below, their heads and front legs burrowed deep in rose blossoms. The lions, separated by rounded leaves and palmettes, lift an enormous bud with large outer petals, their back legs resting on the corner of a four-sided Ionic column. This complex rendering of flora, fauna, and column surmounts a fluted orb and another stylized pinecone.[1] Although Greek art features each of these motifs in many separate forms, their combination in a single ornament is unique.[2]

Like many ancient jewels, this one is composed of dozens of individual parts soldered together. Nearly all of them are made of thin gold sheet, but a few, including the lions' legs and the volutes, were cast first and then added to the larger composition. The multiple, loop-in-loop chain with snake-head terminals beneath the fluted orb may have been attached to a similar pin reportedly found in the same tomb.[3]

1. Herbert Hoffmann and Patricia F. Davidson, *Greek Gold: Jewelry from the Age of Alexander* (Brooklyn, N.Y.: Brooklyn Museum, 1965), 184–87.

2. Berta Segall, "Two Gold Pins in the Classical Collection," *Bulletin of the Museum of Fine Arts* 39, no. 234 (August 1941): 54.

3. Paul Jacobsthal, *Greek Pins and Their Connexions with Europe and Asia* (Oxford: Clarendon Press, 1956), 66. The other pin is 96.718 in the Museum of Fine Arts, Boston.

Belt buckle

Korean, Goryeo dynasty, 11th–12th century
Gilt silver
23 × 6.2 × 0.5 cm (9 1/16 × 2 7/16 × 3/16 in.)
Gift of Robert T. Paine Jr. 60.1321

This Korean Goryeo dynasty belt buckle is an excellent example of the period's sophisticated metalwork. Two cast-silver frames form the buckle's two decorated panels, which probably were attached to a leather belt. The buckle's high-relief work on the right side depicts tree peonies, leaves, branches, and blossoms. The left panel features herbaceous or bush peonies in low relief. Here, the artist worked the metal from behind using a beating and impressing technique similar to repoussé.[1] Peonies are auspicious symbols in Korea associated with prosperity, nobility, feminine beauty, and love.[2]

Goryeo artists produced masterpieces in various media such as celadon-glazed pottery, woodblock-printed texts, including the *Tripitaka Koreana* (Buddhist scriptures composed of eighty thousand characters), lacquer objects, and metalwork. Metalwork ranged from Buddhist bells, temple gongs, and incense burners to such secular items as mirrors, bracelets, hairpins, needle cases, and belt buckles like this one.[3]

1. Museum of Fine Arts, Boston, *Korean Art Collection at the Museum of Fine Arts, Boston* (Deajeon, Korea: National Research Institute of Cultural Heritage and the Museum of Fine Arts, Boston, 2004), 328.

2. Robert Moes, *Auspicious Spirits: Korean Folk Paintings and Related Objects* (Washington, D.C.: International Exhibitions Foundation, 1983), cat. no. 3.

3. Kumja Paik Kim, *Goryeo Dynasty: Korea's Age of Enlightenment, 918–1392* (San Francisco: Asian Art Museum–Chong-Moon Lee Center for Asian Art and Culture in cooperation with the National Museum of Korea and the Nara National Museum, 2003), 168.

Pomander

Probably England, about 1580
Silver gilt
H. 6.4 cm, diam. 3.4 cm (H. 2½ in., diam. 1⁵⁄₁₆ in.)
Bequest of Frank Brewer Bemis 35.1547

Men and women of late-medieval and Renaissance Europe wore pomanders of aromatic substances to eliminate bad odors and prevent infections. The earliest known examples held mixtures of spices, herbs, and blossoms molded into a ball and inserted into simple cases of open metalwork. By the sixteenth century, elaborately decorated containers with separate compartments for individual scents were worn hanging from a girdle or suspended from a long chain around the neck.

This hexagonal pomander has eight hinged compartments that slide open. Inside, each wedge-shaped section is engraved with the name of the substance it was meant to house: *ROSE* (rose), *CEDRO* (cedar), *GESMINI* (jasmine), *AMBRA* (ambergris), *MOSCHETE* (musk), *VIOLE* (violet), *NARANSI* (orange), and *GAROFOLI* (clove). The central container is capped by a grotesque figure atop a second hexagonal sphere, which may be removed to fill the pomander. Under the spool-shaped base is an engraved cartouche that once surrounded a heraldic coat of arms.[1] Pomanders like this one were worn until the last quarter of the seventeenth century, when they were replaced by small bottles of liquid scents or perforated vessels containing aromatic vinegar.[2]

1. Ellenor M. Alcorn, *English Silver in the Museum of Fine Arts, Boston*, vol. 1 (Boston: Museum of Fine Arts, 1993), 60–61.

2. W. Turner, "Pomanders," *Connoisseur* 32 (April 1912): 152.

Fig. 21. Portrait of a woman, Frans Pourbus, the Elder (Netherlandish, 1545–1581), 1581, oil on panel. Pomanders were often worn suspended from a chain around the waist.

MOSCHETE
ROSE

Chatelaine with etui

England, about 1750
Gilt brass
24 × 10 × 2.1 cm (9 7/16 × 3 15/16 × 13/16 in.)
Gift of Miss Emily M. Babcock 51.653

A fashionable eighteenth-century Englishman or -woman wore this elaborate rococo-style chatelaine as an accessory to formal dress. Essentially a hinged hook worn over a belt, the chatelaine in this example is joined to two appendages at the sides in the form of oval boxes and a multipurpose central container called an etui. The ensemble was called an equipage, after the French word for "equipment" or "trappings."

The plaques of the chatelaine are cast in relief with putti and classical goddesses arranged in asymmetrical cartouches. The small oval boxes are made of hammered sheet metal and decorated with ornamental swags and shells. Now empty, at one time they may have held a thimble and thread.[1] The etui, embellished on both sides, hangs from the plaque above by a swivel hoop. On the front, a woman seated in an idyllic garden reads a book; on the back, the Roman goddess of wisdom, Minerva, poses in an outdoor setting. Various gilt-metal implements are inside the etui: a miniature spoon, a pick, a small scoop, and a folding knife with a handle adorned with raised-relief flowers. Several utensils are now missing; most likely one of them was a tiny fork.

The extensive promotion of equipages by fashion writers of the late nineteenth century and their use by royals such as Alexandra, Princess of Wales, in the early twentieth century made them extremely popular with both men and women.[2] They eventually fell out of fashion after the brief appearance of home-made fabric forms around 1910.

1. For similar examples, see Genevieve E. Cummins and Nerylla D. Taunton, *Chatelaines: Utility to Glorious Extravagance* (Woodbridge, Suffolk, UK: Antique Collectors' Club, 1994), 34, 39, 42. See also Genevieve E. Cummins, *How the Watch Was Worn: A Fashion for 500 Years* (Woodbridge, Suffolk, UK: Antique Collectors' Club, 2010), 24.

2. Cummins, *How the Watch Was Worn*, 88–89.

Chatelaine with watch and pendants

Wedgwood Manufactory (English, founded 1758)
About 1790
Gilt metal, steel, carnelian, ceramic, and crystal
20.2 × 4.5 × 1.7 cm (7 15/16 × 1 3/4 × 11/16 in.)
Bequest of George Washington Wales 03.302a–b

The English porcelain manufactory Wedgwood made ceramic cameos that were typically mounted in hair ornaments, necklaces, brooches, rings, and watch fobs. In this late-eighteenth-century chatelaine, the cameo medallions were made for the coronation of Leopold II in 1790, when he became king of Germany. According to an invoice from that year, Wedgwood sent 186 chatelaines with commemorative cameos to Frankfurt for the big event.[1]

The chatelaine's waist hook features Minerva, the Roman goddess of wisdom, placing a crown with an eagle's crest on a bust of Leopold as two other Roman deities, Mars and possibly Charitas, contemplate it. Suspended from chains attached to the hook are three trinkets: an undecorated carnelian fob; a V-shaped container, possibly for snuff; and a swivel mirror in a case with an engraved hammer and anvil, symbols of force and labor. A fourth chain is missing its ornament, which was probably a key for the pendant watch decorated with a second Wedgwood cameo. The watch cameo depicts the radiant head of Phoebus Apollo, the sun god, encircled by a lively border of bows and blossoms.

The classical motifs symbolized hope for peace and enlightenment during troubled times in Europe. Unfortunately, Leopold II, who had brought such peace to Tuscany before his coronation, lived only two years after gaining the German throne. He was succeeded by Francis II, who was defeated by Napoleon.

1. Jean Gorely, *Old Wedgwood* (Wellesley, Mass.: Wellesley Press, 1942), 71.

Shoe buckles

United States or Europe, last quarter of the 18th century
Gold, silver, steel, and glass
2.9 × 7.3 × 6 cm (1⅛ × 2⅞ × 2⅜ in.)
Bequest of Buckminster Brown, M.D. 95.1363–4

Dr. John Warren of Boston, a prominent late-eighteenth-century surgeon and dedicated patriot, wore these sparkling buckles on plain black shoes for formal occasions.[1] Although diamond was the gem of choice for such adornments, Warren's shoes feature faux stones made of colorless glass paste because diamonds were difficult to obtain and usually prohibitively expensive in the American colonies. In the early 1730s, when Georges-Frédéric Strass (of Strasbourg and later Paris) invented a form of lead glass that was transparent, highly refractive, and capable of being faceted and set like diamond, glass paste became a highly popular substitute, especially for buckles, buttons, and brooches.[2]

Paste rosettes set in closed-back silver mounts stud the center of these shoe buckles. Oblong pastes arc away from them and terminate in clusters of four faux gems. Each paste has a dot of black paint at the bottom in imitation of an open culet, a feature of early brilliant-cut diamonds (also known as mine cuts). The interior border is made of gold sheet engraved with a swag motif; the double tongue that secures the buckle to the shoe is made of steel.

1. Warren was appointed senior surgeon of the Continental Massachusetts General Hospital in 1777 and five years later was one of the founding members of Harvard Medical School; see *Sibley's Harvard Graduates* 17:655–69, as reproduced by the New England Historical Society's Colonial Collegians database at http://www.newenglandancestors.org/ebooks/CC/CCIntro.pdf.

2. Martha Gandy Fales, *Jewelry in America, 1600–1900* (Woodbridge, Suffolk, UK: Antique Collectors' Club, 1995), 48–49.

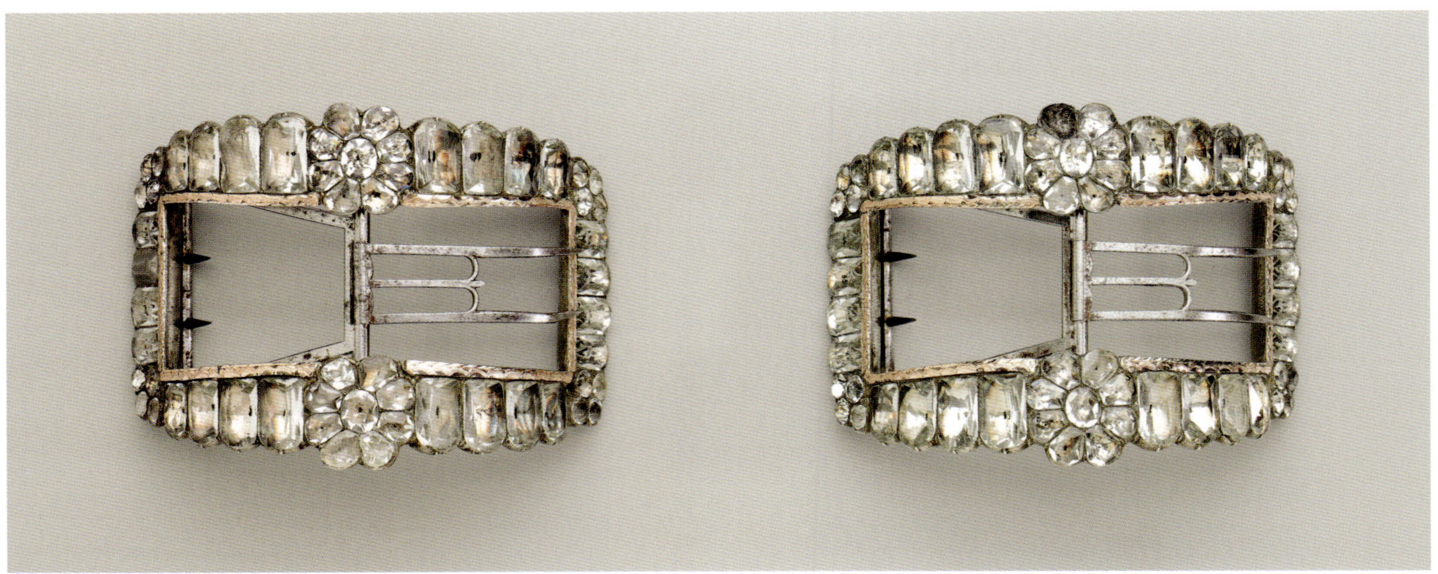

Netsuke in the form of a hare and loquats

Okatomo of Kyoto (Japanese, about 1750–1800)
Late 18th century
Stained ivory and horn
3.1 × 3.9 × 2.1 cm (1¼ × 1$\frac{9}{16}$ × $\frac{13}{16}$ in.)
William Sturgis Bigelow Collection 11.23441

Netsuke, miniature Japanese sculptures, originally functioned as toggles that suspended small stacked boxes from an attached cord tucked under a sash tied at the waist. Highly prized as fashion accessories in seventeenth- and eighteenth-century Japan, they became obsolete as a form of functional adornment when Japanese men began to abandon traditional dress for Western attire in the 1870s.[1] This netsuke, which depicts a squatting hare with its left front paw resting on three loquats, is made of ivory stained in select areas to emphasize the incised fur on the head and body. The animal's eyes and the loquats' calyxes are inlaid with pale horn. In Japan, the hare is the fourth animal of the zodiac and indicates the hours between five and seven in the morning, as well as the month of February.[2]

Netsuke artists passed their skills from father to son, primarily in the cities of Osaka, Kyoto, and Edo (modern Tokyo). They typically carved their diminutive sculptures out of ivory imported from China or out of wood, although they also used buffalo horn, stag antler, and ceramics.

1. Netsuke continue to be made for export and collectors. For a history, see Joe Earle, *Netsuke: Fantasy and Reality in Japanese Miniature Sculpture* (Boston: MFA Publications, 2001), 17–26.

2. Karl M. Schwartz, *Netsuke Subjects: A Study on the Netsuke Themes with Reference to Their Interpretation and Symbolism* (Vienna: Böhlau Verlag Gesellschaft, 1992), 122, no. 341.

Stomacher

France, possibly from Navarre, early 1800s
Gold (about 16kt) and emerald
22.5 × 8.6 × 1 cm (8⅞ × 3⅜ × ⅜ in.)
Bequest of Mrs. Arthur Croft–The Gardner Brewer Collection 01.6495

Men and women in Europe once wore stomachers from the neckline to the waist to cover elaborate lacings on their clothes. The earliest examples, often heavily embroidered, date from the fifteenth century. By the seventeenth century, only women wore stomachers, which could include a lavish, symmetrical, V-shaped framework encrusted with gems. Such a filigree jewel was either sewn onto the garment or attached by ribbon to the bodice.[1] A segmented construction afforded flexibility and aided physical movement. Popular motifs used by jewelers included bows and stylized flowers

This nineteenth-century French stomacher is unusual for its emerald stones, a gem associated with Spain and Portugal. Most provincial French pieces of the period were made of silver or copper gilt highlighted by raised bezel-set glass pastes or small diamonds. In style, the stomacher resembles bodice jewelry worn in several French regions bordering Spain and Portugal, particularly Navarre. Although stomachers fell out of fashion in major French cities by the close of the eighteenth century, they continued to be popular in the provinces well into the next century. They adorned regional dress, and often their bottom segment was either a Christian cross or a Saint-Esprit pendant, reflecting the religious sentiments of the wearer.[2]

1. For more information on stomachers, see Diana Scarisbrick, *Jewellery in Britain, 1066–1837: A Documentary, Social, Literary, and Artistic Survey* (Norwich, UK: Michael Russell, 1994), 287–88.

2. Claudette Joannis, *Bijoux des regions de France* (Paris: Flammarion, 1992), 97, 122, and 123; Rémy Kerténian, *Le bijou Provençal: Parures du quotidien et bijoux de fête* (Geneva: Aubanel, 2003), 62–63.

Posy holder (tuzzy-muzzy)

England or United States, mid-19th century
Silver
14.7 × 6.5 × 4.5 cm (5 13/16 × 2 9/16 × 1 3/4 in.)
Gift of Miss Emily M. Babcock 46.657

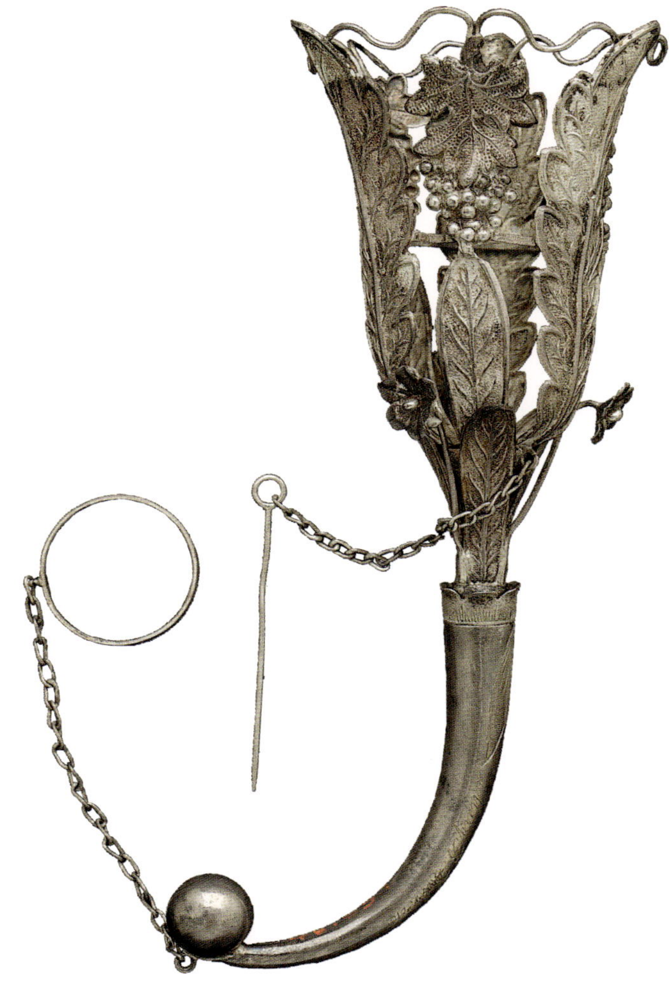

The custom of carrying small bouquets of flowers called nosegays became popular among young upper-class women during the Victorian era. Carried in posy holders (called tuzzy-muzzies in the United States), the nosegays expressed a person's sentiments through a rich and commonly shared language of flowers. Each flower communicated a specific emotion. Roses conveyed exchanges of love, whether platonic (yellow roses), brand new (lavender roses), or passionate (red roses). Morning glories symbolized unrequited love, and yellow carnations conveyed disdain. If a woman's suitor was too shy to communicate his admiration directly, he could offer a symbolic bouquet instead. Women also made bouquets for their friends or for their own use. Popular reference books classified the flowers and their meanings.[1]

Posy holders were typically made of silver with curved handles, sometimes with a chain attached to a ring that could be worn on a finger. A pin secured the bouquet to the posy holder, allowing the arrangement to be held or worn dangling from the finger. This particular example is inscribed on the handle with the name of its owner, Mary B. Babcock.

1. The most popular books on the subject were Charlotte de la Tour's *Le langage des fleurs,* published in 1819, and Kate Greenaway's illustrated book *The Language of Flowers,* which first appeared in 1885. For further information on the history of floral symbolism, see Geraldine Adamich Laufer, *Tussie-Mussie: The Victorian Art of Expressing Yourself in the Language of Flowers* (New York: Workman Publishing, 1993), 6–53.

Headdress (*feng tien*)

Chinese, late Qing dynasty, about 1900

Gilt metal, kingfisher feathers, jadeite, tourmaline, coral, turquoise, lapis lazuli, bone, pearl, glass, resin, silk satin weave, and silk plain weave

21.6 × 24.8 × 19.1 cm (8½ × 9¾ × 7½ in.)

Bequest of Miss Lucy T. Aldrich Res.55.48

The Eurasian kingfisher is known for its radiant, electric blue feathers. In China the bird's iridescent plumes were highly prized and used in the decorative arts, as in this late-Qing-dynasty headdress. Black silk satin covers the ornament's iron-wire framework,[1] attached to which are numerous ornamental motifs, including a central blossom with a jadeite center and pink tourmaline petals. Butterflies, bats, flowers, and two phoenixes amid stylized waves and clouds add to the ornate composition.[2] They are further embellished by kingfisher feathers set in gilt metal mounts nestled between pearls and semiprecious stones. Many of the flowers and creatures were mounted *en tremblant* on small metal springs, so they quivered when the wearer moved or turned her head. The front fringe of pearls with colorful beads and glass adorned the forehead.

Chinese artisans used the kingfisher's feathers as early as the Han dynasty (206 B.C.–A.D. 220) to decorate wall hangings and bedcovers.[3] During the Ming (1368–1644) and Qing (1644–1912) dynasties, they also used the feathers in jewelry and headdresses, especially those worn by brides on their wedding day or by noblewomen on ceremonial occasions. By the early twentieth century, women of lesser rank could afford small ornaments decorated with the feathers, leading to the demise of the once-prolific bird in China's rivers and marshes.[4]

1. Beverly Jackson, *Kingfisher Blue: Treasures from an Ancient Chinese Art* (Toronto: Ten Speed Press, 2001), 97–98.

2. Emily Banis, "The Museum of Fine Arts, Boston Kingfisher Feather Headdress," *Adornment* 7, no. 2 (Summer 2008): 12–13.

3. Victoria Z. Rivers, *The Shining Cloth: Dress and Adornment That Glitter* (New York: Thames and Hudson, 1999), 132.

4. Roland Hartman, "Kingfisher Feather Jewellery," *Arts of Asia* (May–June 1980): 75.

Luckenbooth brooch

England, mid-19th century
Silver, enamel, and agate
38 × 7.8 × 1.4 cm (14 15/16 × 3 1/16 × 9/16 in.)
Gift of Miss Emily M. Babcock 51.1967

This hand-fabricated ornament is a form of the Luckenbooth brooch, a heart-shaped pin surmounted by a crown popular in the Scottish Lowlands during the eighteenth and nineteenth centuries. The name comes from the luckenbooths (street stalls) that sold them in Edinburgh. They were also known as Queen Mary's brooches, which refers to Mary Stuart, whose marriage to Francis, Dauphin of France, cemented the alliance between Scotland and France in 1558 and whose crowned monogram sometimes adorns the brooch's center.[1]

This jewel's two hearts lie horizontally head to head. The materials, both agate and enameling, suggest it was made in England rather than Scotland, where enamels rarely embellish hard-stone adornments. On the pin's reverse is the inscription "Mrs. E. B. Alward/1865/1876."

Many Luckenbooth brooches were love tokens or betrothal gifts, although there is evidence to suggest that some may have also served as amulets to ward off witches.[2] In the eighteenth century silversmiths in rural Scotland made the jewels, but during the nineteenth century city jewelry craftsmen took over the manufacture, creating more elaborate versions sometimes set with stones.

Appreciation for Scottish culture gained momentum in England with the writings of Sir Walter Scott and Queen Victoria and Prince Albert's passion for Scotland. The royal couple first visited their northern neighbor in 1842 and subsequently purchased Balmoral Castle in Aberdeenshire as a summer retreat. They also developed a fondness for Scottish costume and adornment, especially jewels made with local stones called cairngorms, a variety of yellow-brown quartz named for Cairngorms Mountains in the eastern Highlands.[3] It was not long before Scottish "pebble jewelry" became a fad in England. The demand for this novel ornament was so great that jewelers in Birmingham and elsewhere began manufacturing a variety of forms, few of them based on Scottish designs. Although the stones were occasionally set in gold, most of the jewelry was made of silver. When supplies of Scottish cairngorms began to dry up, British metalsmiths obtained agates from Idar-Oberstein, Germany, a centuries-old source for cut stones.

1. Personal communication from Diana Scarisbrick, January 19, 2010.

2. Shirley Bury, *Jewellery, 1789–1910: The International Era*, vol. 2 (Woodbridge, Suffolk, UK: Antique Collectors' Club, 1991), 515–17.

3. Ibid., 514.

Renaissance-revival lady's pocket watch

Case by Tiffany and Company (American, founded 1837)
Movement and dial by Patek Philippe (Swiss, founded 1851)
About 1890
Gold, silver, enamel, diamond, and crystal
5 × 3.5 × 1.3 cm (1 15/16 × 1 3/8 × 1/2 in.)
Museum purchase with funds donated by Susan B. Kaplan in honor of Yvonne J. Markowitz and her decades of service to the MFA 2008.27

Open-face men's pocket watch

American Waltham Watch Company (American, 1851–1957)
1887
Gold-filled metal, enamel, nickel, and crystal
8 × 5.5 × 1.5 cm (3 1/8 × 2 3/16 × 9/16 in.)
Gift of Yvonne J. Markowitz 2008.28

Tiffany and Company was the premier retailer of fine timepieces in the United States during the second half of the nineteenth century. The company's earliest watches included pocket chronometers by Arnold and Frodsham of London and keyless, stem-winding watches from the Geneva firm Patek Philippe. Watches were so important to Tiffany's business that the company began making its own shortly after the Civil War, recruiting the talented British watchmaker Joseph Charles Whitehouse to head its new department.[1] In 1874 Charles Tiffany opened a watchmaking factory in Geneva, where he hoped to combine American technological expertise with the considerable mechanical skills of Swiss artisans, but the factory closed a few years later. He thereafter depended on Patek Philippe to supply watch works for his New York store. Tiffany's relationship with the Swiss watchmaker continues to this day.[2]

The bejeweled Tiffany lady's pocket watch in the Renaissance-revival style features a chased and engraved gold dial with black-enamel Roman numerals separated by blue-enamel fleur-de-lis. The

foliate bezel encloses a lever escapement movement that controls the time. The reverse is decorated with two enamel portraits of elegant women set in oval frames bordered by delicate rose-cut diamonds. A scrolling grillwork with shimmering diamond highlights surrounds each image. The case is unmarked but typical of work fabricated in France for Tiffany during the latter part of the nineteenth century. The watch was owned by the philanthropist Clara B. Snow, of Brockton, Massachusetts, wife of the prominent and civic-minded shoe manufacturer George G. Snow.[3]

Her husband's open-face pocket watch was made by the American Waltham Watch Company, a leading nineteenth-century American watch manufacturer along with the Elgin Watch Company based in Elgin, Illinois. Waltham watches were mass-produced, numbering more than 35 million between 1851 and 1957, when the company closed. Throughout the firm's complex history of nearly one hundred years, it manufactured a wide variety of timepieces, including railroad watches, chronographs, repeaters, and deck watches.

George Snow's watch features a white enamel dial with black Roman-numeral indicators, a subsidiary seconds dial, and a transfer photograph of Clara. The watch has a nickel lever escapement movement and a gold-filled case with an engraved foliate design on the reverse. The case was made by Pioneer, a firm known for supplying gold and gold-filled cases to leading American watch manufacturers.[4]

1. John Loring, *Tiffany Timepieces* (New York: Harry N. Abrams, 2004), 11.

2. Clare Phillips, ed., *Bejewelled by Tiffany, 1837–1987* (New Haven, Conn.: Yale University Press in association with the Gilbert Collection Trust and Tiffany & Co., 2006), 194–97.

3. Meghan Melvin, "A Tale of Two 19th Century Watches at the Museum of Fine Arts, Boston," *Adornment* 7, no. 1 (Spring 2008): 21.

4. Tom Engle, Richard E. Gilbert, and Cooksey Shugart, *Complete Price Guide to Watches* (Mt. Pleasant, S.C.: Tinderbox Press, 2007), 38, 110.

Belt buckle

Peter Carl Fabergé (Russian, 1846–1920)
Fedor Rückert (Russian, 1840–1917)
Early 20th century
Silver gilt and enamel
D. 0.6 cm, diam. 6.5 cm (D. ¼ in., diam. 2 9/16 in.)
Gift of Mrs. Eustace Strong in memory of her mother, Mary K. Wells 30.114

Between 1890 and the First World War, an emphasis on slender waists in Western ladies' fashion spurred the wearing of belts with ornamental buckles.[1] In Russia, buckle designs reflected the sumptuous tastes of the Romanov court, Fabergé's most important patron.[2] Worn with dresses and robes made of imported silk and lush velvets embellished by gold-thread embroidery, Fabergé's colorful buckles from the period were typically rectangular or oval in shape and decorated with transparent enamels over metal with engine-turned patterns.

This cloisonné enameled buckle is unusual for Fabergé because it is in the neo-Russian style, which combines ethnic Russian motifs in abstract, modernist formats very much influenced by the designs of the Austrian and German *stil moderne* and secessionist movements.[3] Such designs were composed of repetitive geometric forms and highly stylized floral motifs. Works in metal were enlivened by enamels in blue, green, white, and brown. Some, including this example, have twisted silver-gilt *cloisons* and painted enamel highlights in gold.

1. Jo-Anne Birnie Danzker, *Art Nouveau Buckles* (Munich: Arnoldsche, 2000), 11.

2. Géza von Habsburg, *Fabergé: Imperial Craftsman and His World* (London: Booth Clibborn Editions, 2000), 30–31.

3. Jelena Milojković-Djurić, *Panslavism and National Identity in Russia and in the Balkans, 1830–1880: Images of the Self and Others* (New York: Columbia University Press, 1994), 54–95. For a better understanding of the neo-Russian style in the arts, see Anne Odom, *Russian Enamels: Kievan Rus to Fabergé* (Baltimore: Walters Art Gallery, 1996), 107.

Maltese-cross brooch

Designed by Maison Gripoix (French, founded 1869) for the House of Chanel (French, founded 1909)

1970–1979

Gilt metal and glass

7.1 × 7.1 × 1.8 cm (2 13/16 × 2 13/16 × 11/16 in.)

Museum purchase with funds donated by Penny Vinik 2008.34

Departing from the prevailing notion that women of position and style should wear fine jewelry made of only precious materials, French couturiers in the 1920s began to recognize nonprecious jewelry as an acceptable accessory for designer clothing. Working with jewelry manufacturers, the fashion houses created *bijoux de couture*, typically whimsical, imaginative ornaments inspired by current fashions and made of inexpensive materials such as gilt metal and glass. The designer usually put his or her firm's name on the jewels and sold them to boutiques in limited numbers.[1]

French clothing designer Gabrielle (Coco) Chanel is frequently credited with having first understood that jewelry played an important role in tasteful, harmonious fashion ensembles.[2] Seeing jewelry more as an expression of a woman's personality than as a symbol of wealth, she often accessorized her understated clothing designs with both fine and faux jewelry, sometimes boldly mixing the two. Chanel was particularly attracted to ropes of faux pearls and chains, as well as designs based on ancient, medieval, Renaissance, and baroque jewels.

This later Chanel brooch is based on the Maltese cross, a sixteenth-century design derived from the emblem of the Knights of Malta. It was fabricated by Maison Gripoix, a multigenerational Parisian firm that made jewelry for leading couturiers, including Chanel, Paul Poiret, Cristóbal Balenciaga, and Jeanne Lanvin.[3] Chanel became interested in the Maltese cross after she befriended Duke Fulco di Verdura. A gifted jewelry designer with an interest in Byzantine art and historic emblems, Verdura made Chanel a pair of enameled cuff bracelets, each of which had a Maltese cross dramatically embellished with scattered diamonds and colored stones in the center. She counted the cuff bracelets among her favorite jewels.

1. Melissa Gabardi, "Bijoux de Couture: France, 1927–1968," in *Jewels of Fantasy: Costume Jewelry of the 20th Century*, ed. Deanna Farneti Cera (New York: Harry N. Abrams, 1992), 225.

2. She was not the first designer to retail couture jewelry; see Florence Müller, *Costume Jewelry for Haute Couture* (New York: Vendome Press, 2007), 16.

3. Ibid., 146.

Halter top

Elsa Peretti (Italian, born 1940)

Whiting and Davis (American, founded 1876) for Tiffany and Company (American, founded 1837)

About 1975

Silver mesh

H. 35.6 cm, w. 76.8 cm (H. 14 in., w. 30¼ in.)

Gift in honor of Elizabeth Ann Coleman 2004.497.1

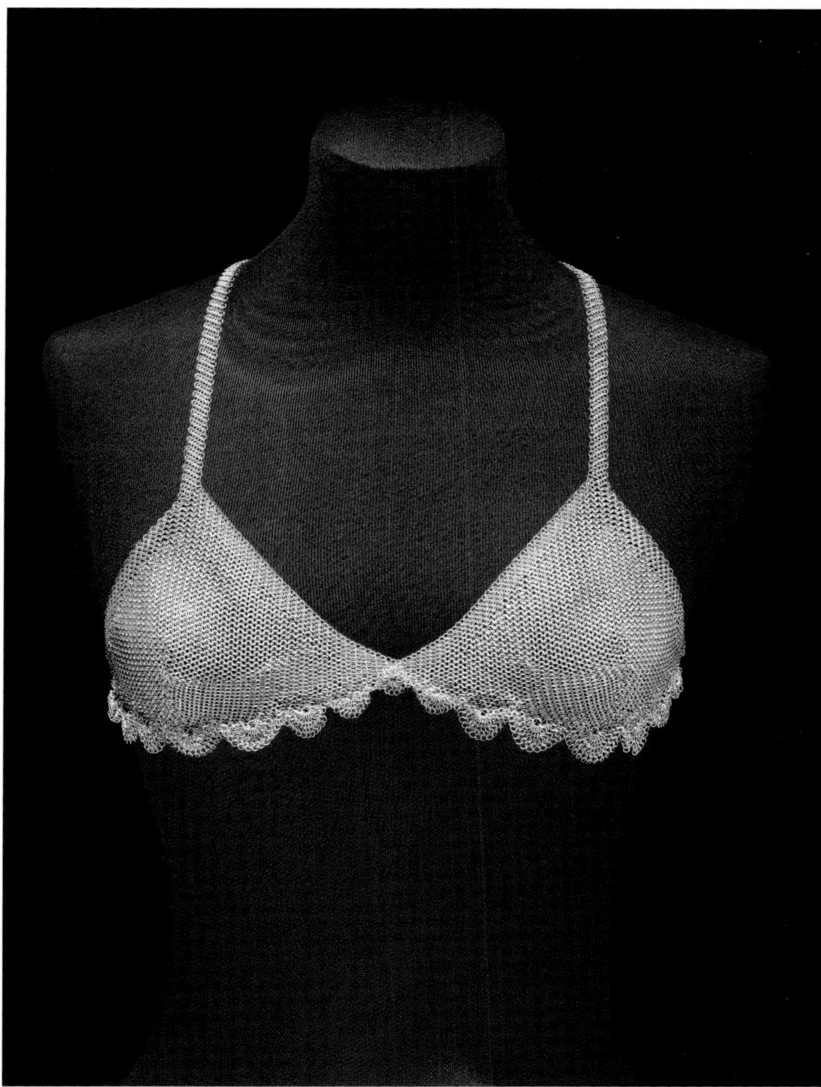

Elsa Peretti earned an interior design degree in Rome before moving in 1969 to New York City, where she modeled for fashion icon Roy Halston Frowick before she began to design silver jewelry. In 1971 she won the prestigious Fashion Critics' Coty Award and in 1974 joined Tiffany and Company, the oldest surviving retailer and manufacturer of jewelry in the United States.

As a complement to the sleek, fluid, and seductive garments in Halston's fall 1974 collection, Peretti contributed a silver-mesh halter top to be worn under a creamy silk shirt open to the waist.[1] The inspiration for the cross between jewelry and clothing came during a trip to Jaipur, India, where Peretti saw woven metalwork and then supervised the creation of a hand-fabricated halter prototype. Back in New York, she consulted Samuel Beizer, the first chairman of the jewelry department at the Fashion Institute of America, about producing such a garment. Beizer contacted the Rhode Island firm Whiting and Davis, a company known for its machine-made mesh purses, and then both Peretti and Beizer worked with the firm to adapt existing machinery to produce Peretti's design. Her silver-and-gold-mesh halters for Tiffany and Company remained fashionable for several years.[2]

Since then, Peretti has designed several jewelry lines with organic, sculptural forms for Tiffany, including bone cuff bracelets and bean-shaped ornaments and accessories. Although she has also designed hollowware and decorative objects made of ceramic and glass, she remains best recognized for her work in silver and is frequently credited with having reintroduced the material to the high-style jewelry market.

1. Elizabeth Ann Coleman, "Tiffany: The Perfect Accessory to Fashion," in *American Luxury: Jewels from the House of Tiffany*, ed. Jeannine Falino and Yvonne J. Markowitz (Woodbridge, Suffolk, UK: Antique Collectors' Club, 2009), 176–77.

2. Louisa W. Bann, "Halter Top," in *Bejeweled by Tiffany, 1837–1987*, ed. Clare Phillips (New Haven, Conn.: Yale University Press, 2006), 289–90.

Bib necklace

Kenneth Jay Lane (American, born 1930)
1980–89
Gold-plated metal, cast resin, and metallic paint
23.5 × 18 × 1.5 cm (9¼ × 7¹⁄₁₆ × ⁹⁄₁₆ in.)
Museum purchase with funds donated by Penny Vinik 2008.120.1

Costume jewelry's popularity in the United States from the 1950s to the mid-1970s had much to do with the personality and creative energy of New York–based jewelry designer Kenneth Jay Lane. In this bib necklace made of large faux gems, Lane purposefully and dramatically alludes to the luxurious opulence of traditional, high-style jewelry. There is no attempt to hide the materials' artificial nature: the "emeralds" and "rubies" are made of cast resin that simulates rough-cut precious stones, and the gold bezels are painted on the stones' perimeters to look like gold settings. The leading fashion magazines *Vogue* and *Harper's Bazaar* frequently featured Lane's costume jewelry, making it the passion of socialites, celebrities, and fashion-conscious women alike.[1]

D. D. (Drew Dixon) Ryan, a noted New York socialite connected to the fashion world, owned this Lane necklace. Ryan began her career as an assistant to fashion photographer Richard Avedon and later became a photo editor at *Harper's Bazaar*. She also designed costumes for Stephen Sondheim's Broadway production of *Company* (1970) and worked as an assistant to the New York fashion designer Halston. According to Ryan's 2007 obituary, she often wore clothing that she made herself and had a keen eye for accessories and "really good costume jewelry."

1. Vivienne Becker, "The Return of the Ornament, 1965–Present," in *Jewels of Fantasy: Costume Jewelry of the 20th Century*, ed. Deanna Farneti Cera (New York: Harry N. Abrams, 1991), 313.

Woman's suit in two parts

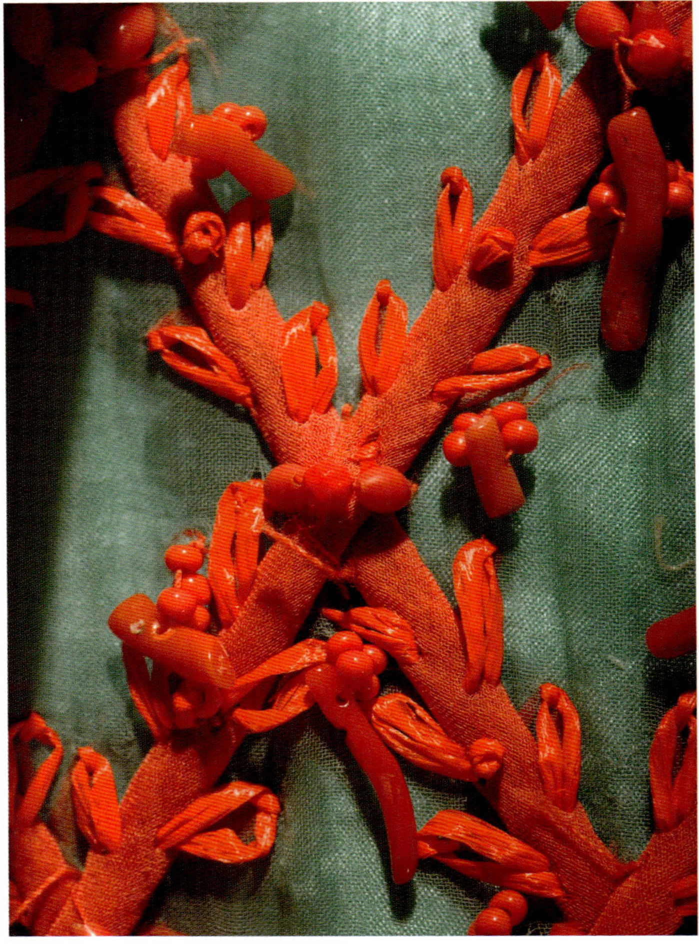

Arnold Scaasi (American, born 1931)

Spring 1968

Silk plain weave, coral, glass, plastic, and metal

Dress: 92.7 cm (36½ in.) center back; 89.5 cm (35¼ in.) center front

Jacket: 41.3 cm (16¼ in.) center back; 29.8 cm (11¾ in.) center front

Arnold Scaasi Collection—Gift of Arnold Scaasi made possible through the generous support of Jean S. and Frederic A. Sharf, anonymous donors, Penny and Jeff Vinik, Lynne and Mark Rickabaugh, Jane and Robert Burke, Carol Wall, Mrs. I. W. Colburn, Megan O'Block, Lorraine Bressler, and Daria Petrilli-Eckert 2009.4060.1–2

Clothing and adornment come together as a single entity in this two-piece dress ensemble created by the leading mid-twentieth-century couturier Arnold Scaasi for Joetta Norban, a New York City socialite and wife of a prominent developer and nightclub proprietor. At the neckline of the turquoise bodice and the cuffs of the coral shantung silk jacket, natural coral, glass, and plastic bead decoration functions as a choker and matching bracelets. Scaasi's use of branched coral beads, which project away from the wearer, reinforces the impression that the decoration is a form of stand-alone jewelry.

Like many of New York City's fashionable women, Norban donated her time and energy to charities, serving on the committee (and later as cochair) of the Lila Motley Cancer Foundation's Peacock Ball. For the 1966 event, Scaasi created an elegant gown embroidered with coral and turquoise beads for Norban. A regular client of the designer, she must have been particularly pleased with the color combination and materials, because the designer created this suit for her soon after that event.

Characterized by exquisite craftsmanship, each of Scaasi's designs takes at least three craftsmen about 120 hours to complete. Many of his luxurious creations are embellished by embroidery, intricate beading, appliqués, or feathers. At various points in his career, Scaasi also designed costume jewelry.[1]

1. The Museum of Fine Arts, Boston, acquired the Arnold Scassi archive in 2009.

Fig. 22. Necklace, Alexander Calder (American, 1898–1976), 1941, silver.

The art nouveau style fell out of fashion by the First World War. The 1920s, which witnessed the emergence of the art deco style, were years of rapid change marked by innovations such as electrical lighting, commercial radio, modern aviation, and the building of skyscrapers. Design in the decorative arts emphasized speed, linear geometries, and abstractions. Platinum, diamond, and other precious materials came back in vogue for jewelry joined by other stones that were deemed unfashionable at the start of the century such as jade, turquoise, onyx, coral, and lapis lazuli. Jewelers, now largely working in high-style houses that relied on the apprenticeship model of training, often combined these

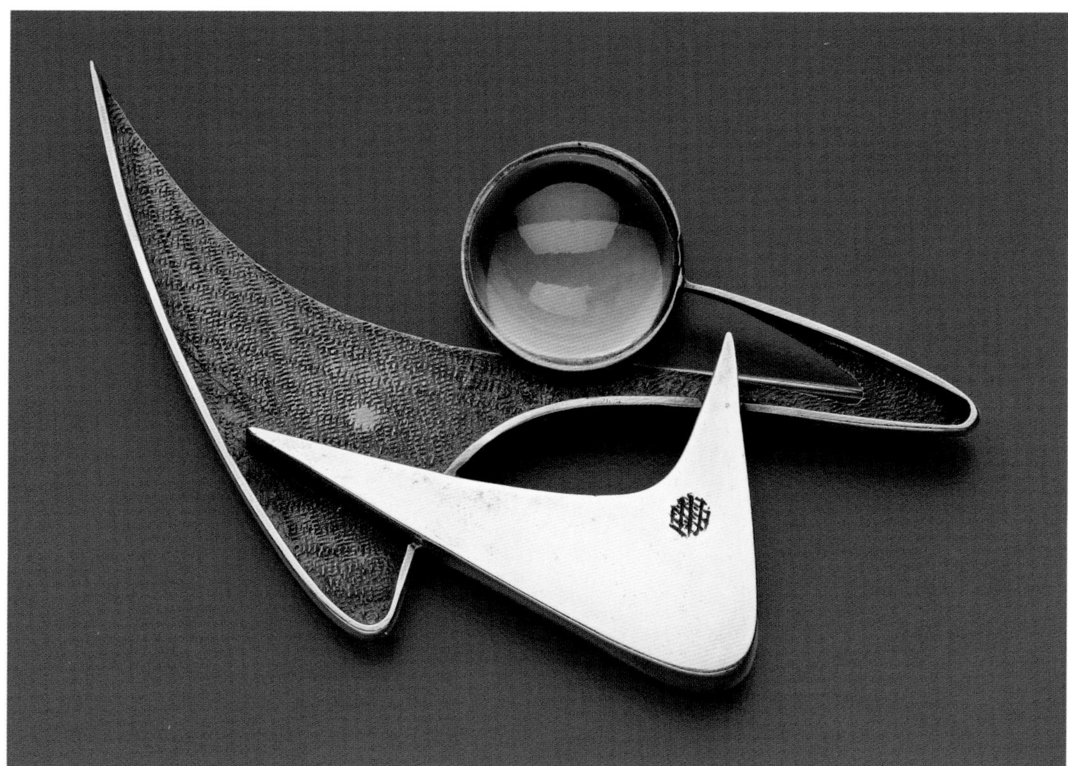

Fig. 23. Brooch, Margaret De Patta (American, 1903–1964), about 1980, silver and quartz.

opaque stones with clear, transparent materials such as rock crystal and diamond to create ornaments with both deep, saturated color and glittering, reflected light. Contrasting, even clashing, colors invigorated the flat, streamlined designs. In summarizing the art deco style in a 1929 article, French jeweler Georges Fouquet stated, "Speed is the characteristic of present-day life. The composition of a piece of jewelry must be readily understood and must be constructed of simple lines, free from affectation and superfluous detail."[1]

The arts and crafts, art nouveau, and art deco movements were part of a larger cultural experience known as modernism, a far-reaching social, economic, and political reform movement with roots in Renaissance humanism, the Enlightenment, and neoclassical idealism. Modernists were passionate agents of transformation in a world revolutionized by advances in science and technology. Confronted by an outdated societal infrastructure, they created new, standardized, and mechanized systems. At the same time, the new platforms were flexible and adaptable to further improvements. Amid this upheaval of change, art was viewed as a vehicle for conveying these transformations to the general public.

Those artists who became part of the early studio jewelry movement saw themselves as such agents of transformation. Some, like Alexander Calder, had achieved success as sculptors and painters. Calder was a seminal figure in the studio jewelry movement; his

Fig. 24. Brooch, Margaret Craver (American, born 1907), about 1945, silver and quartz.

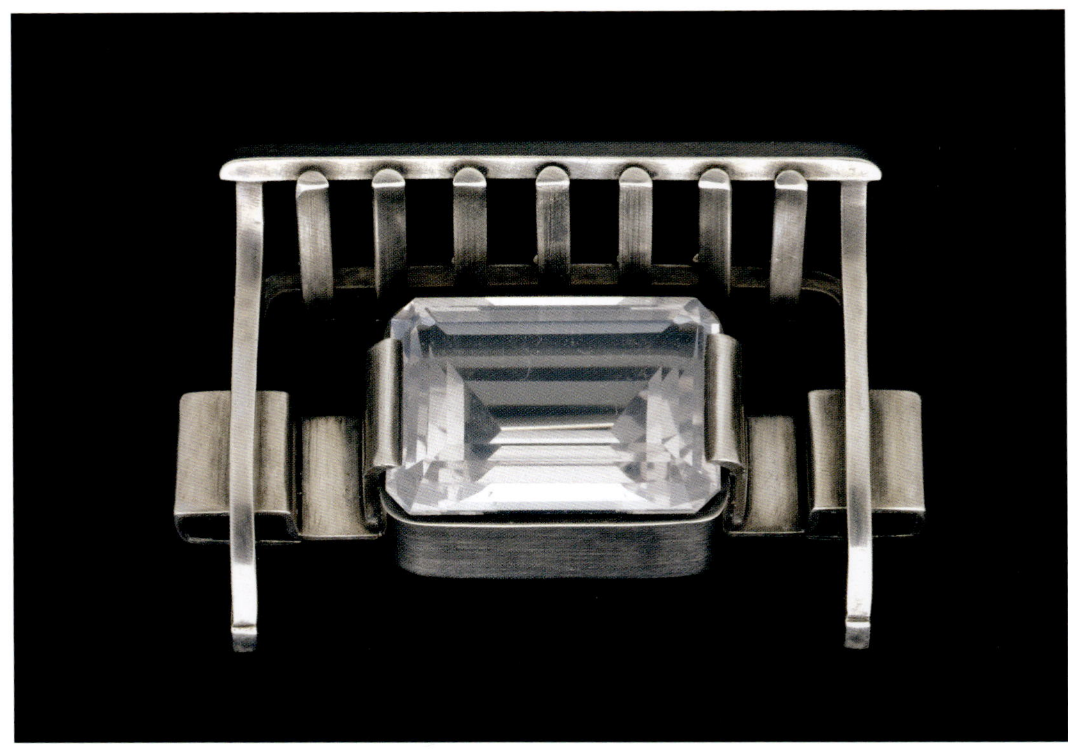

ornaments were simple constructions made of silver or brass and stylistically have much in common with jewelry from ancient cultures (fig. 22). While high-style jewelers of the 1920s, 1930s, and 1940s welcomed scientific advances in the art of lapidary and metalworking, Calder relied on mechanical methods, such as coiling and riveting, to join and secure individual elements. Because each piece was handcrafted, no two pieces were the same—a feature commonly associated with studio jewelry.

While artists like Calder were known primarily for their nonjewelry creations, others experimented almost exclusively with what they called "sculpture to wear." Some of the earliest artist-jewelers were California-based Margaret De Patta (fig. 23) and East Coast jewelers Sam Kramer and Art Smith. De Patta's work was strongly influenced by constructivism and Bauhaus design, whereas Sam Kramer was inspired by surrealism (although he described his own work as "abstract").

In the post–World War II era, Margret Craver emerged as a central figure in the studio jewelry movement (fig. 24). Educated in design at the University of Kansas in Lawrence during the late 1920s, she later sought instruction in traditional metalsmithing in both the United States and Sweden. In 1947 she founded the first of three annual National Silversmithing Workshop Conferences. Several of the instructors came from England and Scandinavia, and the students who attended these programs, such as John Paul Miller, Earl

Pardon, and Alma Eikerman, later became influential jewelers. Many rediscovered ancient and medieval jewelry-making techniques, which added a degree of technical sophistication not present in the earlier work of studio jewelers.

By the 1960s, the studio jewelry movement was international in scope. Many of the jewelers associated with it identified themselves as artists who expressed themselves through the medium of jewelry. International jewelry exhibitions, such as the one held at Goldsmiths' Hall, London, in 1961, resulted in a greater recognition of an approach to jewelry that was described as bold, imaginative, individualistic, and unfettered by the past. Since then, studio jewelers have used the medium to express their personal thoughts and feelings on a range of subjects, including environmental pollution, gender relationships, consumerism, and new technologies. Some create abstract, conceptual works that redefine the relationship of jewelry to the body, whereas others explore the possibilities inherent in new, man-made materials.

1. Georges Fouquet, "La bijouterie et la joaillerie modernes," *Figaro's supplement artistique* (June 13, 1929), as quoted in Sylvie Raulet, *Art Deco Jewelry* (New York: Rizzoli, 1985), 69.

Marsh Bird Hair Ornament (brooch)

Charles Robert Ashbee (English, 1863–1942)

1901–2

Gold, silver, enamel, ruby, moonstone, and freshwater pearl

9 × 10.5 × 1.5 cm (3⁹⁄₁₆ × 4⅛ × ⁹⁄₁₆ in.)

Museum purchase with funds donated by Susan B. Kaplan, Marshall H. Gould Fund, John H. and Ernestine A. Payne Fund, Gift of Linda Fenton, Dorothy-Lee Jones Fund, Gift of Penny Vinik, and Adrienne Iselin Gilbert Memorial Fund 2007.827

A leader of the British arts and crafts movement and one of the first to design jewelry, Charles Robert Ashbee founded the Guild of Handicraft in London, dedicating it to the design and fabrication of decorative objects and running it as a cooperative enterprise.[1] Many of the guild's products were exhibited and sold in Ashbee's gallery on Brook Street, Mayfair, London. By the close of the nineteenth century, Ashbee and the guild had achieved international recognition, with members showing their work regularly with the Arts and Crafts Exhibition Society. They also participated in the Vienna Secession Exhibition of 1902, and images of their work appeared in the prestigious and influential design journals *Studio*, *Art Journal*, and *Dekorative Kunst*.

In 1902 the guild moved to Chipping Camden in Gloucestershire to create an artists' commune.[2] Like many of his colleagues, Ashbee embraced socialist ideals and emphasized teamwork and shared experience. He designed his *Marsh Bird Hair Ornament* (now a brooch) around this time, working with fellow guild members A. Gebhardt to fabricate it and with William Mark to enamel it. The ornament is unusual for its backless plique-à-jour enamel, which allows light to pass through the metal cells. Most jewelry made in the arts and crafts tradition features backed cloisonné or champlevé enamelware, but with this jewel Ashbee and his team sought the effect of stained glass. Six cabochon moonstones shimmer in the space above the bird's head and wings. At each side, freshwater pearls dangle from elegant silver-wire loops. *Marsh Bird* was exhibited at the Woodbury Gallery from 1902 to 1903, and an image of it subsequently appeared in a 1903 article in the prestigious craft journal *Studio*.[3]

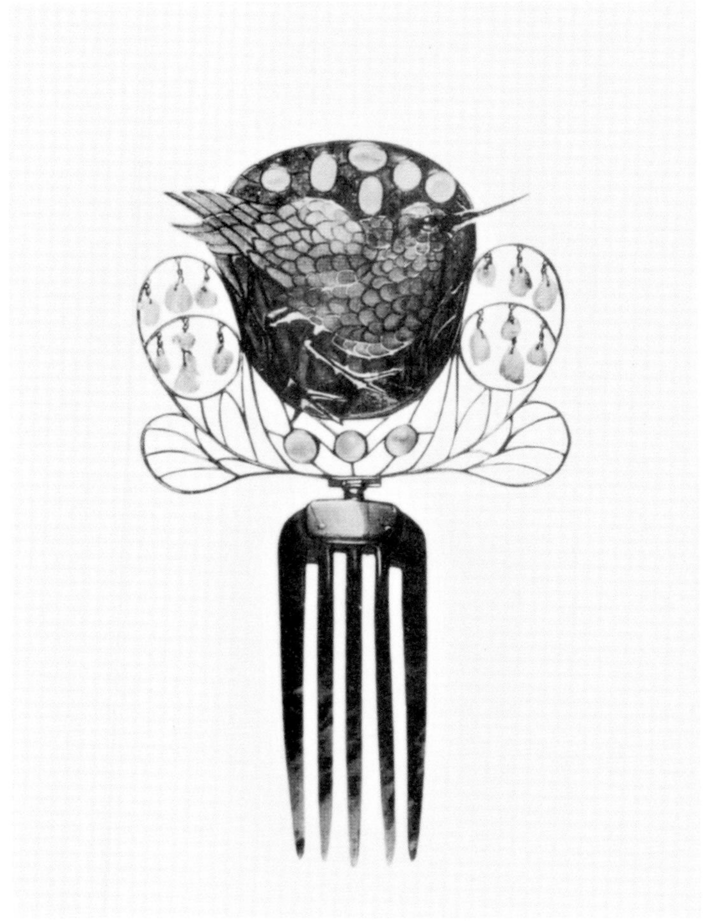

Fig. 25. An illustration of Charles Robert Ashbee's *Marsh Bird* from a 1903 catalogue published by the Guild of Handicraft.

1. Elyse Zorn Karlin, *Jewelry and Metalwork in the Arts and Crafts Tradition* (Atglen, Penn.: Schiffer Publishing, 1993), 38.

2. At the time, the guild consisted of about 150 artists and their families. It remained active until 1908, when it dissolved for economic reasons. See Alan Crawford, *C. R. Ashbee: Architect, Designer, and Romantic Socialist* (New Haven, Conn.: Yale University Press, 1985), 144–48.

3. "Studio-Talk," *Studio* 27 (1903): 209.

Big Double Gold Brooch

John Paul Cooper (English, 1869–1933)
1908
Gold, ruby, moonstone, pearl, amethyst, and chrysoprase
14 × 9.6 × 0.8 cm (5½ × 3¾ × 5⁄16 in.)
Gift of Susan B. Kaplan 2008.264

Architect, designer, and metalsmith John Paul Cooper was a leading figure in the British arts and crafts movement, serving as the head of the metalwork department at the Birmingham Municipal School of Art from 1901 to 1906.[1] His early interest in jewelry design and fabrication began shortly after his association with Henry Wilson, an architect in the office of John D. Sedding, with whom Cooper apprenticed. Wilson's interest in craft, especially metalwork and jewelry, inspired young Cooper to design his own jewelry. And, like Wilson, Cooper eventually employed others to do his fabrication, although occasionally he did his own chasing and repoussé work. Cooper's jewelry was crafted primarily in 15-karat gold, with semiprecious cabochons and mother-of-pearl. His method of designing his work based on a selection of stones (rather than creating a design and then finding suitable gems) distinguished Cooper from other arts and crafts artists. He once commented that stones should "play on one another as two notes of music."[2]

This brooch is a major work by Cooper, created during a period when the artist relied on stones rather than representational imagery. Inspired by medieval and Celtic designs, the jewel is airy and graceful and conveys a sense of refined opulence. Its gold work features finely chased leaves and tendrils, and its bezel-set stones include ruby, pearl, moonstone, amethyst, and chrysoprase. Cooper's chief craftsman, Lorenzo Colarosi, spent 273 hours making this piece, which Cooper entitled *Big Double Gold Brooch*. Cooper may have executed the chase work himself.[3]

1. N. Natasha Kuzmanović, *John Paul Cooper: Designer and Craftsman of the Arts and Crafts Movement* (Gloucestershire: Sutton Publishing, 1999), 57–58.

2. Cooper described his design approach in an undated paper delivered to students at the Birmingham Municipal School of Art; see ibid., 101.

3. The drawing for the brooch, dated December 3, 1908, can be found in *Stockbook I*, page 81, in the Cooper Family Archives, UK.

Hair ornament with antennae

René Lalique (French, 1860–1945)
About 1900
Gold, silver, steel, diamond
8.8 × 12.5 × 7 cm (3 7/16 × 4 15/16 × 2 in.)
Gift of the Sataloff and Cluchey Family 2008.68

Art nouveau jewelers valued the craftsmanship and artistry of an object over the inherent worth of its materials. This hair ornament made of white diamonds is therefore atypical for an art nouveau jewel, though it was made by the movement's preeminent jeweler, René Lalique. Lalique usually preferred plique-à-jour enamel, cast glass, or less precious stones because he felt they brought more color and light into his works than did diamonds. Often he embellished his designs with cabochon cuts rather than brilliants, particularly stones that had a natural sheen or iridescence such as moonstone or opal. He also used ivory or translucent natural horn in lieu of gold, platinum, and other precious metals.

In this whimsical piece, two antennae made of hollow silver cubes, each set with a graduated brilliant secured by four prongs, rise gracefully from the gold-wire headband. A steel wire runs through the stacked cubes, allowing the antennae to arc and the cubes to tremble freely when the wearer moves, thereby accentuating the gemstones' sparkle. Although made of precious materials, the ornament's motif is fanciful—a free-form fragment of a butterfly that would have appealed to avant-garde French ladies.

Like other art nouveau artists, Lalique tended to choose natural plant and animal motifs with curves and sinuous movements. His work also sometimes featured the darker side of nature—serpents, beetles, thorns, withering flowers—reflecting the period's mood as expressed by his contemporaries Baudelaire and Rimbaud. The wide-ranging images and complexity of Lalique's compositions were matched by the meticulous craftsmanship of each piece.

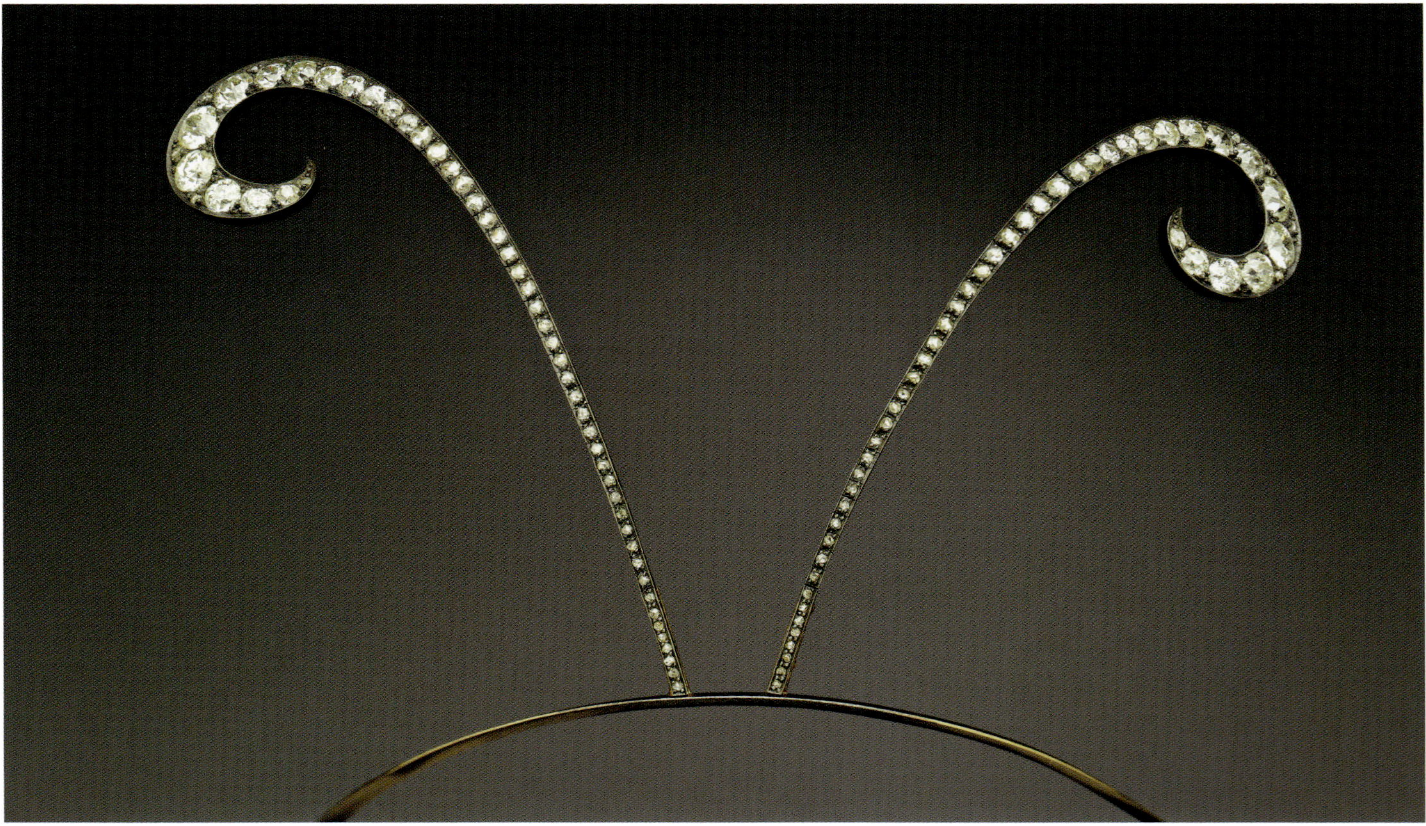

Seaweed brooch

Paul Liénard (French, 1849–unknown)
About 1908
Gold and mabe pearl
5.4 × 11 × 1 cm (2 1/8 × 4 5/16 × 3/8 in.)
Gift of Joe and Ruth Sataloff in honor of Susan B. Kaplan 2007.892

Art nouveau jewelry is often described as the most tantalizing, exotic, and technically sophisticated adornment ever created. The elegant simplicity of this brooch by art nouveau proponent and jeweler Paul Liénard understates its fine workmanship. The brooch features a central mabe pearl flanked by two clusters of cast-gold seaweed fronds with a remarkable undulating quality. The seaweed's stems form elegant ellipses joined to plant-shaped prongs that hold the luminous pearl in place. Similar to other art nouveau ornaments, the decoration on the underside of this jewel reiterates the design elements on the front. Liénard created several ornaments using the seaweed motif; he also used it for his border design for the jewelry magazine *La revue de la bijouterie, joaillerie, orfèvrerie.*

Liénard trained with the Swiss-born decorative arts designer Eugène Grasset, whose teachings and publications inspired many jewelers weary of mainstream historicism and its prevailing emphasis on gem-set platinum adornments. Little else is known about Liénard's early career, except that shortly after the Paris Exposition of 1900, he registered his own mark and opened a studio at 7 rue Joubert in Paris. By 1906 he was exhibiting regularly at the Paris salons and designing jewels for Bolin, a Russian firm in Moscow.[1] His known work, which draws heavily on plant and insect forms, is elegant, graceful, and sinuous.

1. Yvonne J. Markowitz and Elyse Zorn Karlin, *Imperishable Beauty: Art Nouveau Jewelry* (Boston: Museum of Fine Arts, 2008), 149.

Necklace

Josephine Hartwell Shaw (American, 1865–1941)
1910–18
Gold, jade, and colored glass
50.8 × 9.2 cm (20 × 3⅝ in.)
Gift of Mrs. Atherton Loring 1984.947

The Society of Arts and Crafts, Boston (SACB), was the first arts and crafts reform organization in the United States. Its membership included professional craftspeople, educators, social reformers, and philanthropists whose goal was to "stimulate in workmen an appreciation of the dignity and value of good design and to counteract . . . over-ornamentation and specious originality."[1] To achieve this end, its members gave lectures, published their activities, organized juried exhibitions, and created beautiful objects in keeping with arts and crafts philosophy.

Some of the earliest members of SACB were women, among them Master Craftsman Josephine Hartwell Shaw, a Massachusetts native. She both designed and fabricated her creations, including this necklace, a private commission for Mrs. Atherton Loring of Boston. The central elements in the ornament are two pale green antique jades complemented by green-toned gold and polished rectangular plaques of green glass. A sophisticated composition and one of Shaw's most important pieces, this jewel demonstrates a harmonious interplay of forms, colors, and contrasting textures. Shaw's work was highly acclaimed, and it was exhibited at the Cleveland Decorative Arts Club (1908) and the Art Institute of Chicago (1911 and 1918).[2] Although Shaw also produced hollowware in silver and copper for a time, she eventually focused exclusively on jewelry.

1. Mission Statement, 1897, Boston Society of Arts and Crafts Archives, Archives of American Art, Boston Public Library, Boston, Massachusetts.

2. For further information on the life of the artist, see Kaitlin Shinnick, "The Jewelry of Josephine Hartwell Shaw" (master's thesis, Bard Graduate Center, 2008).

Brooch

Frank Gardner Hale (American, 1876–1945)
About 1920
Gold, diamond, sapphire, peridot, and zircon
6.6 × 5 cm (2⅝ × 1 15/16 in.)
Gift of Joseph B. and Edith Alpers 1998.569

Frank Gardner Hale's career owes much to Boston's heightened awareness of the arts at the turn of the twentieth century. The city's leadership in arts and crafts education and design came about as a result of a worker shortage in art-related industries, such as printing and textile production. To remedy the problem, the state legislature passed a law in 1870 requiring the incorporation of art education in the public schools; however, few skilled instructors could be found to train future artisans. As a result, the Massachusetts Normal Art School was founded in 1873 (renamed the Massachusetts College of Art and Design in 1959), followed by the School of the Museum of Fine Arts, Boston, in 1876. The principles of John Ruskin formed the foundation of the curriculum at these institutions, and several of their graduates, including Hale, later emerged as important Boston arts and crafts jewelers.

Hale studied with Henry Hunt Clark, an outstanding instructor in design theory at the School of the Museum of Fine Arts, Boston, during the late 1890s, and with Charles Robert Ashbee's Guild of Handicraft in Chipping Camden, England, in 1906.[1] When Hale returned to the United States in 1907, he was well prepared to open his own studio in Boston. He became a force in the Society of Arts and Crafts, Boston, and won numerous awards for his designs, including the silver medal at the Panama Pacific Exposition in San Francisco (1915) and both the Frank Logan Prize and the bronze medal at the Exhibition of Applied Arts at the Chicago Art Institute (1917). Hale's jewelry is known for its outstanding craftsmanship and distinctive designs. Stylized blossoms, curved stems, sensuous vines, and delectable berries characterize his works, in addition to an acute attention to color, both in stones and in enamels. Similar to his other work, this sumptuous brooch follows a symmetrical, openwork arrangement with colored stones.

1. Hale also spent time in London with noted arts and crafts jeweler Frederick Partridge.

Jeweled casket

Edward Everett Oakes (American, 1891–1960)
1929
Silver, gold, amethyst, pearl, onyx, and wood
13.5 × 20.1 × 16.1 cm (5⁵⁄₁₆ × 7¹⁵⁄₁₆ × 6⁵⁄₁₆ in.)
Museum purchase with funds donated anonymously 2000.628.1a–b

Brooch

Edward Everett Oakes (American, 1891–1960)
About 1920
Gold, silver, sapphire, and moonstone
3.8 × 0.8 cm (1½ × ⁵⁄₁₆ in.)
Benjamin Pierce Cheney Fund 1986.265

In 1926 Boston-based arts and crafts jeweler Edward Everett Oakes embarked on a project that he considered his crowning achievement, this jeweled casket.[1] It took him months to acquire the stones, which amounted to 143 Siberian amethysts, 5 South American amethysts, 86 pearls, and 86 pieces of onyx. When the casket was exhibited at the Society of Arts and Crafts, Boston (SACB) in 1929, the press described it as "architecture in miniature."[2]

Oakes's jewelry designs are drawn from the natural world and typically consist of foliate patterns arranged asymmetrically. Many of his ornaments have notched frames that enclose openwork arrangements of serrated leaves, blossoms, and coiled stems. Oakes was a skilled metalsmith and utilized a variety of metal techniques, including repoussé, chasing, and carving, to execute his designs. He rarely worked in platinum, preferring gold and silver, often combining the two in a single ornament. Oakes also preferred bezel-set cabochons in soft hues, especially moonstones from India and small Montana sapphires.

Oakes was part of a second wave of U.S. arts and crafts jewelers in the early decades of the twentieth century who profited from apprenticeships with established artists. He spent five years with Boston metalsmith Frank Gardner Hale and three years with jeweler Josephine Hartwell Shaw. Oakes opened his own shop in 1917, the same year the SACB named him a master craftsman. By then he had exhibited his work at the Art Institute of Chicago and the SACB. Although Oakes's clientele was based in Boston, his work was highly regarded throughout the country. He was honored by the SACB in 1923 with a bronze medal, the most prestigious award for American craftsmen. By the 1930s Oakes had nine men and women working in his shop, including the talented Eddie Nelson, who had studied with Louis Comfort Tiffany.[3] The shop's jewelry, including this brooch, was handwrought and usually of an original design. The work was sold at SACB shops or at Oakes's atelier, where clients seeking custom-made ornaments worked directly with the artist.

1. Nonie Gadsden, "Reaction and Reform: The Late Nineteenth and Early Twentieth Centuries," in *MFA Highlights: American Decorative Arts and Sculpture* (Boston: MFA Publications, 2006), 175.

2. The Siberian amethysts were cut in the workshop of William A. Mercer in New York City, whereas the four amethyst balls that form the feet of the box and the large oval amethyst in the lid were cut in Idar-Oberstein, Germany. For more information on the materials, see G. H. C., "Silver and Precious Stones Make an Exquisite Jewel Casket," *Boston Evening Transcript*, October 16, 1929, 7.

3. Edith Alpers, "Edward Everett Oakes (1891–1960), a Master Craftsman from Boston, Massachusetts," *Jewellery Studies* 3 (1989): 74–75.

Brooch

Harry Bertoia (American, 1915–1978)
1941
Silver
8.6 × 13.3 × 1 cm (3⅜ × 5¼ × ⅜ in.)
Promised gift of The Daphne Farago Collection L-SE 1057.1.7

Harry Bertoia is best known as a mid-twentieth-century sculptor and industrial designer, but from 1938 to 1943 he created abstract ornaments of hammered brass and silver while in charge of the metalworking studio at the Cranbrook Academy of Art in Bloomfield Hills, Michigan. His jewelry from that period is similar in style to that of Alexander Calder, with whom he occasionally exhibited in the early 1940s.[1] The textured metal surfaces of this brooch by Bertoia resemble asymmetrical and overlapping olive leaves or sea anemones and lend the ornament a soft, organic sensation.

In 1943 Bertoia largely abandoned jewelry making to join Cranbrook designer Charles Eames in California, where he began a successful career as an industrial designer. His contribution to the U.S. studio jewelry movement occurred during his years at Cranbrook, where he replaced old-style interpretations of the historical past with modernist ideals.

1. Two of the galleries were the Alexander Girard Gallery in Detroit and the Nierendorf Gallery in New York; see Toni Lesser Wolf, "Harry Bertoia," in *What Modern Was: Design, 1935–1965*, ed. Martin Eidelberg (New York: Harry N. Abrams, 1991), 253.

Lovers

Sam Kramer (American, 1913–1964)
Carol Enners Kramer (American, 1918–1986)
1949
Silver, turquoise, and garnet
11.4 × 8.3 × 2.5 cm (4½ × 3¼ × 1 in.)
The Daphne Farago Collection 2006.288

Influenced by the surrealist movement in the arts, a few early studio jewelers created ornaments that probe the unconscious through visually nonsensical, disquieting, and occasionally bizarre forms. The most articulate of these jewelers was Sam Kramer, a Greenwich Village bohemian whose promotional material advertised "Fantastic Jewelry for People Who Are Slightly Mad: We have things to titillate the damnest ego—utter weirdities conceived in moments of semi-madness."[1]

Odd materials, such as taxidermy eyes and found objects, were trademarks of Kramer's distinct style of jewelry. He also used shells, semiprecious stones, and unusual minerals to contextualize his designs. For the *Lovers* brooch, Kramer collaborated with his wife, Carol Enners Kramer, a talented jeweler in her own right. The artists fabricated three metal planes and riveted and hinged them together. Bezel-set cabochon stones strategically placed on the male figure add color and dimensionality to the dynamic, erotic ornament, which has been described as "a battle of the sexes . . . a Rorschach Test in metal—deliberately ambiguous, multivocal, and provocative."[2]

Sam Kramer studied literature and art at the University of Pittsburgh and the University of Southern California. In Pittsburgh he apprenticed for several months with Dave Heller, owner of a commercial jewelry establishment. He learned how to work silver and quickly discovered he had no interest in creating traditional jewelry. His imagination was ignited by the aboriginal fetish, the dreamscape, and the inchoate form, which became the bases for his edgy and unprecedented body of work.

1. Sam Kramer, quoted in Mark Foley, "Fantastic Jewelry for People Who Are Slightly Mad," *Metalsmith* 6, no. 1 (Winter 1986): 11.

2. Foley, "Fantastic Jewelry," 14.

Necklace

Ed Wiener (American, 1918–1991)
About 1949
Silver
19.7 × 12.7 × 0.5 cm (7¾ × 5 × 3⁄16 in.)
The Daphne Farago Collection 2006.595

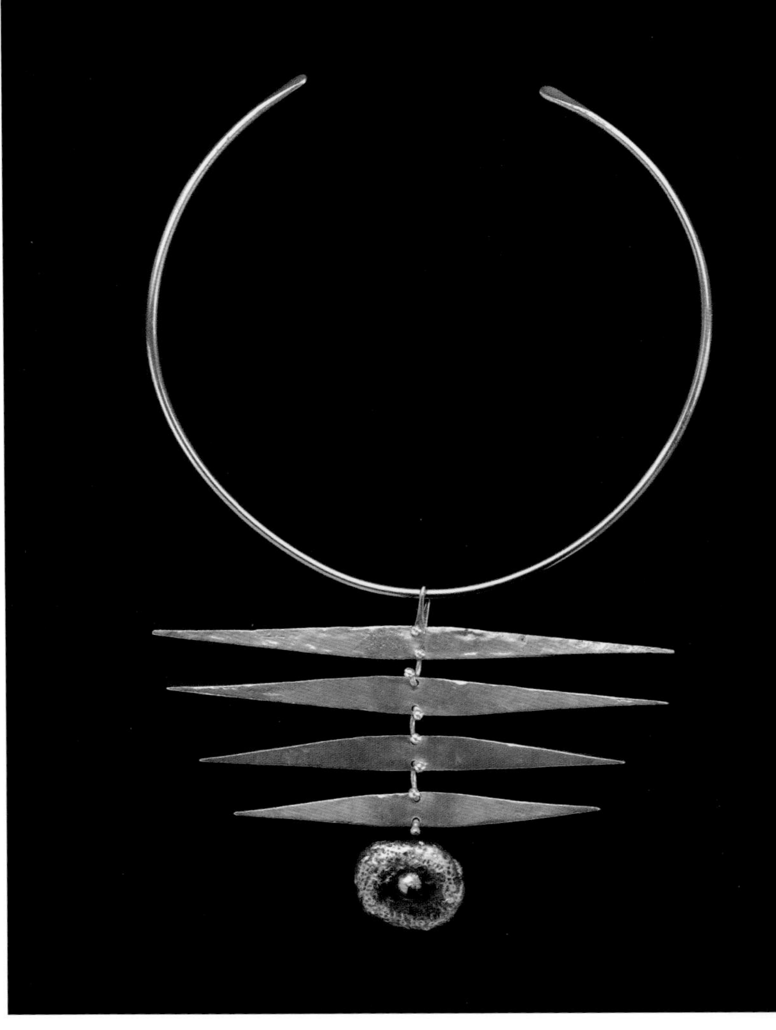

Self-taught jeweler Ed Wiener was part of the United States' post–World War II studio jewelry phenomenon. The field at the time was wide open to experimentation, and specialized training was largely unavailable. As a result, those interested in applying modernist ideals to jewelry approached the subject in novel ways. They often chose nontraditional materials for their works and techniques, such as wire twisting, which did not require sophisticated metal skills.

Therefore, like other early studio jewelers, Wiener's career in jewelry making was an explorer's journey. In the mid-1940s, Wiener and his wife, Doris, operated a studio and shop in New York City's East Village, where they initially made minimalist, twisted-wire brooches for friends.[1] Wiener's designs soon evolved into abstract representations suggestive of specific forms or physical movements, such as a five-pointed star that evoked a flying bird or dancer. The artist took an eclectic approach to his work, drawing inspiration from the flat, two-dimensional planes of cubist art as well as the sculptural, rough-hewn jewelry and graceful mobiles of Alexander Calder.[2] Wiener was also influenced by avant-garde artists, such as Hans Hoffman and Adolph Gottlieb, who visited his shops in New York and Provincetown, Massachusetts.[3] Although Wiener's early jewelry was primarily fabricated from silver and semiprecious stones, he later created ornaments in gold with more costly gems.

Throughout his career, Wiener preferred simple, elegant forms and flat planes. He is known for experimenting with the effects of oxidation on silver when he wanted to manipulate contrast, and with negative spaces when he wanted to control depth and volume. The basic shape of this necklace is that of an open torque made of heavy round wire with plain hammered terminals. Suspended from the center are four graduated horizontal bars with tapered ends and rough surfaces. Contrasting with the flat bars is a sculptural round pendant with a bulbous center. The horizontal bars, which move slightly when worn, were probably inspired by Calder's kinetic sculptures.

1. Ed Wiener, Milton W. Brown, and Blanche R. Brown, *Jewelry by Ed Wiener: Retrospective Exhibition, December 1, 1988–January 7, 1989* (New York: Fifty/50 Gallery, 1988), 13.

2. Tony Lesser Wolf, "Ed Wiener's Arts and Ends," *Metalsmith* 8, no. 3 (Summer 1988): 27–28; see also Toni Greenbaum, *Messengers of Modernism: American Studio Jewelry, 1940–1960* (Paris: Flammarion, 1996), 143.

3. Wiener, Brown, and Brown, *Jewelry by Ed Wiener,* 21.

Necklace

Art Smith (American, born in Cuba, 1917–1982)
About 1958
Silver, turquoise, chrysoprase, rhodochrosite, and amethyst
43.8 × 26 × 1.9 cm (17¼ × 10¼ × ¾ in.)
The Daphne Farago Collection 2006.537

Art Smith created bold, biomorphic ornaments made of silver, copper, brass, and semiprecious stones. He was fascinated by the human body and believed that "a good piece of jewelry literally caresses the body and . . . plays with it."[1] He also artfully employed negative space so his jewelry revealed parts of the body, making them part of his compositions.[2] His typically large-scale ornaments of hammered sheet metal and twisted or hammered wire were influenced by the jazz musicians and modern dancers with whom he was close friends, as well as by surrealist painting, African art forms, the kinetic sculpture of Alexander Calder, and the jewelry of Harry Bertoia. When Smith used stones, he usually selected bezel-set semiprecious cabochons for their color harmonies, as in this ornament where three undulating, asymmetrical panels are embellished by colored stones of different hues.

While Smith was a formative artist in the avant-garde studio jewelry movement, he was also an excellent marketer in the world of traditional women's magazines, achieving considerable recognition in his lifetime. During the 1950s and 1960s, his jewelry appeared in *Vogue* and *Harper's Bazaar,* and in 1969 he was given a one-man exhibition at the Museum of Contemporary Crafts (currently the Museum of Arts and Design) in New York. He was also a frequent lecturer at colleges, universities, and art schools.

1. Art Smith, quoted by Brooke Kamin Rapaport and Kevin L. Stayton in *Vital Forms: American Art and Design in the Atomic Age, 1940–1960* (Brooklyn, N.Y.: Brooklyn Museum of Art in association with Harry N. Abrams, 2001), 201.

2. Kelly H. L'Ecuyer, with contributions by Michelle Tolini Finamore, Yvonne J. Markowitz, and Gerald W. R. Ward, *Jewelry by Artists: In the Studio, 1940–2000* (Boston: MFA Publications, 2010), 64.

Galaxy Necklace

Art Smith (American, born in Cuba, 1917–1982)
About 1960
Silver
26.4 × 17.8 × 6 cm (10⅜ × 7 × 2⅜ in.)
The Daphne Farago Collection 2010.590

In an interview at his studio in 1971, Art Smith said that his jewelry was composed of sheet metal, wire, and space. He emphasized that space as a design element was cheap and "tangible" and of importance for how his work related to the body.[1] This relationship is apparent in *Galaxy Necklace*, which Smith composed using oxidized branches made of curved, flattened wires terminating in shining silver balls. Attached to a hammered silver wire, these branches curve around the back of the neck without any closure. The contrast between the dark wire and the polished balls creates the illusion that the spheres are suspended in midair, hence the title *Galaxy Necklace*. An elegant and distinctive adornment, this piece is one of four "stick and ball" necklaces that Art Smith considered one of his most successful designs.[2] It came from the estate of Blanche Calloway, sister of Cab Calloway, the well-known jazz musician.

Smith ultimately achieved recognition as one of the most important American studio jewelers working in the postwar United States. Along with Alexander Calder, Harry Bertoia, Paul Lobel, Margaret De Patta, and Sam Kramer, he represented the revolutionary modernist movement that flourished in New York City during the mid-twentieth century. As a Cuban-born black man of Jamaican descent growing up in Brooklyn at a time when racial discrimination was pervasive, Smith's journey to becoming an artist was not always easy. In the early forties, Cooper Union in Manhattan was one of the few art schools to admit black students, and Smith was fortunate to obtain a four-year scholarship there.[3] His transition from an architecture student to a jewelry designer began when he met a jeweler named Winifred Mason while working part-time at the Children's Aid Society in Harlem.[4] After operating within her studio for four years, he set up his own shop in Greenwich Village in 1944. A victim of vandalism and heckling due to racial prejudice, he became a vocal and active advocate for human justice. He remained in his last studio and shop on Fourth Street—known as a lively meeting place for conversation and music—for about thirty years, until 1979, when his health deteriorated.

1. Art Smith, interview by Paul Cummings in Smith's studio in Greenwich Village, August 24 and 31, 1971, Archives of American Art, Smithsonian Institution, Washington, D.C., 11; also quoted in Toni Greenbaum, "Goldsmith, Silversmith, Art Smith," *Echoes Magazine* 6, no. 3 (Winter 1997): 42.

2. Charles L. Russell, *Art Smith: His Life and Work* (unpublished manuscript draft as of May 3, 2009).

3. Marbeth Schon, *Modernist Jewelry, 1930–1960* (Atglen, Penn.: Schiffer Publishing, 2004), 70.

4. Barry Harwood, *From the Village to Vogue: The Modernist Jewelry of Art Smith* (Brooklyn, N.Y.: Brooklyn Museum, 2008), 5.

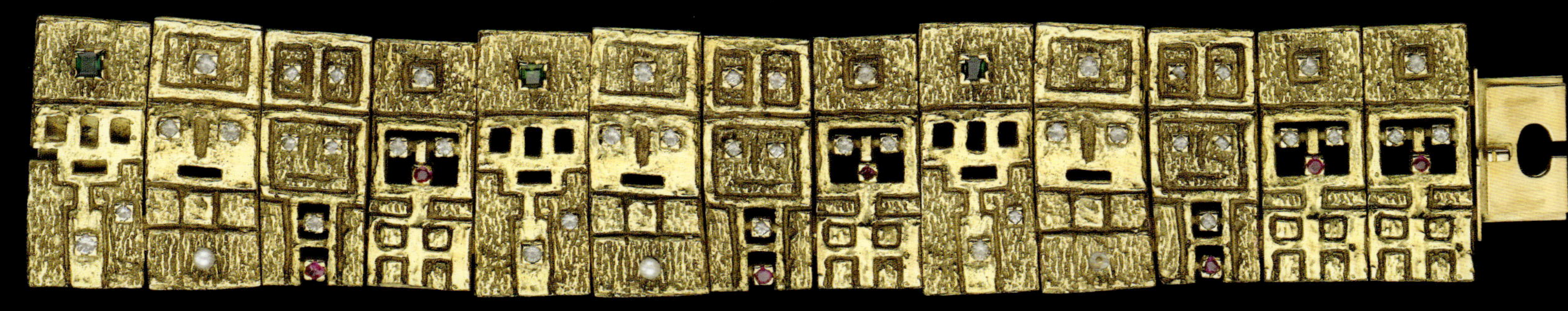

King's Bracelet

Anton Frühauf (Italian, 1914–1999)
1959
Gold, ruby, sapphire, tourmaline, and pearl
L. 17.1 cm, w. 3 cm, d. 0.2 cm (L. 6¾ in., w. 1³⁄₁₆ in., d. ¹⁄₁₆ in.)
Gift of Karen Sethur Rotenberg in honor of the jeweler Anton Frühauf 2007.410

Anton Frühauf was one of the first European jewelers to experiment with avant-garde styles. Born into an Italian family of highly successful metalsmiths, he was steeped in a tradition of goldsmithing that had long been regarded as a fine art.[1] Initially trained according to a classic apprenticeship model, Frühauf enhanced his education and broadened his outlook by attending the Academy of Applied Art in Munich. Afterward he moved to Rome, where he worked for several years as a goldsmith, returning to his hometown of Merano in 1946 at the age of thirty-two. He opened a studio there and soon gained a reputation for avant-garde jewelry design that has much in common with modernist sculpture.

His early work, which often features raised, textured surfaces and stylized patterning, reflects an interest in petroglyphs, cave paintings, ancient script, and Greek mythology. By the late 1950s, when this bracelet was created, his work had become more abstract and three-dimensional, and it incorporated gemstone highlights. While he cast some of his adornments, he assembled many others that resemble large-scale metal wall hangings out of gold sheet. Other works show a distinct architectural aspect reminiscent of building facades dating to the 1960s. Although Frühauf is best known for his creations in gold, he also worked in alternative materials such as wood and acrylic.

1. Ralph Turner, *Jewelry in Europe and America: New Times, New Thinking* (New York: Thames and Hudson, 1996), 24–25.

Janus (necklace)

Björn Weckström (Finnish, born 1935)
Lapidary artist: Bernd Munsteiner (German, born 1943)
1965
Gold and smoky quartz
Length of necklace: 43.2 cm (17 in.)
Pendant: L. 4.5 cm, w. 2.2 cm, d. 1 cm (L. 1¾ in., w. ⅞ in., d. ⅜ in.)
Gift of Karen and Michael Rotenberg 2007.422

Mid-twentieth-century Finnish studio jewelry was dominated by modernist ideals. Most avant-garde jewelers eschewed gold in favor of silver in simple, bold, and geometric shapes, sometimes embellishing it with indigenous semiprecious stones.[1] However, one metalsmith, Björn Weckström, was fascinated by gold, especially the folds, crevices, and rough textures of gold nuggets. The artist felt that matte and rough surfaces enhanced the mystique of the metal.[2]

Weckström set this highly sculptural rectangular gold pendant with two pyramidal quartzes at a 110-degree angle. He named the work *Janus*, after the Roman god associated with doors, beginnings, and transitions. The stones are gateways, reflecting one another and leading the eye in opposite directions. They were cut by Bernd Munsteiner, a lapidary artist celebrated for his innovative fantasy cuts and stone sculptures. Like Weckström's, Munsteiner's work often contrasts both polished and rough-textured surfaces. Weckström has also experimented with silver and nontraditional jewelry materials such as patinated bronze and acrylic. He also creates large-scale bronze sculptures, glass decorative objects, and acrylic furniture.

1. John Haycraft, *Finnish Jewellery and Silverware* (Helsinki: Kustannusosakeyhtiö Otavan Kirjapaino, 1962), 7–10. For a discussion of Finnish gold and local stones, see Marianne Aav, "Simplicity and Materialism in the Design of Finnish Jewelry and Metalwork," in *Finnish Modern Design: Utopian Ideals and Everyday Realities, 1930–1997*, ed. Marianne Aav and Nina Stritzler-Levine (New Haven, Conn.: Bard Graduate Center for Studies in the Decorative Arts and Yale University Press, 1998), 167.

2. Marianne Aav and Eeva Viljanen, eds., *Björn Weckströrm* (Helsinki: Designmuseo, 2003), 10.

Man with Bee

Robert W. Ebendorf (American, born 1938)
1968
Copper, silver, tintype photo, brass, aluminum, stones, and other found objects
17.1 × 11.1 × 1.3 cm (6¾ × 4⅜ × ½ in.)
The Daphne Farago Collection 2006.150

Robert Ebendorf was strongly influenced by Scandinavian design early in his career, having studied in Norway on a Fulbright scholarship in 1963. The scholarship and subsequent grants gave him the opportunity to apprentice with master Scandinavian craftsmen who worked in both traditional and modernist formats.[1] Ebendorf's early work therefore reflects his mastery of precise metalworking, stonecutting, and enameling, as well as the Scandinavian preference for simple, abstract design.

During the late 1960s, however, Ebendorf moved away completely from those early influences, experimenting instead with assemblage techniques and nontraditional materials such as vintage photographs, Plexiglas, scraps of tin cans, and found objects. Many of his works since then have been rich in texture and surrealist in content, and they often incorporated slogans or puns that are deliberately enigmatic.[2] The artist feels that the found objects he recycles into jewelry evoke emotional responses from the viewer, triggering old memories and lending an ornament a personal narrative. His method of construction is playful. He recently explained, "I really enjoy sitting down and looking at the materials and saying, 'I'll take this piece, I'll take that piece. I will set the pearl here. Oh, let us put a gemstone here!' Or I'll just take this piece of wire I found on the way home and look at it . . . and just see what it looks like."[3]

1. Robert Ebendorf, interview by Tracey Rosolowski at the artist's home in Greenville, North Carolina, April 16–18, 2004, Archives of American Art, Smithsonian Institution, Washington, D.C., 27–28.

2. Glen R. Brown, "Robert Ebendorf's Pilgrimage to Paradox," *Metalsmith* 27, no. 3 (2008): 31.

3. Ebendorf, interview by Rosolowski, 45–46.

Goldfinger

Bruno Martinazzi (Italian, born 1923)
1969
Gold
7.3 × 6.4 × 5.7 cm (2⅞ × 2½ × 2¼ in.)
The Daphne Farago Collection 2006.346

Bruno Martinazzi follows an Italian tradition that includes the Renaissance masters Lorenzo Ghiberti, Filippo Brunelleschi, and Benvenuto Cellini, all of them sculptors trained in the goldsmith's art.[1] Martinazzi views the acts of chiseling a block of stone or hammering a sheet of gold as opposites that mirror one another. In both his stone sculpture and his gold jewelry, he favors minimalist anatomical renderings, which he sees as symbolizing the human condition. Some of his imagery—an eye, a clenched fist, a set of brooding lips, or an accusatory finger—has aggressive and even sinister overtones. Isolated from the body, the fragments have a power greater than an ordinary gesture. According to the artist, they represent an expansion of recognizable forms into reflections and ideas.[2] The hand in this bracelet represents the creative urge and the point of contact between two individuals.

1. Ellen Maurer Zilioli, "Gold and Stone: Bruno Martinazzi, Jewelry and Myth," in *Bruno Martinazzi*, ed. Karl Bollmann et al. (Stuttgart: Arnoldsche, 2007), 58.

2. Paolo Fossati, "Martinazzi: Creator of Precious Objects," in *Martinazzi*, ed. Carla Gall Barbisio et al. (Stuttgart: Arnoldsche, 1997), 19.

Sun, Moon, Stars, Rain Wedding Crown

Merry Renk (American, born 1921)
1974
Silver, gold, pearl, and plique-à-jour enamel
H. 8.5 cm, diam. 27 cm (H. 3⅜ in., diam. 10⅝ in.)
Gift in honor of Rose R. Jockwig 1984.739

New Jersey–born Merry Renk attended the School for Industrial Arts in Trenton, New Jersey, before studying photography, sculpture, and art history at the Institute of Design in Chicago in 1946. She and two of her classmates opened 750 Studio, an avant-garde gallery featuring the works of contemporary artists and craftspeople, including László Moholy-Nagy, Margaret De Patta, and Lenore Tawney. The space included a studio where Renk experimented with enamel and jewelry, creating linear ornaments made from wires that were bent, forged, cast, and arranged in groups.[1] By the 1950s, Renk had settled in San Francisco, where she became a full-time jewelry artist and a founding member of the San Francisco Metal Arts Guild.

Renk has always been interested in jewelry for the head. She decorates some of her crowns and hair ornaments with gemstones, and others with plique-à-jour enameling. Enameling in the form of blue raindrops and green crescent moons, as well as openwork gold suns and seed pearl stars, decorates the tips of overlapping silver-wire points in this crown. Renk completed this piece shortly after being awarded a grant by the National Endowment for the Arts in 1974. The grant inaugurated a period in which Renk fully explored the potential of enamel color applied to metalwork.

The artist describes her jewelry up to that point as "nonobjective art" that often incorporated interlocking design elements, V-shaped forms, and folded metal in the overall design. Around that time, Renk began drawing portraits and images from her dreams. She later commented that this experience transformed her jewelry. It came to express complex and multilayered ideas through what she calls a "symbolic realism" based on memories, family, nature, and ecological concerns.[2] Such expressions required that she add a number of new techniques, such as gem setting, to her standard metalsmithing practices.

1. Renk, interview by Arline M. Fisch, January 18–19, 2001, Archives of American Art, Smithsonian Institution, Washington, D.C., 4–5.

2. Joel Clemons, "Jewelry as Art: A Retrospective of Renk's Work," *Peninsula Times Tribune,* March 24, 1981, C-5.

Autumn Twilight

Yoshiko Yamamoto (American, born in Japan, 1932)
1992
Gold, diamond, and boulder opal
3.8 × 6.8 × 0.6 cm (1½ × 2¹¹⁄₁₆ × ¼ in.)
Gift of the Seminarians 1992.425

Although Yoshiko Yamamoto originally trained in Japan in traditional flower arranging and the art of the tea ceremony, she demonstrated an interest in modernist design rather than past traditions when she became a metalsmith in the United States, graduating from the School of the Museum of Fine Arts (SMFA) in 1973. During her early career, while working for her teacher and mentor Miyé Matsukata at Matsukata's Boston-based atelier and gallery, Janiyé, Yamamoto focused on asymmetrical, abstract forms, the effects of mixing metals, and the texturing of metal surfaces.

After Matsukata's death in 1981, Yamamoto shifted to combinations of high-karat gold, enamel, and colored stones, occasionally incorporating found objects and artifacts from Asian and Western cultures. She also incorporated references to historic jewelry in her work, as in a fibula brooch she created in 1985 based on an ancient Roman clothing fastener. Since the 1990s, the artist has experimented with kinetic sculptures and adornments that incorporate removable brooches.

This abstract brooch represents Yamamoto's later work, in which she seeks unusual minerals, natural crystals, and partly polished stones instead of cut stones. Among her favorites are boulder opals, a form of precious opal cut to retain some of the surrounding brown matrix, which the artist associates with the earth. She frequently allows a stone's shape to inform her designs.[1] The rainbow iridescence of the softly polished stone in this brooch contrasts with the textured matte finish of the gold sheet and the highly polished forged wires. More recently, Yamamoto has worked with found materials and monofilament, which she crochets into lightweight colorful adornments.

1. Yvonne Markowitz, *Quiet Ripples: The Creative Journey of Yoshiko Yamamoto* (Tokyo: Yoshiko Yamamoto, 2009), 16.

Polyp Colony

John Paul Miller (American, born 1918)
1995
Gold and enamel
Pendant: 5.7 × 5.1 × 1.6 cm (2¼ × 2 × ⅝ in.)
Length of chain: 41.3 cm (16¼ in.)
The Daphne Farago Collection 2006.361

A 1940 industrial design graduate of the Cleveland School of Art, John Paul Miller began his career teaching basic art courses at the school after serving in the military. In the evenings, he and his lifelong friend and fellow metalsmith Fred Miller made jewelry. John Paul also worked with enamels, experimenting with various metal alloys, fluxes, and techniques. He eventually developed a distinctive enamel style in which he melded 18kt gold circles, triangles, and rectangles onto a 24kt gold sheet in raised abstract patterns and then placed multilayered enamels in a variety of tints and shades in the negative spaces.

Miller eventually directed all of his creative energies to jewelry making. He became fascinated by granulation, an ancient Etruscan technique in which tiny gold granules are fused to high-karat gold sheet. Although Allesandro Castellani revived the technique in Italy during the nineteenth century, he wrote little about the mechanical aspects of the process. Miller set out to master this form of decoration on his own, consulting archaeological references and conducting numerous experiments with different alloys, after seeing photographs of granulated gold jewelry by the contemporary German artist Elisabeth Treskow.[1] By the 1950s Miller had succeeded in this endeavor, and over the next several decades he created an extraordinary menagerie of wearable sea creatures, all delicately enameled and embellished with gold granules. This exquisite pendant, with its hand-wrought loop-in-loop chain, is an outstanding example of Miller's unique style of enameling, his ability to create imaginative and whimsical animal forms, and his highly sophisticated gold work.

1. Frances Taft, "John Paul Miller: Infusing Form with Feeling," *Metalsmith* 26, no. 3 (Fall 2006): 49.

Ram's Horn Necklace

Linda MacNeil (American, born 1954)
1998
Gold-plated silver and optical glass
Diam. of exterior: 13.7 cm (5⅜ in.)
Gift of The Seminarians in memory of Stephen D. Paine 1998.190

Linda MacNeil is both a sculptor and a studio jeweler with a keen interest in architecture, industrial design, and functional as well as decorative objects.[1] Her deep appreciation for jewelry's historical past has led to Egyptian, Celtic, and nineteenth-century European influences in her work. MacNeil often uses humble, nonprecious materials to create ornaments that are precise, carefully balanced, and decidedly modern. In this necklace, she used optical glass, a bubble-free jewel-like substance with perfect clarity. The "*Ram's Horn*" of the jewel's title harks back to the past—horned rams' heads were popular motifs representing certain divinities in the ancient Near East and the Mediterranean world. Here, the rams' heads are stylized triangular glass forms with subtle, gently curved horns.

MacNeil devotes much of her time to experimenting with materials, including enamel and glass. Her interest in the French art nouveau jeweler René Lalique and the creative possibilities of enamel and glass began during her undergraduate years at the Rhode Island School of Design. She furthered her explorations while a guest artist at the British Society of Glass (1985) and as a faculty member at the Pilchuck Glass School (1989). As a result, MacNeil has greatly expanded the repertoire of glass techniques that Lalique used during his jewelry-making years. In addition to glass engraving, casting, acid polishing, and *pâte de verre*, MacNeil has explored the properties of optical glass, commercial glass plate, and Vitrolite, an opaque glass used during the 1930s to 1950s.

1. Karen S. Chambers, "Linda MacNeil: A Detailed Look," *Metalsmith* 16, no. 3 (Summer 1996): 27. See also Suzanne Ramljak and Helen Drutt English, *United in Beauty: The Jewelry and Collectors of Linda MacNeil* (Atglen, Penn.: Schiffer Publishing, 2002), 15.

Cuff bracelet

Angelita (Angie) Reano Owen (Native American, born 1946)
Santo Domingo Pueblo, New Mexico
1995
Tiger cowrie, turquoise, spiny oyster, mother-of-pearl, jet, and epoxy
W. 5.4 cm, diam. 4.3 cm (W. 2⅛ in., diam. 1⅔ in.)
Museum purchase with funds donated by Lois and Stephen Kunian and The Seminarians 1998.57

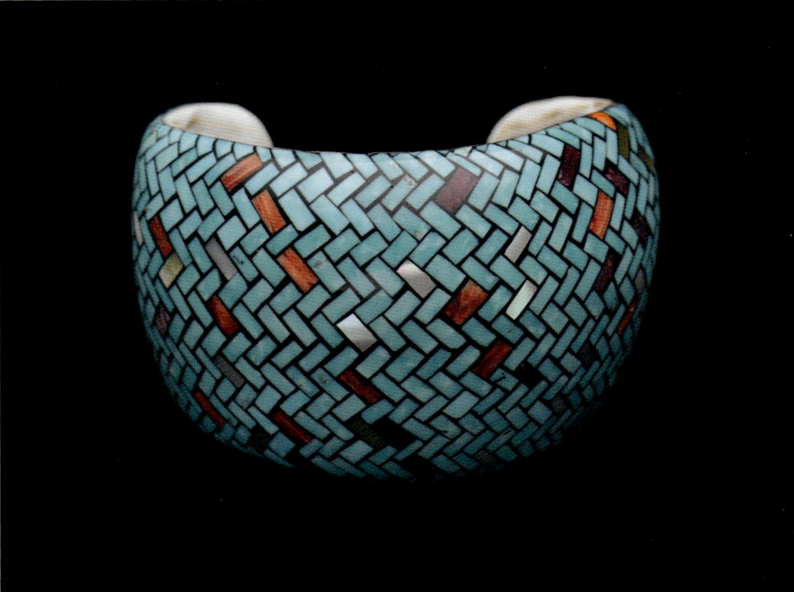

Angelita (Angie) Reano Owen continues a long tradition of jewelry making by the people of Santo Domingo Pueblo. This tradition incorporates turquoise, stone, shells, coral, and silver, but Owen combines those traditional materials with modern lapidary equipment and epoxies to integrate prehistoric and postmodern design elements.[1] For this mosaic bracelet, Owen created a shell substrate, over which she applied small rectangles of turquoise and shell in a herringbone pattern. The ornament's flat patterning is modernist in design, but its form and materials are rooted in her culture's rich past.

Owen grew up a third-generation Santo Domingo Pueblo artist. She was particularly inspired by her mother, who made mosaic jewelry out of recycled automobile parts during the Depression.[2] Santo Domingo Pueblo jewelers have used materials native to the Four Corners region of the United States (where southern Utah, northern Arizona, northwestern New Mexico, and southwestern Colorado meet) for centuries. Turquoise, for example, an auspicious stone associated with the sky and sacred personages, comes from the nearby Los Cerrillos Hills. Shells of the spiny oyster, clam, abalone, and Conus from the Gulf of California and the Pacific Coast were acquired by trade with other Native American peoples and then with European settlers beginning in the nineteenth century.

1. Paula Baxter, "Cross-cultural Controversies in the Design History of Southwestern American Indian Jewellery," *Journal of Design History* 7, no. 4 (1994): 241. William A. Turnbaugh and Sarah Peabody Turnbaugh, *Indian Jewelry of the American Southwest* (Atglen, Penn.: Schiffer Publishing, 1996), 65–66.

2. Linda Foss Nichols, *Voice of Mother Earth: Art of the Puebloan Peoples of the American Southwest* (Nagoya, Japan: Nagoya/Boston Museum of Fine Arts, 2000), cat. 104.

Paisley Necklace

Kiff Slemmons (American, born 1944)
1998
Silver and wooden rulers
22.9 × 18.4 × 0.6 cm (9 × 7¼ × ¼ in.)
The Daphne Farago Collection 2006.527

Recycling has been a common practice in jewelry making since antiquity. Traditional jewelry materials are too precious to discard when ornaments fall out of fashion, and they can be another way of preserving wealth. Studio jewelers play with a different notion of recycling when they include discarded or found objects in their work. Some artists are conscious of the importance of recycling discarded, and occasionally toxic, materials, whereas others see an abandoned item as an intriguing form of found object.

Kiff Slemmons recycles an old-fashioned ruler by incorporating it into this bold and contemporary neck ornament. She explained that "the old ruler is a beautiful tool in itself," and that such implements give her jewelry a new dimension because of "the references they bring over from their previous use."[1] While growing up, Slemmons spent time in her father's print shop, where steel rulers were used for proofreading and lining up columns of type. The curved patterns of ruler parts in this necklace completely transform the original hard-edged tool into a lyrical medley of abstract forms. In addition, the color of the wooden parts, the hinged arabesques, and the carefully balanced numerals contribute to the work's dynamic synergy. In both form and title the necklace suggests the ornamentation of India and an exoticism far removed from a workman's technical instrument.[2] The necklace is at once nostalgic and playful, recalling school-day memories in the predigital age.

1. Susan Cummins, *Beyond the Obvious: Rethinking Jewelry* (San Francisco: Craft and Folk Art Museum, 1999), 54.

2. Signe Mayfield, *The Thought of Things: Jewelry by Kiff Slemmons* (Palo Alto, Calif.: Palo Alto Art Center, 2000), 7, 10.

Pendant necklace

Jean Vendome (French, born 1930)
About 2000
Gold, diamond, and ametrine
23 × 14 × 1.8 cm (9 1/16 × 5 1/2 × 11/16 in.)
Anonymous promised gift

Pendant-brooch

Jean Vendome (French, born 1930)
About 1997
Gold, chrome diopside, and aquamarine
18.5 × 3.8 × 3 cm (7 5/16 × 1 1/2 × 1 3/16 in.)
Anonymous promised gift

The French jeweler Jean Vendome (born Jean Tuhdarian) once said, "Stones have always been part of my life. It is difficult to understand why I have always been obsessed by them. They somehow resonate within me; they are always there; they torment me."[1] After opening his first shop in Paris in 1948, Vendome created high-style jewelry (*haute joaillerie*) to order for leading jewelry retailers. By the mid-1950s, however, he tired of this work and opted to create one-of-a-kind or limited-production pieces based on his own designs. Cuts of exotic, semiprecious stones and natural specimens aroused his interest the most.[2]

Around this time, Vendome developed a lifelong friendship with the French polar explorer Paul-Émile Victor, whose exploits inspired the jeweler to create the Aurore, Boréale, Horizon, and Éclipse jewelry series, imaginative works that are romantic, otherworldly, and modernist. In the 1970s Vendome introduced another line of jewelry called Vitrail (Stained Glass Window), for which he cut semitranslucent gems into slices and assembled the slices—often from a single crystal—in designs that showcase subtle hues, natural inclusions, and harmonies.

Vendome created this striking necklace as part of the Vitrail series, using four irregularly shaped slices of ametrine in gold, open-back bezels arranged as a cascade. Two asymmetrical gold elements with pave-set diamonds surmount the pendant. It is a remarkable ornament with an artful interplay between color, light, and geometric adjacencies.

The pendant-brooch is a good example of the artist's use of natural specimens. A vibrant green chrome diopside enhanced by five cabochon and step-cut aquamarines dominates the center; aquamarine crystal adorns the bottom. The jewel is a medley of gem textures with sleek, clean planes and bumpy outgrowths. Similar to many of Vendome's adornments, the colors and shapes inform the design.

1. Marlène Crégut-Ledué, *Jean Vendome: Les voyages précieux d'un créateur* (Dijon: Éditions Faton, 2008), 158.

2. Sophie Lefèvre, *Jean Vendome* (Paris: Somogy éditions d'art, 1999), 7–12.

Dandelion Brooch (from the City Flora / City Flotsam series)

Jan Yager (American, born 1951)
2001
Silver and auto glass
14 × 14.6 × 1.9 cm (5½ × 5¾ × ¾ in.)
The Daphne Farago Collection 2006.634

Jan Yager pursues the found-object genre of studio jewelry in a run-down warehouse district of Philadelphia. Her jewels incorporate crack vials, shattered auto glass, and spent bullet casings as, in the artist's own words, "tangible evidence of poverty, exploitations, drugs, and violence."[1] Her series of crack-vial neck ornaments from the 1990s, for example, confronts and exposes the hidden world of addiction in American cities.

Yager links her neglected environment to her artwork in another way in her City Flora series, which includes this dandelion brooch. Here she seeks to celebrate nature's resilience rather than showcasing humankind's destructive tendencies. The series is a testament to survival, poignantly illustrating the adaptive power of nature and the lessons it can teach us.[2] The brooch re-creates the dandelion, an unwelcome plant in formal gardens but a common, even charming presence in ordinary cityscapes.

Yager fabricated this brooch using real dandelion leaves, gently separating each frond from the stem and gluing it to a silver sheet. She then ran both the silver sheet and the leaves through a rolling mill. This process resulted in an embossed, textured surface that reflects the veins and patterns of the plant. In the center, a glass shard from a car shimmers like a diamond in the rough. With this series, the artist continues a long tradition of jeweled botanicals—flowers and plants that communicate moral, spiritual, or emotional messages.

1. Quoted in Jan Yager, "City Flora / City Flotsam," Daphne Farago Lecture on Craft Jewelry series at Museum of Fine Arts, Boston, September 19, 2004.

2. Tracey Rosolowski, "Intervening in Amnesia: Jan Yager's Mnemonic Adornment," *Metalsmith* 21, no. 1 (Winter 2001): 18.

Cuff bracelet

Michael Zobel (German, born in Morocco, 1942)
Lapidary artist Tom Munsteiner (German, born 1968)
2003
Gold, silver, rutilated quartz, and diamond
5 × 6.5 × 7 cm (1 15/16 × 2 9/16 × 2 3/4 in.)
Gift of Peter Schmid 2008.265

Michael Zobel creates flamboyant jewelry that combines wearable forms with a theatrical, larger-than-life aesthetic. He achieves this effect through the sculptural nature of his work and frequent use of unusual, bold gemstones. The artist is also known for his complex surface treatments on metals, as in this example, where he fused 22-karat and 24-karat gold streaks onto a silver surface that he then oxidized. The gold is slightly raised, giving the impression of spontaneous splashes of gold on a dark field. In the ornament's center, a large (182.38 karat) bezel-set, square-cut, and rutilated quartz specimen overlays tiny diamonds embedded in metal. Zobel developed both techniques, the fusing of gold on silver and the setting of small diamonds under transparent or translucent stones, in the 1980s.

Tom Munsteiner, a third-generation lapidary artist known for his unusual cuts, executed the cuff's lapidary work. Although Munsteiner usually creates gem sculptures that inspire artists to create exceptional jewels, he carved the quartz for this bracelet to fit Zobel's design. Zobel has described his jewels as "a concept, an idea. If on the one hand such a concept has to be subordinated to the material, it is on the other also deeply inspired by it. Through the connection of precious metals, stones, and unconventional materials I create unique objects, which make the extraordinary wearable. For almost forty years, this has been the stimulus and demand of my creative work."[1]

Zobel trained as a goldsmith in Pforzheim, Germany, at the Kunst und Werkschule in the early 1960s. After his studies, he worked as a designer in Henry Denys' studio in France and in 1968 established his own shop in Constance, Germany.[2] In 2005 Zobel and his design and business partner, Peter Schmid, transferred the studio's title to Schmid, and it is now known as Atelier Zobel.

1. Yvonne J. Markowitz, "Michael Zobel: A Retrospective," *Adornment: The Magazine of Jewelry and Related Arts* 7, no. 3 (Fall 2008): 29.

2. Michael Zobel, *Zobel: Das rote Buch* (Konstanz: Michael Zobel, 2004), 20–21.

Choker #88

Mary Lee Hu (American, born 1943)
2005
Gold
20.3 × 21.6 × 1.3 cm (8 × 8½ × ½ in.)
Promised gift of The Daphne Farago Collection

Mary Lee Hu's fascination with wire began during her graduate-school days at Southern Illinois University, when she attempted to adapt macramé knotting to metal wire. As her talent developed, she borrowed other techniques from the textile world, producing large, openwork adornments inspired by her appreciation of ethnic jewelry.[1] Since the 1980s, Hu has worked primarily in gold, a metal historically prized for its warm color, durability, and mystical associations. These later, more geometric pieces show tighter construction and reflect the artist's interest in pattern, rhythm, and repetition.[2]

Hu's complex gold adornments, including this neck ornament, require many hours of intense labor to craft.[3] The dense wirework composition rests gently on the shoulders when worn. Like many of Hu's ornaments, this neck piece has fluid, dynamic lines reminiscent of the whiplash curves common to art nouveau jewelry. Negative spaces that allow the wearer's skin to peek through also inform the composition.

In antiquity, metalsmiths experimented with the decorative potential of precious metal wire, particularly in ancient Greek and Etruscan civilizations, where wire filigree was used, often in conjunction with granulation to embellish sheet metal. Artisans also used wire braiding and loop-in-loop chains but to a lesser extent. It was not until the studio-jewelry movement of the mid-twentieth century that artists fully explored wirework techniques, basing their research on baskets and textiles.

1. Ettagale Blauer, *Contemporary American Jewelry Design* (New York: Springer, 1991), 54.

2. Carolyn L. E. Benesh, "Mary Lee Hu," *Ornament* 6, no. 3 (1983): 4.

3. Cindy Strauss et al., *Ornament as Art: Avant-garde Jewelry from the Helen Williams Drutt Collection* (Houston: Arnoldsche in association with the Museum of Fine Arts, Houston, 2007), 480.

Brooch in Two Parts: Flower and Sparkling Pink Petal

Linda Kindler Priest (American, born 1946)
2009
Gold, silver, sapphire, and cobaltocalcite druse
Top brooch: 5.5 × 4.9 × 0.3 cm (2³⁄₁₆ × 1¹⁵⁄₁₆ × ⅛ in.)
Bottom brooch: 6.5 × 4.1 × 0.5 cm (2⁹⁄₁₆ × 1⅝ × ³⁄₁₆ in.)
Gift of Mary-Lark Dupont 2010.673.1–2

Few contemporary studio jewelers have mastered the difficult and labor-intensive metalworking technique of repoussé (also known as repoussage) with the subtlety and sensitivity of Linda Kindler Priest. For this traditional method, the artist uses tools to punch or hammer sheet metal from the back to produce raised areas on the front.[1] Priest depicts a delicate 'Wargrave Pink' (*geranium endressii)* bloom, its petals and stamens directed upward, in repoussé relief on the soft, matte gold top of this two-part brooch. The stem, flanked by two leaves with scalloped borders and adorned with a twist of bezel-set pink sapphires, links the top jewel to the lower one. The second ornament is a vibrant, hot pink cobaltocalcite druse stone bezel-set in silver. Two modeled leaves surmount it, along with a cluster of three bezel-set pink sapphires and one bezel-set green sapphire. When the brooches are worn together as shown here, the tips of the stems create a continual organic unit, at once sensual and elegant. The parts can also be worn separately.

Priest imbues her work with personal meanings, some deeply significant, others more whimsical. Her inspiration comes from the natural world and the beauty of its stones, plant life, and creatures, but her perspective is all her own—very unlike the shared language of flower and animal symbols in the eighteenth and nineteenth centuries. Insects, birds, fish, backyard animals, and exotic beasts appear frequently in her work, along with ordinary and exotic flowers. Her rare talent to manipulate metal results in a poetic rendering of blossoms, delicate dragonfly wings, bird feathers, and the hair and musculature of mammals. Each piece of jewelry is unique to the object it captures and interprets, and the ornament's outer shape either echoes this essence or works synergistically with the design.[2]

1. For a full description of this technique, see Nancy Mēgan Corwin, *Chasing and Repoussé: Methods Ancient and Modern* (Brunswick, Me.: Brynmorgen Press, 2009), ix.

2. Carl Little, "Linda Kindler Priest: A Classic Menagerie," *Ornament* 31, no. 1 (2007): 50–53.

Citron Cascade Ruffle

Elise Winters (American, born 1947)
2009
Polymer clay
22.9 × 20.3 × 2.5 cm (9 × 8 × 1 in.)
Gift of Aaron Winters 2010.354

Contemporary studio jeweler Elise Winters embraces modern, manmade substances instead of the precious materials of traditional high-style jewelry. Her polymer clay jewelry is influenced by her training and experience in other media, particularly photography. She has said that during her photography years she examined "the ephemeral quality of light and color in nature . . . the reflective shimmer off a rippling stream . . . the iridescences of creatures in a tidal pool, [and] the blush of color on the skin of ripe fruit."[1] As a studio jeweler, she continues to explore the relationship between light and color through specially formulated metallic acrylic paints and iridescent glazes over polymer.

The rhythmic shifting of colors in this neck piece from her Ruffle series enhances the dynamic flow of the ornament's highly sculptural form. When worn, the decorative strip of polymer curls around the neck, and the undulating, ribbonlike effect in the center lies at the throat. The blues and greens shimmer and morph into one another, catching the light as the wearer moves. The ingenious clasp, or closure, is composed of two interlocking curls at the end of the cascade. Winters always deals with color in combinations, and it is the dynamics of their interaction that inform her jewelry.

1. Artist's statement, 2010, as reproduced on her Web site at http://www.elisewinters.com/new/index.php/artists-statement. Winters actively promotes polymer clay as an art material, and to this end she created the Polymer Art Archive Web site, which offers resources for students, artists, collectors, and the general public; see http://www.polymerartarchive.com.

GLOSSARY

BY TONI STRASSLER

agate. A fine-grained fibrous variety of chalcedony quartz with colored bands or irregular clouding. It is found in many colors and is translucent to semi-transparent. Those with lacelike inclusions are called dentritic.

alloy. A homogeneous mixture of two or more metals.

ambergris. A grayish substance secreted by the intestines of sperm whales that can be used to retard the evaporation of perfume.

ametrine. A quartz with the combined mineral properties of both amethyst and citrine.

armorials. Pertaining to coats of arms.

assay. A test of the purity of an alloy to determine its percentage of gold or silver.

bail. The metal loop on top of a pendant through which a chain or cord passes.

basse-taille. Translucent enameling over a low-relief design cut into gold, silver, or copper.

bazuband. In Indian jewelry, a common form of upper-arm ornament, generally consisting of one, three, or five parts hinged together and tied on the arm with cords. In the late Mughal period, it was also worn at the front of a turban.

bezel-set. A descriptive term for a gem, enamel, or other object that is surrounded and held in place by a perfectly fitted rim of metal (the bezel) attached to a metal base and bent over slightly.

bodhisattva. In Buddhism, an enlightened being who out of compassion forgoes nirvana to save others; a follower of Buddha.

boulder opal. Mostly found in Australia, this form of precious opal appears as a thin layer on ironstone in veins in boulders. It is exposed on one side, and the natural stone is left on the back.

broad collar. An ancient Egyptian neck ornament worn in life and death; it is composed of rows of beads strung on linen. Such ornaments were amuletic and served to protect the wearer.

cabochon. An unfaceted stone, domed and highly polished, usually with a flat bottom.

cameo. A gemstone with varicolored layers, carved in relief to show the design and background in contrasting colors.

cannetille. A type of jewelry decoration in which coiled and twisted gold wires achieve a delicate scrolling effect sometimes enhanced with a gemstone or enameling; it is named after an embroidery technique made with fine twisted gold or silver thread.

carnelian. A translucent red or orange chalcedony.

cartouche. An ornament in the form of an oval shield or oblong scroll that bears a design or inscription.

caryatid. A supporting column sculpted in the form of a draped female figure.

casting. The process of forming an object by pouring molten metal or glass into a mold, which can then be removed from the mold after hardening.

cat's eye. A fibrous mineral exhibiting the quality of chatoyancy, which is the changeable, wavy sheen seen on some cabochon gemstones. Examples are cat's eye chrysoberyl, cat's eye tourmaline, and cat's eye quartz.

caul. The fetal membrane.

chalcedony. A transparent or translucent milky gray or blue quartz; also a family of different varieties of colored quartz stones such as agate, onyx, carnelian, and sard.

champlevé. An enameling technique in which the metal background is dug out by etching, carving, or casting, forming recessed compartments into which enamels are placed, fused by heat, and then polished to produce a flat surface.

chasing. A metalwork technique in which tools such as hammers, chisels, and punches push away and indent the surface metal.

chiton. A tunic worn by men and women in ancient Greece.

chrysoprase. A clear green or apple-green gemstone that is a variety of chalcedony (a type of quartz).

cinnabar. A heavy reddish mercuric sulfide that is the principal ore of mercury, often used as pigment or as an inlay.

cloisonné. An enameling technique in which the design is outlined by flat metal wires attached to a metal back. These wire compartments are filled with colored enamels, which are then fused by heat.

cloisons. The partitions that form the compartments in a cloisonné enamel.

conus. A type of sea-snail shell that is more or less in the shape of a cone; some have colorful patterning.

culet. The tiny flat facet on the tip of the pointed section of a cut stone.

depletion gilding. A method of producing a layer of nearly pure gold on an object made from a gold alloy by removing the other metals from its surface with acids or salts, usually in combination with heat. This subtractive process is also referred to as "surface enrichment."

diadem. An ornamented band worn around the brow, usually signifying elevated status or royalty.

diopside. A crystallized silicate of lime and magnesia found in a variety of metamorphic rocks. It is used as a gemstone and ranges in color from clear, grayish green to almost black.

enamel. A material made from powdered glass or grains that have been colored by metal oxide, then heat-fused to metal or glass to produce a shiny surface. Enamels range from opaque to transparent.

engraving. A technique of incising lines or patterns with a sharp tool into the front surface of a hard material to produce a design.

en résille. A highly specialized enameling technique in which the enamel is fused into sunken gold-lined cells or incisions in translucent glass and then polished to a smooth surface.

escapement. The mechanism that controls the watch movement.

faience. In Egypt, a quartz-based ceramic covered with a vitreous glaze, usually green to dark blue.

fibula. An ancient, often ornamented, clasp or brooch used to fasten garments; the precursor of the safety pin.

filigree. Plain, twisted, or plaited fine wire, usually gold or silver, bent into an intricate design, which is then soldered to metal sheet or left as openwork.

flux. The liquid or paste applied to metal surfaces to inhibit the production of oxides during heating.

forging. The technique of hammering metal on a smooth, hard surface in order to form, thin, or shape it.

fusion. The merging of different elements by liquefying or melting them by applying heat.

garnet. A group of minerals differing in color and composition. Six common varieties of this gemstone are pyrope, almandine, spessartite, uvarovite, andradite, and grossular.

gaud. A large ornamental bead on a rosary.

girandole. A style of earring or brooch in which a large stone or decorative element suspends three smaller pear-shaped pendants of similar design; popular during the seventeenth and eighteenth centuries.

Gorgon. In Greek mythology, this refers to Medusa and her two monstrous sisters, who had snakes for hair; they were so horrible that looking into their eyes turned the beholder into stone.

granulation. An ancient technique in which tiny gold granules are adhered to a metal surface, in groups or lines to produce a delicate design.

guilloché. A style of continuous engraved decoration made on metal by an engine-turning lathe and often covered by transparent enamel to reveal the engraved pattern below.

heishi. A Native American word originally meaning "shell," now used as a term to describe tiny handmade, cylindrical beads.

himotōshi. The channel or hole in a netsuke through which the cord passes to attach it to the sash (obi) of a garment.

hollowware. Metal objects that serve as receptacles or containers such as bowls, pitchers, and teapots.

intaglio. The incised design carved into or beneath a hard stone or metal.

jabot pin. A pin with removable decorative elements on both ends.

jadeite. One of the minerals known as jade; the other is called nephrite. It is a hard fibrous stone that in its most valued form is white or intensely green and translucent.

jasperware. A fine, hard-grained, and unglazed stoneware introduced by Josiah Wedgwood in the eighteenth century; often colored with metallic oxides, with a raised design remaining white.

kundan. Translated from a Hindi word meaning "pure gold," a stone-setting technique found in Indian jewelry in which a gem is set by using a tool to compress, shape, and polish the surrounding metal, leaving a ridge that serves as the bezel.

lapidary. The art of cutting, shaping, and polishing stones; also a person who employs these techniques.

loop-in-loop chain. An ancient method of chain making that in its simplest form uses each round link, which is pinched and bent, to thread through the previous bent link.

mabe pearl. A cultured, half-spherical pearl created by inserting a similarly shaped mother-of-pearl nucleus into an oyster and attaching it to the flat part of the shell's inner surface.

maharatnani. In Hindu cosmology, the term for the "great stones"—diamond, ruby, sapphire, emerald, and pearl. The "lesser stones" (the *uparatuani*) are topaz, cat's eye, coral, and zircon. These gems were known as the *nava-ratna,* which traditionally had the symbolic meaning of good fortune.

matrix. The natural rock or mineral in which any crystal or gemstone is embedded.

narwhal. An Arctic whale; the male is characterized by a long twisted ivory tusk projecting from the left side of his head.

netsuke. A Japanese toggle at the end of a cord that suspends a pendant from a sash.

niello. A black metallic alloy of sulfur, copper, silver, or lead that in powdered form is heated, fused in place, and polished flat to become an inlay in incised lines or areas on a metal surface, usually silver and sometimes gold.

old mine cut. An early style of diamond cutting in which the gem has a variety of facets. There is a large flat table on the top of the stone and a small flat surface on the bottom. Old mine cut diamonds were often used in the Georgian and Victorian eras.

organic gems. Materials used as stones that were once living organisms such as pearl, amber, coral, and jet.

oxidized. The result of combining a metal, often silver, with oxygen, to produce a dark "antique" finish.

parure. A matching set of jeweled ornaments intended to be worn at the same time; also called a suite. It usually includes a necklace, bracelets, earrings, brooches, and hair ornaments. A "demiparure" refers to a less than full set.

pâte de verre. Glass, usually opaque, formed by grinding glass that is refired into a mold. The glass may be lightly enameled.

patination. The staining of metal, glass, horn, or other surface by the application of chemicals, sometimes colored enamels.

pectoral. A decorative ornament worn on the chest, suspended, sewn, or pinned to a garment, such as the funerary adornments found on Egyptian mummies.

peridot. A relatively soft, transparent gem colored in a range of greens, sometimes brilliant, depending on the proportion of iron in the mineral.

plique à jour. A technique of enameling that, like cloisonné, uses metal partitions between the enamels, but in this case without the metal backing, thereby allowing light to pass through.

posy rings. A type of finger ring inscribed with a short love poem or sentimental expression.

precious-stone rough. An uncut diamond, emerald, sapphire, or ruby.

quartz. A common mineral that is very hard, composed of silicate, and found in many different rocks and stones, such as agate, amethyst, chalcedony, citrine, and rock crystal.

repoussé. The process of producing a relief design in a thin piece of metal by using tools to stretch the metal from the back; often used with chasing.

resin. A solid, organic, and yellow to brown substance exuded from pine or fir trees.

rhodium. A durable and expensive metal that is part of the platinum family; unlike platinum, it is liquid in its raw natural state.

rhodochrosite. A rather soft material characterized by a bright pink color, generally banded; some have transparent crystals, which are typically carved into cabochons.

rock crystal. A usually colorless and transparent quartz, differentiated from glass by its greater hardness, coldness, and double refraction.

rose cut. A cut of diamond that was most popular in the eighteenth and nineteenth centuries and that was round like a rosebud. The crown is dome shaped; the facets, which vary in number, meet in a point at the center; and the bottom is flat. There are single, double, and even triple rose-cut diamonds, depending on the number of horizontal layers of facets.

rutilated quartz. A variety of rock crystal that has fine needlelike inclusions. It is often of cabochon cut.

sablé. An eighteenth-century French beadwork technique that was used to decorate bags, boxes, and other small objects to commemorate events or express sentiments. The opaque and translucent beads were strung one horizontal row at a time and then were joined together by looped stitches.

sard. A clear or translucent deep orange-red to brown-red variety of chalcedony.

sardonyx. A variety of onyx with alternating brown and white bands of sard and other minerals.

signet. A seal, often placed on a ring, used to impress an official mark of identification.

silicious. Relating to or consisting of silica.

suite. A parure, that is, a matching set of ornaments.

talisman. A protective jewel to which magical properties are attributed.

tesserae. The small, usually square, individual parts of different colored materials such as stone, marble, glass, and so on, which, when placed side by side, create a design. In antiquity, they formed mosaics that were used as architectural decorations on walls and floors. This technique was miniaturized and adapted to jewelry during the nineteenth century in Italy, where they were known as micromosaics. The tesserae were cut from glass rods and combined into compositions that were then mounted.

torque. A type of metal collar or armband formed by a strip of twisted metal.

tsavorite. A green (grossular) garnet discovered in Tanzania in the late 1960s.

tumbaga. An alloy of mostly gold and copper that was widely used by pre-Columbian cultures in Central and South America to make fine ornaments.

twining. Interweaving or interlacing two or more threads, strings, or wire.

vinaigrette. A small decorative receptacle with a perforated top used for scented vinegar or an aromatic substance.

zircon. A common, moderately hard, brittle stone that is sometimes colorless and also occurs naturally in a wide range of blues, greens, and browns. Other colors can be produced artificially by heat treatment. Zircons are usually cut as round brilliants when used as gems.

FURTHER READING

Andrews, Carol. *Ancient Egyptian Jewelry.* New York: Harry N. Abrams, 1997.

Bainbridge, Henry Charles. *Peter Carl Fabergé: Goldsmith and Jeweller to the Russian Imperial Court.* London: Spring Books, 1949.

Becker, Vivienne. *Antique and Twentieth Century Jewellery: A Guide for Collectors.* Colchester, Essex, UK: N.A.G. Press, 1987.

——. *Art Nouveau Jewelry*. New York: E. P. Dutton, 1985.

Brunhammer, Yvonne, ed. *The Jewels of Lalique.* Paris: Flammarion, 1998.

Bury, Shirley. *Jewellery, 1789–1910: The International Era.* Vol. 1, *1789–1861.* Vol. 2, *1862–1910.* Woodbridge, Suffolk, UK: Antique Collectors' Club, 1991.

Cera, Deanna Farneti. *Jewels of Fantasy: Costume Jewelry of the 20th Century.* New York: Harry N. Abrams, 1992.

Cipriani, Curzio, and Alessandro Borelli. *Simon and Schuster's Guide to Gems and Precious Stones.* New York: Simon and Schuster, 1986.

Dietz, Ulysses Grant, Jenna Weissman Joselit, Kevin J. Smead, and Janet Zapata. *The Glitter and the Gold: Fashioning America's Jewelry.* Newark, N.J.: Newark Museum, 1997.

Fales, Martha Gandy. *Jewelry in America, 1600–1900.* Woodbridge, Suffolk, UK: Antique Collectors' Club, 1995.

Falino, Jeannine, and Yvonne J. Markowitz. *American Luxury: Jewels from the House of Tiffany.* Woodbridge, Suffolk, UK: Antique Collectors' Club, 2009.

Falk, Fritz. *Schmuck/Jewellery, 1840–1940: Highlights Schmuckmuseum Pforzheim.* Stuttgart: Arnoldsche, 2004.

Foskett, Daphne. *Miniatures: Dictionary and Guide.* Woodbridge, Suffolk, UK: Antique Collectors' Club, 1987.

Garside, Anne, ed. *Jewelry: Ancient to Modern.* New York: Viking Press in cooperation with the Walters Arts Gallery, Baltimore, 1980.

Gere, Charlotte, and Judy Rudoe. *Jewellery in the Age of Queen Victoria: A Mirror to the World.* London: British Museum Press, 2010.

Karlin, Elyse Zorn. *Jewelry and Metalwork in the Arts and Crafts Tradition.* Atglen, Penn.: Schiffer Publishing, 1993.

Koch, Michael, et al. *The Belle Epoque of French Jewellery, 1850–1910.* London: Thomas Heneage, 1990.

L'Ecuyer, Kelly H., with contributions by Michelle Tolini Finamore, Yvonne J. Markowitz, and Gerald W. R. Ward. *Jewelry by Artists:In the Studio, 1940–2000.* Selections from the Dapne Farago Collection. Boston: Museum of Fine Arts, 2010.

Lewin, Susan Grant. *One of a Kind: American Art Jewelry Today.* New York: Harry N. Abrams, 1994.

Munn, Geoffrey C. *Castellani and Giuliano: Revivalist Jewellers of the 19th Century.* New York: Rizzoli, 1984.

Newman, Harold. *An Illustrated Dictionary of Jewelry.* London: Thames and Hudson, 1981.

Ogden, Jack. *Jewellery.* London: Intelligent Layman Publishers, 2006.

——. *Jewellery of the Ancient World.* New York: Rizzoli, 1982.

Peltason, Ruth. *Living Jewels: Masterpieces from Nature.* New York: Vendome Press, 2010.

Phillips, Clare. *Jewels and Jewellery.* London: V & A Publishing, 2008.

Proddow, Penny, and Debra Healy. *American Jewelry: Glamour and Tradition.* New York: Rizzoli, 1987.

Richter, Anne. *Jewelry of Southeast Asia.* New York: Harry N. Abrams, 2000.

Soros, Susan Weber, and Stephanie Walker, eds. *Castellani and Italian Archaeological Jewelry.* New Haven, Conn.: Bard Graduate Center for Studies in the Decorative Arts, Design, and Culture, 2004.

Tait, Hugh. *7000 Years of Jewellery.* London: British Museum Press, 2006.

Untracht, Oppi. *Jewelry Concepts and Technology.* New York: Doubleday, 1985.

——. *Traditional Jewelry of India.* New York: Harry N. Abrams, 1997.

Williams, Dyfri, and Jack Ogden. *Greek Gold: Jewelry of the Classical World.* New York: Henry N. Abrams, 1994.

FIGURE ILLUSTRATIONS

All illustrations in this book were photographed by Michael Gould and Greg Heins of the Imaging Studios, Museum of Fine Arts, Boston, except where otherwise noted.

p. 10: *The New Necklace*
William McGregor Paxton
(American, 1869–1941)
1910
Oil on canvas
25.2 × 38.7 cm (9 15/16 × 15 1/4 in.)
Zoe Oliver Sherman Collection 22.644

p. 18: Statue of a bodhisattva
Gandharan, Northwest Pakistan, late 2nd century
Gray schist
109.5 × 38.1 × 22.9 cm (43 1/8 × 15 × 9 in.)
Helen and Alice Colburn Fund 37.99

p. 48: *Portrait of a Woman in a Pearl Necklace*
Lorenzo Costa (Italian, 1460–1535)
About 1485–95
Oil on canvas
44.1 × 34 cm (17 3/8 × 3 3/8 in.)
Bequest of Mrs. Thomas O. Richardson 25.227

p. 98: Mourning embroidery
United States, about 1807
Ink and pigment on silk plain weave embroidered with silk
62 × 58.3 cm (24 7/16 × 22 15/16 in.)
Bequest of Marion Austin Greene 1980.424

p. 120: *Indoor Party Scenes*
Japanese, Edo period, about 1661–73
Panel with ink, color and gold on paper
25.2 x 38.7 cm (9 15/16 × 15 1/4 in.)
Denman Waldo Ross Collection 06.283

p. 150: Untitled (mobile)
Alexander Calder (American, 1898–1976)
About 1942
Wire, painted sheet metal, and painted linen cords
173.4 cm (68 1/4 in.)
Decorative Arts Special Fund 60.241

1. Cameo with Livia holding a bust of Augustus
Roman, early Imperial period, A.D. 14–37
Turquoise with modern gold setting
3.1 × 3.8 cm (1 1/4 × 1 1/2 in.)
Henry Lillie Pierce Fund 99.109

2. Miniature portrait of Mrs. Paul Revere (Rachel Walker)
Attributed to Joseph Dunkerly
(American, active 1784–1788)
About 1784
Gold and watercolor on ivory
4.5 × 3.5 cm (1 3/4 × 1 3/8 in.)
Bequest of Mrs. Pauline Revere Thayer 35.1850

3. Wedding ring
Paul Revere Jr. (American, 1734–1818)
1773
Gold
1.7 cm (11/16 in.)
Gift of Mrs. Henry B. Chapin
and Edward H. R. Revere 56.585

4. Brooch
Josephine Hartwell Shaw (American, 1865–1941)
About 1913
Gold and blister pearl
2.9 × 2.5 × 1 cm (1 1/8 × 1 × 3/8 in.)
Gift of John Templeman Coolidge, Jr.
and others 13.1698

5. *Choker #48*
Mary Lee Hu (American, born 1943)
1979
Gold, silver, and lacquered copper
23.5 × 17.8 × 4.4 cm (9 1/4 × 7 × 1 3/4 in.)
The Daphne Farago Collection 2006.257

6. Beaded collar with amulets
Egyptian, Middle Kingdom, Dynasty 11–13, 2061–1640 B.C.
From Sheikh Farag, tomb SF 43
Glazed steatite, gold, and electrum
L. 18.5 cm (7 5/16 in.)
Harvard University–Boston Museum of Fine Arts Expedition 13.3609

7. Reliquary pendant
Meuse (Germany), third quarter of the 12th century
Gilt copper, vernis brun, sapphire, wood, rock crystal, and bone
16.9 × 10.6 × 3.7 cm (6 5/8 × 4 3/16 × 1 7/16 in.)
William Francis Warden Fund 49.480

8. Funerary monument of Aththaia, daughter of Malchos
Palmyrene, Imperial period, A.D. 150–200
Limestone
55 × 42 cm (21 5/8 × 16 9/16 in.)
Museum purchase with funds donated by Edward Perry Warren in memory of his sister 22.659

9. Charm bracelet
United States, about 1945
Silver
18.5 × 1.8 cm (7 5/16 × 11/16 in.)
Gift of Mindy Markowitz Setzen 2011.145

10. *Bhim Singh of Jodphur*
Northwest India (Rajasthan), early 19th century
Opaque watercolor and gold on paper
31.7 × 21.9 cm (12 1/2 × 8 5/8 in.)
Gift of John Goelet 66.136

11. Photographer unknown, Elizabeth Balletta's dogs from the early 20th century, Art of Europe object file 1980.649, Museum of Fine Arts, Boston.

12. *Portrait of Marjorie Merriweather Post*
Douglas Chandor (English, 1897–1953)
1952
Oil on canvas
95.3 × 71.1 cm (37½ × 28 in.)
Hillwood Estate, Museum & Gardens
Bequest of Marjorie Merriweather Post, 1973
Photo by E. Owen

13. Lover's eye brooch
England, about 1820
Gold, ruby, watercolor on ivory and crystal
2.8 × 1.9 × 0.5 cm (1⅛ × ¾ × 3⁄16 in.)
Promised gift of Susan B. Kaplan

14. Heart-shaped earrings
England, about 1880
Gold, silver, diamond, emerald, amethyst, ruby, sapphire, and topaz
4.4 × 1.9 × 0.7 cm (1¾ ×¾ ×¼ in.)
Promised gift of Susan B. Kaplan

15. Mourning band for George Washington
United States, 1799
Silk plain weave (ribbon and crepe), ink
31.5 × 7 cm (12⅜ × 2¾ in.)
Gift of Emily Welles Robbins (Mrs. Harry Pelham Robbins) and the Hon. Sumner Welles, in memory of Georgiana Welles Sargent 49.1012

16. *Levi Willard*
Winthrop Chandler (American, 1747–1790)
About 1770–75
Oil on canvas
67.94 × 59.69 cm (26¾ × 23½ in.)
The M. and M. Karolik Collection of Eighteenth-Century American Arts 37.42

17. *Mrs. Levi Willard (Catherine Chandler)*
Winthrop Chandler (American, 1747–1790)
About 1770–75
Oil on canvas
67.94 × 59.69 cm (26¾ × 23½ in.)
The M. and M. Karolik Collection of Eighteenth-Century American Arts 37.43

18. *Infanta Maria Theresa*
Studio of Diego Rodríguez de Silva y Velázquez (Spanish, 1599–1660)
1653
Oil on canvas
128.6 × 100.6 cm (50⅝ × 39⅝ in.)
Gift of Charlotte Nichols Greene in memory of her father and mother, Mr. and Mrs. Howard Nichols 21.2593

19. Woman's jacket
England, about 1610 with later alterations
Linen plain weave, embroidered with silk and metallic threads and spangles; metallic bobbin lace
Center back: 43 cm (16 15⁄16 in.)
The Elizabeth Day McCormick Collection 43.243

20. Necklace
Elsa Schiaparelli (Italian, active in France, 1890–1973)
About 1950–1959
Silver-colored metal and colored glass
43.2 × 5.1 cm (17 × 2 in.)
Gift of Susan B. Kaplan 2006.1994.1

21. Portrait of a Woman
Frans Pourbus, the Elder (Netherlandish, 1545–1581)
1581
Oil on panel
142.9 × 78.4 cm (56¼ × 30⅞ in.)
Willliam Sturgis Bigelow Collection 27.176

22. Necklace
Alexander Calder (American, 1898–1976)
1941
Silver
H. 1.3 cm, l. 86.4 cm (H. ½ in., l. 34 in.)
Promised gift of The Daphne Farago Collection

23. Brooch
Margaret De Patta (American, 1903–1964)
About 1980
Silver, quartz
5.1 × 8.9 × 1.3 cm (2 × 3½ × ½ in.)
The Daphne Farago Collection 2006.121

24. Brooch
Margret Craver (American, born 1907)
About 1945
Silver and quartz
3.8 × 4.4 × 1.9 cm (1½ × 1¾ × ¾ in.)
Gift in memory of Eleanor Hodge Pough, Wellesley '30 1991.1050

25. Illustration of Charles Robert Ashbee's *Marsh Bird* from a 1903 catalogue published by the Guild of Handicraft (Bury, 1991, plate 341)

INDEX

Page numbers in *italics* refer to illustrations.

Achaemenid (Persian Empire), 28–29, *29*
agate, 20, 55, *55*, 86, *86*, 93, *93*, 139, *139*, 193
alloy, defined, 193
amber, 19–20, 40–42, *41*, 42, 84–87, *85*, *87*, 195
ambergris, 130, 193
American Requiem 3047.9.11.2001 (Jocz), 103, 118, *119*
American Waltham Watch Company, 140–41, *141*
amethyst, 69, *69*, *158*, 159, 164, *165*, 169, *169*
ametrine, 184, *185*, 193
amulet cases, 23, *23*, 26, *27*, 44, *44*, 46, *46*
amulets, *18*, 19, *20*, 22, *22*, 25, 35, *35*, 36, *36*, 139, *139*
aquamarine, 45, *45*, 184, *185*
archaeological revival style, 74, *75*, 82, *82*, 84–86, *84–86*, 114, *114*
armbands, 62, *62*, *63*, 102, *102*, 193
armlets, 45, *45*, 54, *54*
armorials, 130, *130*, *131*, 193
art deco, 92, *92*, 152–53
art nouveau, 12, 86, 92, 94, 151–53, 160, *160*, 161, *161*, 180, 189, *189*
arts and crafts movement, 92, 94, 151, 159; Boston, 15, *16*, 162–64, *162–65*; England, 12, 15, 151, 156, *156–58*, 159
Ashbee, Charles Robert, 156, *156*, *157*, 163
assay, 193
Autumn Twilight (Yamamoto), 178, *178*
avant-garde jewelry, described, 151–55

bails, 28, 35, 38, *39*, 40, *40*, 62, *62*, 193
Balletta, Elizabeth, 93, *93*
bangles, 13, 49, *50*, 115, *115*. *See also* bracelets
basse-taille, 40, *40*, 193
bazuband, 193
bead-net dress (Egypt), 126, *126*
belt buckles, 83, *83*, 94, 129, *129*, 142, *143*
Berlin iron jewelry suite, 77, *77*
Bertoia, Harry, 15, 166, *166*, 169, 170
betrothal jewelry, 106, *106*, 111, 139, *139*
bezel-set, 55, *55*, 76, *76*, 86, *87*, 104, *104*, 106, *106*, 135, 136, *158*, 159, 184, *185*, 188, *188*, 190, *190*, 193; cabochons, 55, 164, *165*, 167, *167*, 169, *169*
Bhim Singh of Jodphur (India), 62, *63*
Big Double Gold Brooch (Cooper), *158*, 159
bijoux de couture, 124, 144, *144*
Bissinger, Georges, 86, *86*
bodhisattva, *18*, 19, 193
Boone, Jeremiah, 113, *113*
Boston, 14, *15*, 76, 78, *78*, 108, *108*, 134, *134*, *140*, 140–41, 178; arts and crafts movement, 15, *16*, 162–64, *162–65*
boulder opal, 178, *178*, 193
bracelet clasps, 76, *76*, 86, 99–100, 115, *115*
bracelets, 32, *32*; avant-garde, 172, *172*; bangles, 49, *50*, 115, *115*; in demiparure, 69, *69*, 83, *83*; dress and adornment jewelry, 148, *149*; *King's Bracelet* (Frühauf), 172, *172*; revival-style, 84, *84*; sentimental jewelry, 115, *115*; wealth and power emblems, 49, *50*, 55, *55*, 57, *57*, 64, *64*, 66, *67*, 69, *69*, 76, *76*, 77, *77*, 83, *83*, 84, *84*
bracelets, charm, 51–52, *52*, 103
bracelets, cuff, 144, 182, *182*, 188, *188*
Brazil, 69, *69*, 70, *71*, 78, *78*
broad collars, 25, *25*, 126, 193
Brogden, John, 86
brooches: *American Requiem 3047.9.11.2001* (Jocz), 118, *119*; *amorini* on doves suite, 114, *114*; arts and crafts style, 15, *16*, 156, *156*, *158*, 159, 163, *163*, 164, *164*; avant-garde, 139, *139*, *153*, 154, *154*, 156, *156*, *157*, *158*, 159, 161, *161*, 163, *163*, 184, *185*, 186, *187*, 190, *190*; bicycle brooch, 89, *89*; *Big Double Gold Brooch* (Cooper), *158*, 159; *Brooch in Two Parts* (Priest), 190, *190*; *Dandelion Brooch* (Yager), 186, *187*; in demiparure, 74, *75*, *77*, *77*, 79, *79*; dress and adornment jewelry, 139, *139*, 144, *144*; *Fish Lunching on a Pearl* (Cooperman), 97, *97*; as garment-fastener (*See* fibula); Japanesque-style, 92, *92*; "lover's eye," 100, *100*; Luckenbooth brooch, 139, *139*; Maltese-cross brooch, 144, *144*; *Marsh Bird Hair Ornament* (brooch) (Ashbee), 156, *156*, *157*; mourning, 49, *50*, 79, *79*, 113, *113*; owned by Post, 94, *94*, *95*; Queen Mary's brooches, 139; revivalist-style, 74, *75*; seaweed brooch (Liénard), 161, *161*; sentimental jewelry, 100, *100*, 113, *113*, 114, *114*, 118, *119*; and "sweetheart" jewelry, 52; wealth and power emblems, 49, *50*, 52, 66, *67*, 74, *75*, 77, *77*, 78, *78*, 79, *79*, 82, *82*, 89, *89*, 92, *92*, 94, *94*, *95*, 97, *97*, 114, *114*. *See also* pendant/brooches
Brooch in Two Parts (Priest), 190, *190*
Buddhism, *18*, 19, 38, *39*, 129, 193
Buffum, William Arnold, 84–85, 86
Bulgari (company), 56, 96, *96*
bulldog sculpture (Fabergé), 93, *93*
bust of Augustus (Roman Imperial), 14, *14*
bust of George IV (England), 68, *68*
Butler and Wilson, 16
Byzantine Empire, 57, *57*, 80, 106, *106*

cabochons, 159, 160; amber, 86, *87*; aquamarine, 184, *185*; bezel-set, 55, 164, *165*, 167, *167*, 169, *169*; defined, 193; emerald, 73, *73*; garnet, 31, *31*, 104, *104*; moonstone, 156, *157*; pearl, 64, *64*; rhodochrosite, 195; ruby, 72, *72*, 73, *73*, 93, *93*; rutilated quartz, 196; sapphire, 21, *21*; turquoise, 61, *61*
cairngorms, 139
Calder, Alexander, 15, *150*, 151, *152*, 153–54, 166, 168, 169, 170
cameos, 14, *14*, 57, *57*, 65, *65*, 76, *76*, 86, *86*, 105, *105*, 106, *106*, 133, *133*, 193; *Death of Meleager*, 14, 60, *60*; *nicolo*, 84, *84*
cameo suite, 74, *75*
Campana, Giovanni Pietro, 114
cannetille, 69, *69*, 88, *88*, 193
Carnegie, Hattie, 16, 124
carnelian, 22, *22*, 23, *23*, 28, *29*, 133, *133*, 193
Cartier, 93, 94
cartouche, 130, *130*, *131*, 132, *132*, 193
caryatid, 87, *88*, 193
caskets, jewelry, 61, *61*, 86–87, *87*, 153, 164, *165*
Castellani firm, 80, 82, *82*, 114, 179
Castellani firm (possibly), 84–85, *85*
casting, defined, 193
cat's eye, 45, 90, *91*, 193, 195
caul, 46, *46*, 193
Ceylon, probably, 61, *61*
chains, 25, *48*, 51, 69, *69*, 86, *86*; double loop-in-loop, 25, *25*; loop-in-loop, 128, *128*, 179, *179*, 189, 195
chalcedony, 57, *57*, 84, *84*, 193. *See also* agate; carnelian; chrysoprase; sard
champlevé, 34, *34*, 43, *43*, 62, 156, 193
Chanel, Gabrielle (Coco), 16, 124, 144, *144*
Charles I, King, 108
charm bracelets, 51–52, *52*, 103
charms, 44; Egypt, 19, *20*; U.S., 46, *46*, 115, *115*
chasing, defined, 194
chatelaines, 12, 121, *122*, 132, *132*, 133, *133*
China, 138, *138*
chitons, 128, 194
Choker #48 (Hu), 15, *17*
Choker #88 (Hu), 189, *189*
chokers, 15, *17*, 86, *86*, 189, *189*
Christesen, Vilhelm, 83, *83*
chrysoberyl, cat's eye, 45, 90, *91*, 193

chrysoprase, *158*, 159, 169, *169*, 194
cinnabar, 194
Citron Cascade Ruffle (Winters), 191, *191*
Civilotti, Antonio, 80, *80*
Clark, Henry Hunt, 163
clasps, jewelry, 76, *76*, 84, *84*, 86, 99–100, 115, *115*; fibula, 68, *68*, 178, 194; Heracles-knot motif, 31, *31*; interlocking curls, 191, *191*; tongue-and-groove, 115, *115*
cloisonné, 28, 34, 142, *143*, 156, 194, 195
cloisons, 22, *22*, 28, 142, *143*, 194
Codman, Martha Catharine, 69, *69*
collars, beaded (Egypt), 19, *20*, 126, *126*
collars, broad (Egypt), 25, *25*, 126, 193
Colombia, 37, *37*
Colt family jewelry, 70, *71*
combs, 125, *125*
conus (shell), 182, 194
Coomaraswamy, Ananda, 13
Cooper, John Paul, *158*, 159
Cooperman, Marilyn, 97, *97*
coral, 20, 45, *45*, 74, 138, *138*, 148, *149*, 152, 182, 195
coral revivalist suite, 74, *75*
Costa, Lorenzo, *48*, 49
costume jewelry, 16, 122–24
Craver, Margret, 15, *154*, 154–55
cuff bracelets, 144, 182, *182*, 188, *188*
cuff links, 108, *108*, 121
culet, 194

Dandelion Brooch (Yager), 186, *187*
Death of Meleager, probably Italian Renaissance, 14, 60, *60*
demiparure, 69, *69*, 70, *70*, *71*, 74, *75*, 77, *77*, 79, *79*, 83, *83*, 114, *114*, 195
Denmark, 49, *50*, 83, *83*
De Patta, Margaret, 15, *153*, 154, 170, 176
depletion gilding, 194
Devaranne and Son, 77, *77*
diadems, 28, 31, *31*, 49, *50*, 51, 194
diamond cuts: brilliant, 78, *78*, 79, *79*, 89, *89*, 134, 160, *160*; cutting centers (Europe), 49; old mine cut, 70, *71*, 78, *78*, 79, *79*, 86, *86*, 134, 195; rose cut, 73, *73*, *140*, 141, 196; rough, 195
diamond (gem): in Hindu cosmology, 45, 195; lab-grown, 103; talismanic powers of, 20
diamond jewelry, 68, *68*, 70, *71*, *140*, 140–41, 160, *160*, 188, *188*; brooches, 78, *78*, 89, *89*, 94, *94*, *95*, 97, *97*, 163, *163*, 178, *178*; necklaces, 70, *71*, 86, *86*; pendant necklaces, 184, *185*; pendants, *42*, 42–43, *43*
diamonds, faux, 51. *See also* glass paste; rhinestone
diamonds, pavé, 184, *185*
diamond trade, 49, 70
diopside, 184, *185*, 194
dress, bead-net, 126, *126*
dress and adornment jewelry, described, 12, 121–24
Dunkerly, Joseph, 14, *15*
earrings, 28–29, *29*, 30, *30*, 66, *67*, 70, *70*, *71*, 101, *101*, 104, *104*, 106, *106*, 114, *114*; archaeological revival style, 84–85, *85*; in demiparure, 79, *79*, 114, *114*; *girandole*-style, 66, *67*, 194; heart-shaped, 101, *101*
Ebendorf, Robert W., 15–16, 174, *174*
ebony, 47, *47*, 86–87, *87*
Edward VII , King, 81
Egypt, 12, 19, *20*, 31, 35; amulet cases, 23, *23*, 26, *27*, 44; amulets, 35, *35*; bead-net dress, 126, *126*; combs, 125, *125*; gods and goddesses, 19, *20*, 22, *22*, 25, *25*, 26, *27*, 32, 33, 35, *35*, 36; influences, 36, 82, 104, *104*, 180; pectorals, 22, *22*; pendant necklaces, 25, *25*; and trade, 23, *23*, 26, *27*, 55; tricolor design scheme, 22, *22*, 25, *25*, 32, *32*
Egypt, possibly: bracelets, 55, *55*
Egypt, probably: amulets, 36, *36*
Egypt Exploration Fund, 13
Eikerman, Alma, 155
Elizabethan revival style, 86, *86*
emerald (gem): cabochon, 73, *73*; in Hindu cosmology, 45, 195; imitation, 51, 146, *147*; rough-cut, 146, 195; talismanic powers of, 20
emerald jewelry, *42*, 42–43, *43*, 45, *45*, 55, *55*, 62, *62*, 68, *68*, 72, *72*, 73, *73*, 86, *86*, 90, *91*, 94, *94*, *95*, 97, *97*, 101, *101*, 136, *136*
emerald trade, 49, 55, 94
enamel, defined, 194
enameling (technique): basse-taille, 40, *40*, 193; *en résille*, 34, 194. *See also* cloisonné; guilloché; plique-à-jour
England: arts and crafts movement, 12, 15, 151, 156, *156–58*, 159; *cannetille* (technique), 88; dress and adornment jewelry, 132, *132*, 133, *133*, 139, *139*; mourning rituals, 102; sentimental jewelry, *100*, 100–101, *101*, 108, *108*; wealth and power emblems, 68, *68*, 86, *86*, 89, *89*
England, probably: dress and adornment jewelry, 130, *130*, *131*; wealth and power emblems, 64, *64*, 65, *65*, 66, *67*
England or America: dress and adornment jewelry, 137, *137*
England or France: wealth and power emblems, 69, *69*
engraving, defined, 194
en résille, 34, 194
en tremblant, 138, *138*
epoxy (material), 182, *182*
equipage (ensemble), 132, *132*
escapements, watch, *140*, 141, 194
etui, 132, *132*
Europe. *See specific country*
Europe or United States: shoe buckles, 134, *134*
expositions and exhibitions, 77, 82, 83, 86, 90, 155, 156, 162, 163, 164, 169

Fabergé, Peter Carl, 93, *93*, 142, *143*
faience, 23, *23*, 36, 126, *126*, 194
Farago, Daphne, 15
Farnham, G. Paulding, 90, *91*
fasteners, 31, *31*, 54, 55, *55*. *See also* clasps, jewelry
Ferlini, Giuseppe, 33
fibula, 68, *68*, 178, 194
filigree, defined, 194
finger rings. *See* rings, finger
Finland, 173, *173*
Fish Lunching on a Pearl (Cooperman), 97, *97*
flux, 179, 194
forging, defined, 194
found-object jewelry, 167, 174, *174*, 178, 186, *187*
Fouquet, Georges, 153
France, 76; art nouveau, 12, 151–52, 153, 160, *160*, 161, *161*; avant-garde jewelry, 160, *160*, 161, *161*, 184, *185*; *cannetille*, 88; costume jewelry, 124, 144; dress and adornment jewelry, 121, *122*, 136, *136*, *140*, 141, 144, *144*; equipage, 132, *132*; and *sablé*, 110, *110*, 196; sentimental jewelry, 109, *109*, 110, *110*; wealth and power emblems, 64, 74, *75*, 86, *86*
France (or England): wealth and power emblems, 69, *69*
Franklin, Benjamin, 65, 111
Frühauf, Anton, 172, *172*
funerary jewelry. *See* mourning and funerary jewelry
funerary monument of Aththaia (Palmyra), 49, *50*, 51
funerary portrait reliefs, 49, *50*, 51
fusion, 179, *179*, 188, *188*, 194

Galaxy Necklace (Smith), 170, *171*
garnet (gem), 45, 55, 194; cabochon, 31, *31*, 104, *104*; grossular garnet, 45, *45*, 196. *See also tsavorite*
garnet jewelry, 31, *31*, 45, *45*, 57, *57*, 104, *104*, 166–67, *167*
gauds, rosary, *41*, 42, 194
gem-set necklace (Bulgari), 96, *96*
gemstones, "organic," 19–20, 195
George IV, bust of, 68, *68*
Germany, 21, *21*, 77, *77*, 86–87, *87*, 93, 139, 142, 188, *188*
Gibson, Rosamond Warren, 78
girandole, 66, *67*, 194
glass paste, 51, 57, *57*, 134, *134*, 136
gold: talismanic powers of, 11, 19, 23, 26, *27*, 44. *See also specific jewelry pieces*
gold and copper alloy. *See tumbaga*
Goldfinger (Martinazzi), 175, *175*
Gorgon, 86, *87*, 194
Gothic-style jewelry, 77, *77*
Gralnick, Lisa, 15–16, 116, *116*, *117*
granulation, defined, 194
Grasset, Eugene, 161
Greece: Byzantine Empire, 57, *57*; classical, 53, *53*, 128, *128*; gods and goddesses, 30, *30*, 31, *31*, 53, *53*, 55, *55*, 57, *57*, 86, 99, *104*, 104–6, *106*, 111, *111*; Hellenistic, 31, *31*, 55, *55*, 104, *104*; Hellenistic, or classical, 53, *53*; Hellenistic, or Roman Imperial, 30, *30*, 55, *55*

Greece, East, 28, *28*
Greece, northern, 30, *30*
Gucci, 16
Guild of Handicraft (England), 156, *156*, 163
guilds, jeweler, 12, 151, 156, 163, 176
guilloché, 113, *113*, 194

hair accessories, 66, 121, 125, *125*
hair ornaments, 49, *50*, 66, 99, 102, 108, 111–13, *112*, *113*, 115, *115*, 133, 156, *156*, *157*, 160, *160*, 176, *177*, 195. *See also* diadems; headbands; headdresses
Hale, Frank Gardner, 163, *163*, 164
halter top (Peretti), 145, *145*
hand ornament *(hathphul)*, 72, *72*
Harper's Bazaar (pub.), 146, 169
Harsaphes amulet (Egypt), 35, *35*
Harvard-Boston Expedition, 13, 23, 32, 33
Harvard University, 13, 15, 23, 32, 33
Haskell, Miriam, 16
Hathor (goddess), 26, *27*, 32, *32*
hat jewels, *48*, 51
haute couture jewelry, 16, 123, 124, 184
headbands, 73, *73*. *See also* diadems
headdresses, 53, *53*; *feng tien*, 138, *138*
head of a pin, *128*, 129
heart-shaped jewelry, 46, *46*, 101, *101*, 103, 108, 139, *139*
heishi, 194
Heracles-knot (motif), 31, *31*
Hinduism, 44, 45, 62, 73, *73*, 195; avatars of Vishnu, *42*, 42–43, *43*
hollowware, 94, 145, 162, 194
Howard, Thomas (Earl of Arundel), 60, 105
Hu, Mary Lee, 15, *17*, 189, *189*
Hunt, William Morris, 76, *76*

India, 13, 43; gods and goddesses, *42*, 42–43, *43*, 45, *45*, 73, *73*; influences, 145, 183; Mughal Empire, 62, *62*, 88, *88*, 94, *94*, *95*; Rajasthan, *42*, 42–43, *43*, 62, 63, 72, *72*; tiger-claw jewelry, 20, 58, *59*, 81, *81*; and trade, 49, 62, 70, 88, 94
India, northern, *42*, 42–43, *43*, 81, *81*, 88, *88*
India, northwest (possibly), 44, *44*
India, South, 73, *73*
Indonesia. *See* Java, East
Indoor Party Scenes, *120*, 121
Infanta Maria Theresa, 122, *122*
inlay, defined, 194
inscriptions, 80, 193; England, 99, 139; France, 109, *109*; Germany, 40–42, *41*, 77, *77*; on mourning jewelry, 102, 112, *112*; Roman Imperial, 56, *56*, 106, *106*; U.S., 14, *15*, 46, *46*, 100, 112, *112*, 113, *113*, 115, *115*; wedding jewelry, 14, *15*, 106, *106*
intaglio, 33, *33*, 40, 57, 60, 86–87, *87*, 106, *106*, 194
Ireland (Bronze Age), 54, *54*
iron jewelry suite, 77, *77*
Italian Renaissance, *48*, 49, 105, 107, *107*, 175
Italian Renaissance, probably, 60, *60*
Italy: avant-garde jewelry, 172, *172*, 175, *175*; dress and adornment jewelry, *123*, 124, 145, *145*; sentimental jewelry, 107, *107*; wealth and power emblems, *48*, 49, 74, *75*, 80, *80*, 82, *82*, 84–87, *85*, *87*, 96, *96*. *See also* Roman Imperial
ivory, 109, *109*, 113, *113*, 125, *125*, 135, *135*, 195; painted miniatures, 14, *15*, 88, *88*, 100, 110–11, *111*
ivory-paneled caskets, 61, *61*, 86–87, *87*

jabot pins, 194
jackets, women's, 121, *122*, 148, *149*
jade, 162, *162*
jadeite, 19, 20, 24, *24*, 138, *138*, 195
Janus (Weckström), 173, *173*
Japan, 51, *120*, 121, 135, *135*, 151, 178. *See also* netsuke
Japanesque style, 92, *92*
jasperware, 65, *65*, 105, 195
Java, East, 58, *59*
jet (material), 20, 182, *182*, 195
Jocz, Daniel, 103, 118, *119*
Jones, Ball and Poor, 78, *78*

King's Bracelet (Frühauf), 172, *172*
Korea, 129, *129*
Kramer, Sam, 15, 154, 166–67, *167*, 170
kundan, *42*, 42–43, 62, 72, *72*, 73, *73*, 195
Künzli, Otto, 15–16

Lacloche Frères, 92, *92*
Lalique, Rene, 160, *160*, 180
Lane, Kenneth Jay, 16, 146, *147*
lapidary, 94, 154, 188, 195; France, 86, *86*; Germany, 173, *173*, 188, *188*; Italy, 84, *84*; Russia, 93, *93*; U.S., 78, *78*, 94, *94*, *95*, 182, *182*
lapis lazuli, 22, *22*, 28–29, *29*, 86–87, *87*, 138, *138*, 152
Leopold II, King, 133
Liénard, Paul, 161, *161*
limited-edition jewelry, 97, *97*, 144, 151
Lincoln, Mary Todd, 79
lockets, 99, 115, *115*, 116, *116*
Longfellow, Henry Wadsworth, 76, 77
loop-in-loop chains, 25, *25*, 128, *128*, 179, *179*, 189; defined, 195
lost-wax process, 35, *35*, 37, *37*
Lovers brooch (Kramer), 166–67, *167*
"lover's eyes" jewelry, 100, *100*
Lowell, Judge John, 110–11, *111*
Luckenbooth brooch, 139, *139*
Luck necklace (Slemmons), 47, *47*

mabe pearl, 161, *161*, 195
MacNeil, Linda, 180, *181*
magical power, jewelry for: described, 19–21. *See also* amulets; amulet cases; talismans
maharatnani, 94, *94*,195
Maison Gripoix, 144, *144*
Maltese-cross brooch, 144, *144*
Man with Bee (Ebendorf), 174, *175*
Marcus and Company, 94, *94*, *95*
Marlborough, Duke of, 14, 60, 105
marriage and wedding jewelry, 14, *15*, 31, *31*, 72, *72*, 73, *73*, 105, *105*, 106, *106*, 107, *107*, 138. *See also* betrothal jewelry
marriage pendants, 107, *107*
Marsh Bird Hair Ornament (Ashbee), 156, *156*, *157*, *cover*
Martinazzi, Bruno, 175, *175*
Mary, Queen, 92
masks, jadeite, 24, *24*
Massachusetts, 110–12, *111*, *112*, 122. *See also* Boston
Massachusetts College of Art and Design, 163
matrix, 195
McConnell, Ruth, 113, *113*
medallions, 77; England, 65, *65*, 68, *68*, 133, *133*; Germany, *41*, 42; Italy, 107, *107*
Melillo, Giacinto (attributed to), 114, *114*
Melos, 28
memento mori jewelry, 101–3, 108, *108*. *See also* mourning and funerary jewelry
Meröe (Nubia), 32–34, *32–34*
micromosaics, 80, *80*, 84
Miller, Fritz von, 86–87, *87*
Miller, John Paul, 15, 154–55, 179, *179*
miniature pendant/brooch, painted, 88, *88*
miniatures, portrait, 14, *15*, 99–100, *100*, 101, 108, *108*, 110, *111*
mobile (Calder), *150*, 151
modernism movement, 153, 166, 168, 170, 172–74, 182, 184
Moffatt, Samuel R. C., 46, *46*
monograms, 80, 111, 112, *112*
moonstone, 156, *157*, *158*, 159, 164, *164*, *165*
mosaics, 182, *182*; micromosaics, 80, *80*, 84; and tesserae (*see* tesserae)
mother-of-pearl, 64, *64*, 182, *182*, 195
mourning and funerary jewelry, 12, 101–3, 111; pectorals as, 195; reliquary pendants, 21, *21*; Stuart crystals, 108; U.S., 79, *79*, *98*, 99, 102, *102*, 112, *112*, 113, *113*, 118, *119*; wreath (Hellenistical or classical Greece), 53, *53*. *See also* amulets; amulet cases
mourning bands, 102, *102*
mourning embroidery, *98*, 99
Munsteiner, Bernd, 173, *173*
Munsteiner, Tom, 188, *188*
Museum of Fine Arts, Boston: first works of jewelry acquired by, 13; and Harvard-Boston Expedition, 13, 23, 32, 33; School of the Museum of Fine Arts, Boston (SMFA), 163, 178
Musgrave, James, 113, *113*

narwhal, 195
National Silversmithing Workshop Conferences, 154–55
Native American jewelry, 182, *182*, 194
necklace, bib (Lane), 146, *147*
necklace and brooches (cameo suite), 74, *75*
necklaces, 23, *23*, 44, *44*, 47, *47*; archaeological revival style, 84–85, *85*; arts and crafts, 162, *162*; avant-garde, 152, *152*, 154, *154*, 162, *162*, *168*, 168–70, *169*, 170, *171*, 173, *173*, 180, *181*, 183, *183*, 191, *191*; *Citron Cascade Ruffle* (Winters), 191,

191; Colt family, 70, *70*, *71*; demiparure, 69, *69*, 70, *70*, *71*; dress and adornment, *123*, 124, 148, *149*; *Galaxy Necklace* (Smith), 170, *171*; *Janus* (Weckström), 173, *173*; *Paisley Necklace* (Slemmons), 183, *183*; parure, 66, *67*, 74, *75*; *Ram's Horn Necklace* (MacNeil), 180, *181*; revivalist style, 74, *75*; wealth and power emblems, 49, *50*, 56, *56*, 58, *59*, 59, 66, *67*, 69, *69*, 70, *70*, *71*, 74, *75*, 80, *80*, 81, *81*, 84–85, *85*, 86, *86*, 96, *96*. *See also* chokers; collars; pendant necklaces
neck ornaments, 90, *91*
neo-Russian style, 142, *143*
netsuke, *120*, 121, 135, *135*, 195; and *himotōshi*, 194
Newman, Charlotte, 86, *86*
New Necklace, The (Paxton), *10*, 11
New York City, and modernist movement, 166, 168, 170
New York Sunday World (pub.), 89
niello, 107, *107*, 195
Norban, Joetta, 148
Norton, Charles Eliot, 15
Nubia, 13, 23, *23*, 26, *27*, 32–34, *32–34*
numismatic jewelry, 56, *56*

Oakes, Edward Everett, 164, *164*, *165*
Okatomo of Kyoto, 135, *135*
Olbia Treasure, 57
old mine cut, 70, *71*, 78, *78*, 79, *79*, 86, *86*, 134, 195
Olmec, 24, *24*
onyx, 164, *165*. *See also* sardonyx
opal, boulder, 178, *178*, 193
"organic" gems, 19–20, 195
Oscar Heyman and Brothers, probably, 94, *94*, *95*
Osirian triad amulet, 36
Owen, Angelita (Angie) Reano, 182, *182*
oxidized finishes, 168, 170, *171*, 188, *188*, 195; and flux, 194

Paisley Necklace (Slemmons), 183, *183*
Pakistan, *18*, 19
Palmyra, 49, *50*, 51
Pardon, Earl, 154–55
Parry, Rowland, 113, *113*
parure: archaeological revival style, 84–85, *85*, 114, *114*; coral revivalist, 74, *75*; cut-steel (England), 66, *67*; defined, 195, 196
paste. *See* glass paste
patch boxes, 110, *110*
pâte de verre, 180, 195
Patek Philippe, *140*, 140–41
patination, 97, *97*, 173, 195
patriotic jewelry, 12, 51–52, *52*, 77, 80, 83, *83*
Paxton, William McGregor, *10*, 11
Peale, Charles Willson, 100, 110–11, *111*
pearl, baroque, *48*, 51
pearl, faux, 64, 144
pearl, freshwater, 64, 156, *157*
pearl, mabe, 161, *161*
pearl-adorned clothing, 121
pearl (gem): in Hindu cosmology, 45, 195; mother-of-pearl, 64, *64*, 182, *182*, 195; as "organic," 195
pearl jewelry, 45, *45*, *48*, 49; arts and crafts, *158*, 159; avant-garde, *158*, 159, 164, *165*, 172, *172*, 176, *177*; dress and adornment jewelry, 138, *138*; *Fish Lunching on a Pearl* (Cooperman), 97, *97*; *osmena*, 64, *64*; sentimental jewelry, 100; *Sun, Moon, Stars, Rain Wedding Crown* (Renk), 176, *177*; wealth and power emblems, 55, *55*, 64, *64*, 73, *73*, 86, *86*, 90, *91*, 97, *97*, 100
"pebble" jewelry, 139
pectoral, 12, 22, *22*, 28, 195
penannular armlets, 54, *54*
pendant/brooches, 88, *88*, 113, *113*, 184, *185*
pendant charms, 46, *46*
pendant necklaces, 25, *25*, 58, *59*, 184, *185*
pendants, 14, *15*, *42*, 42–43, *43*; avant-garde, 179, *179*; and bails, 28, 35, 38, *39*, 40, *40*, 62, *62*; ball-bead (Hellenistic Greece), 31, *31*; Elizabethan revival style, 86, *86*; *Polyp Colony* (Miller), 179, *179*; sentimental jewelry, 107, *107*, 116, *116*, *117*; *Tragedy of Great Love (size 6), The* (Gralnick), 116, *116*, *117*; wealth and power emblems, *48*, 51, 66, *67*, 86, *86*, 133, *133*
pendants, forehead, 73, *73*
pendants, mourning, 113, *113*
Peretti, Elsa, 145, *145*
peridot, 96, *96*, 163, *163*, 195
Persia, 28, *29*, 49
Petrie, Sir Williams Flinders, 35
Pierret, Ernesto, 85
pin catch (brooch, U.S.), 78, *78*
pin head (classical Greece), *128*, 129
pinned hinge (Greek Hellenistic or Roman Imperial), 55, *55*
pins, 51, 52, 121, 137; and fibula, 194; jabot pins, 194. *See also* brooches
Pioneer (firm), 141, *141*
Pitt Rivers, Augustus Henry, 54
platinum, 94, *94*, *95*. *See also* rhodium
plique à jour, 151, 156, *156*, 160, 176, *177*; defined, 195
polymer clay (material), 191, *191*
Polyp Colony (Miller), 179, *179*
pomanders, 130, *130*, *131*
portrait mask (Olmec), 24, *24*
portrait miniatures, 14, *15*, 99–100, *100*, 101, 108, *108*, 110, *111*
Portrait of a Woman in a Pearl Necklace (Costa), *48*, 49
Portrait of Marjorie Merriweather Post (Chandor), 94, *94*
Portugal, 49, 61, 94
Post, Marjorie Merriweather, 94, *94*, *95*
posy holder (tuzzy-muzzy) (England or U.S.), 137, *137*
posy rings, 137, 195
prayer beads, 21. *See also* rosaries
precious-stone rough, 146, *147*; defined, 195
Priest, Linda Kindler, 190, *190*
propaganda, jewelry as, 12, 51, 65, *65*. *See also* patriotic jewelry

quartz, 23, *23*, 108, *108*, 153, *153*, 154, *154*; cairngorms, 139; defined, 105, 195; Stuart crystals, 108, *108*; talismanic powers of, 23, 26, 45. *See also* ametrine; chalcedony; rock crystal
quartz, rose, 45, *45*
quartz, rutilated, 188, *188*, 196
quartz, smoky, 173, *173*
Queen Mary's brooches, 139

Ram's Horn Necklace (MacNeil), 180, *181*
Reisner, George A., 33
relief decoration: and basse-taille, 40, *40*, 193. *See also* repoussé
religious jewelry: talismanic powers of, 21, 107. *See also* Roman Catholic jewelry
reliquary pendants, 21, *21*
Renaissance Europe, 20–21, 151; common jewelry forms, 51; and goldsmithing, 175; and sentimental jewelry, 99; wealth and power in, 49. *See also* Italian Renaissance
Renaissance revival style, 86–87, *87*, 90, *90*, *140*, 140–41
Renk, Merry, 176, *177*
repoussé, 34, 36, *36*, 38, *39*, 44, *44*, *57*, 58, *59*, 74, *75*, 129, 159, 164, 190, *190*; defined, 195
resin, 44, *44*, 138, *138*, 146, *147*, 195
Revere, Rachel Walker, 14, *15*
revivalist style, 74, *75*, 82, *82*, 94; Elizabethan revival, 86, *86*; Renaissance revival, 86–87, *87*, 90, *90*, *140*, 140–41. *See also* archaeological revival style
rhinestone, 123
Rhodes, probably, 28, *28*
rhodium, 123, 195
rhodochrosite, 169, *169*, 195
rings, finger: France, 109, *109*; *Goldfinger* (Martinazzi), 175, *175*; Italy, 175, *175*; memento mori, 102; *mudri* (Northwest India), 72, *72*; Nubia, 34, *34*; Palmyra, 49, *50*, 51; posy ring, 137, 195; Renaissance Europe, *48*, 51; Roman Imperial, 106, *106*; U.S. (Boston), 14, *15*
rings, mourning, 112, *112*
rings, signet, 33, *33*, 196
rings, wedding, 14, *15*
rock crystal, 20, 21, *21*, 23, *23*, 26, *27*, 153; defined, 196
rococo style, 132, *132*
Roma jewelry, 80
Roman Catholic jewelry: marriage pendants, 107, *107*; reliquary pendants, 21, *21*; Requiem Mass-inspired, 118; rosaries, 21, 40–42, *41*; stomachers, 136; triptych pendants, 40, *40*
Roman gods and goddesses, 74, *75*, 104, 105, *105*, 109, *109*, 114, *114*, 132, *132*, 133, *133*, 173
Roman Imperial, 14, *14*, 36, *36*, 55, *55*, 56, *56*, 68, 80, 105, *105*, 106, *106*

Roman Imperial (or Greek Hellenistic), 30, *30*, *54*, 55, *55*
Roman Imperial (or Republican), 105, *105*
Roman *nicolo* cameo, 84
rosaries, 21, 40–42, *41*; and gauds, *41*, 42, 194
rose cut (gemstone cut), 73, *73*, *140*, 141, 196
rosette (East Greek), 28, *28*
Ross, Denman Waldo, 13
ruby (gem): cabochon, 72, *72*, 73, *73*, 93, *93*; in Hindu cosmology, 45, 195; imitation, 51; talismanic powers of, 20
ruby jewelry, 61, *61*, 68, *68*, 72, *72*, 73, *73*, 89, *89*, 93, *93*, 156, *157*, *158*, 159, 172, *172*
Ruckert, Fedor, 142, *143*
Ruffle series (Winters), 191, *191*
Rundell, Bridge, and Rundell, 68, *68*
Ruskin, John, 151, 163
Russia, 93, *93*, 142, *143*, 161
rutilated quartz, 188, *188*, 196
Ryan, D. D. (Drew Dixon), 146, *147*

sablé, 110, *110*, 196
sapphire, Montana, 164
sapphire (gem), 20, 45, 51; cabochon, 21, *21*; in Hindu cosmology, 45, 195; imitation, 51, 146, *147*; talismanic powers of, 20, 21, *21*; yellow sapphire, *42*, 42–43, *43*
sapphire jewelry, 21, *21*, *42*, 42–43, *43*, 97, *97*, 163, *163*, 164, *164*, 172, *172*, 190, *190*
sard, 193, 196
sardonyx, 14, 105, *105*, 106, *106*, 196
Scaasi, Arnold, 16, 148, *149*
Schiaparelli, Elsa, 16, *123*, 124
School of the Museum of Fine Arts, Boston (SMFA), 163, 178
"sculpture to wear," 154
seaweed brooch (Liénard), 161, *161*
sentimental jewelry, described, 12, 99–101
September 11 terrorist attacks, 118
shaman effigy pendants, 37, *37*
Shaw, Josephine Hartwell, 15, *16*, 162, *162*, 164
shell jewelry, 14, 60, *60*, 64, *64*, 74, *75*, 76, *77*, 182, *182*
shell (material): conus, 182, 194; *Cypraea tigris*, 14, 60, *60*; *Nautilus Pompilius*, 64, *64*; spiny oyster, 182, *182*
shoe buckles, 134, *134*
Siberia, 164, *165*
signet rings, 196; Nubia, 33, *33*
silicious, defined, 196
silver: and modernist movement, 173; and patination, 97, *97*, 195. *See also specific jewelry*
silver, oxidized, 168, 170, *171*, 188, *188*, 195
silver mesh halter top (Peretti), 145, *145*
silver trade, 49
"Slave in Chains" medallion (England), 65, *65*
Slemmons, Kiff, 47, *47*, 183, *183*
Smith, Art, 15, 151, 154, 169, *169*, 170, *171*
Snow, George and Clara, *140*, 140–41
Sobral, 16
South America, 37, *37*, 49, 164, *165*, 196
Spain, 92, *92*, 94
spinel, 45, 51, 97, *97*
spiny oyster, 182, *182*
Sri Lanka, 49, 61
Stanford, Jane, 84
star sapphire, 20
statue (Gandharan), *18*, 19
statuette (Egypt), 35, *35*
stil moderne movement, 142
stomachers, 136, *136*
Strass, Georges-Frederic, 134
Stuart crystals, 108, *108*
Studio 27, 156
studio jewelry, 12, 15–16; described, 151–55
Studio (journal), 156
suit, woman's (Scaasi), 148, *149*
suite, defined, 196. *See also* demiparure; parure
Sun, Moon, Stars, Rain Wedding Crown (Renk), 176, *177*
"surface enrichment," 194
surrealism, 151, 154, 166, 169, 174, *174*
sutra case (Korea), 38, *39*
"sweetheart" jewelry, 51–52, *52*
Switzerland, 140, *140*
Syria, 28, 49. *See also* Palmyra

Tairona culture (Colombia), 37, *37*
talismans, 19, 42, 57, 107; defined, 196
Tanzania, 196
tesserae, 80, 196
textiles: and influences, 189; patch boxes, 110, *110*; silk weave, 138, *138*; Stuart crystals, 108, *108*
tiaras, 66
Tiffany, Charles Lewis, 70, 81, 90
Tiffany, Louis Comfort, 164
Tiffany and Company, 81, 145, *145*; "archaeological style," 82, 84, *84*; Renaissance-revival style, 90, *91*, *140*, 140–41; "sweetheart" jewelry, 52
Tiffany and Company, probably: Colt family jewelry, 70, *70*, *71*
tiger-claw jewelry, 20, 58, *59*, 81, *81*
Tiger cowrie, 182, *182*
tool marks, 34, *34*
topaz, 78, *78*, 101, *101*; in Hindu cosmology, 45, 195
topaz, pink, 78, *78*
torque, 28, *29*, 54, 196
tourmaline, 96, *96*, 138, *138*, 172, *172*, 193
Tragedy of Great Love (size 6), The (Gralnick), 116, *116*, *117*
triptych pendant (Germany), 40, *40*
Tryphon (Roman gem carver), 105, *105*
tsavorite, 97, *97*, 196
tumbaga, 37, *37*, 196
turquoise (gem), 148, 152; cabochon, 61, *61*; imitation, 22
turquoise jewelry, 14, *14*, 28, *29*, 45, *45*, 61, *61*, 138, *138*, 166–67, *167*, 169, *169*, 182, *182*
Tutankhamen, King, 82
twining, defined, 196

United States: arts and crafts movement, 126, 162, *162*, 163, *163*; avant-garde jewelry, 151–55, *152–54*, 162–70, *162–71*, 174, *174*, 176–83, *177–83*, 186, *187*, 189–91, *189–91*; and costume jewelry, 122, 146, 148; dress and adornment jewelry, 121–24, 134, *134*, 137, *137*, *140*, 140–41, *141*, 146, *147*, 148, *149*; Native American, 182, *182*; sentimental jewelry, 99–103, *102*, 108, *108*, 110–13, *111–13*, 115, *115–17*, 116, 118, *119*; wealth and power emblems, 49–52, *52*, 70, *70*, *71*, 76, *76*, 78, *78*, 79, *79*, 84, *84*, 90, *91*, 94, *95*, 97, *97*
United States or Europe: shoe buckles, 134, *134*
urn-shaped element *(kalathos)*, 55, *55*

Velázquez, Diego Rodríguez de Silva, 122, *122*
Vendome, Jean, 184, *185*
Victorian era, 56, 89, 137, 195
vinaigrettes, *122*, 196
Virgin and Child with Saints, The (Germany), 40
votive offerings: Egypt, 35, *35*; Greece, 53, *53*

Walters, Henry, 90
Warren, Dr. John, 134, *134*
Warren, Edward Perry, 14
Washington, George, 102, *102*, 111
Washington, Martha Custis, 99–100
watches, 12, 78, 133, *133*; design evolution of, 121; and escapement, *140*, 141, 194
watches, pocket, *140*, 140–41, *141*
watch fobs, 65, 133
wealth and power emblems, described, 11–12, 49–52
Weckström, Björn, 173, *173*
wedding jewelry. *See* marriage and wedding jewelry
Wedgwood Manufactory, 65, *65*, 105, 133, *133*, 195
white sapphire, 45, 51
Whiting and Davis, 145, *145*
Wiener, Ed, 151, 168, *168*
Willard, Levi and Catherine, 112, *112*
Winston, Harry, 94
Winters, Elise, 191, *191*
woman's suit in two parts (Scaasi), 148, *149*
wreath (Hellenistic or classical Greece), 53, *53*

Yager, Jan, 186, *187*
Yamamoto, Yoshiko, 178, *178*

zircon, 45, 51, 163, *163*, 195, 196
Zobel, Michael, 188, *188*